Path Dependence and Regional Economic Renewal

This book investigates the mechanisms that may stimulate or hamper the renewal of the regional industry structure. Recent years have witnessed a strong interest in, and need for, the modernization and upgrading of existing industries and the introduction of new industries. Informed by the evolutionary perspective this book argues that innovations within existing industry paths and the creation of new industries are strongly rooted in the established economic practice. Historically developed skills, existing industrial structure and regional and extra-regional networks form the basis for future regional growth. This volume consists of 11 chapters studying different aspects of regional industrial path development illustrated with cases from Norway, Sweden and Spain. The book also looks into the role of policy for regional economic renewal, and argues that economic renewal is fostered by policies that incorporate both actor-based and system-based elements. Such policy mix will provide a vital push towards renewal and new path development.

This book was originally published as a special issue of *European Planning Studies*.

Arne Isaksen is Professor of Economic Geography at the Department of Work Life and Innovation at the University of Agder, Norway. He is an expert in studies of regional innovation system and innovation policy, and has published a large number of articles in international journals.

Stig-Erik Jakobsen is Professor of Innovation Studies at the Western Norway University of Applied Sciences, Bergen, Norway. He is experienced in studies of industrial development, innovation and innovation policy, and has an extensive publication record in international journals. He is also Associate Editor of *European Planning Studies*.

Path Dependence and Regional Economic Renewal

Edited by
Arne Isaksen and Stig-Erik Jakobsen

Routledge
Taylor & Francis Group

LONDON AND NEW YORK

First published 2018
by Routledge

2 Park Square, Milton Park, Abingdon, Oxfordshire OX14 4RN
52 Vanderbilt Avenue, New York, NY 10017

Routledge is an imprint of the Taylor & Francis Group, an informa business

First issued in paperback 2019

British Library Cataloguing in Publication Data
A catalogue record for this book is available from the British Library

ISBN 13: 978-1-138-57698-8 (hbk)
ISBN 13: 978-0-367-89264-7 (pbk)

Typeset in Minion
by RefineCatch Limited, Bungay, Suffolk

Publisher's Note
The publisher accepts responsibility for any inconsistencies that may have
arisen during the conversion of this book from journal articles to book chapters,
namely the possible inclusion of journal terminology.

Disclaimer
Every effort has been made to contact copyright holders for their permission to
reprint material in this book. The publishers would be grateful to hear from any
copyright holder who is not here acknowledged and will undertake to rectify
any errors or omissions in future editions of this book.

Contents

CONTENTS

Citation Information

The chapters in this book were originally published in *European Planning Studies*, volume 25, issue 3 (March 2017). When citing this material, please use the original page numbering for each article, as follows:

For any permission-related enquiries please visit:
http://www.tandfonline.com/page/help/permissions

Notes on Contributors

Jarle Aarstad is Professor of Innovation and Entrepreneurship at the Western Norway University of Applied Sciences, Bergen, Norway. Aarstad's research focuses on the role of entrepreneurs and innovating firms in a regional context, and he has published extensively in numerous highly ranked international journals.

Heidi Wiig Aslesen is Professor at the Department of Strategy and Entrepreneurship, Norwegian Business School, Norway. Her research is related to regional industrial development and studies of innovation dynamics in specific sectors, global innovation networks and structural determinants for such activity.

Mary Genevieve Billington is Associate Professor at the Norwegian Reading Centre, University of Stavanger, Norway. Her research interests are in the areas of innovation, adult learning, workplace learning, professional development and digital technologies.

David Doloreux is a Professor at the Department of International Business at HEC Montréal, Canada. His research looks at the assumption linking entrepreneurship, creativity and innovation with the idea of territory and population cluster.

Aitziber Elola is a Researcher at Orkestra-Basque Institute of Competitiveness (Deusto Foundation) and Lecturer at Deusto Business School, Spain. Her research is mainly centred on the analysis of sectors and clusters, with special focus on cluster life cycles and global value chains.

Rune Dahl Fitjar is Professor of Innovation Studies at the Centre for Innovation Research and the UiS Business School, University of Stavanger, Norway. His research interests include innovation, regional development, regional politics and policy.

Arnt Fløysand is Professor at the Department of Geography, University of Bergen, Norway. His research interest is investigations of knowledge-network-capital dynamism in different time-spatial settings by combining theories and concepts from economic geography, cultural geography and political-ecology.

Jens Kristian Fosse is Associate Professor at the Mohn Center for Innovation and Regional Development, Western Norway University of Applied Sciences. His research looks at innovation processes in networks and regional clusters, regional innovation systems, and facilitating innovation in private and public sectors.

Susana Franco is a Researcher at Okestra-Basque Institute of Competitiveness and Deusto Business School, Spain. Her research focuses on analyzing the factors that affect clusters, governance, regional competitiveness and sustainable socio-economic progress.

Martin Gjelsvik is Research Manager at the International Research Institute of Stavanger and Professor II at the Stavanger Centre for Innovation Research, Norway. His main research interests are related to innovation management both at the firm and regional level.

Igone Porto Gomez is a Postdoctoral Researcher at the Competitiveness and Economic Development Research Team of the University of Deusto-Deusto Business School, Spain. Her research interest dips into regional innovation systems, focusing on the stakeholders located in the territory. Igone Porto has received financial support from the Basque Government Department of Education, Language Policy and Culture (IT885-16) on the research published in her chapter.

Elisabet S. Hauge is a Postdoctoral Research Fellow at the Department of Working Life and Innovation, University of Adger, Norway and a senior analyst at Oxford Research. Her research interests are on regional development, entrepreneurship and innovation.

Ann Karin T. Holmen is Professor at the Department of Media, Culture and Social, University of Stavanger, Norway. Her research areas look at organization of tasks and services across institutional and geographic boundaries, innovation of tasks and services in municipalities, and co-management and leadership.

Katja Maria Hydle is Head of the Innovation and Industry Research Group at the International Research Institute of Stavanger, Oslo, Norway. Her research concentrates on innovation, strategy, professional service work, organizational practices and multinational companies.

Arne Isaksen is Professor of Economic Geography at the Department of Work Life and Innovation, University of Agder, Norway. He is an expert in studies of regional innovation system and innovation policy, and has published many articles in international journals.

Stig-Erik Jakobsen is Professor of Innovation Studies at the Western Norway University of Applied Sciences, Bergen, Norway. He is experienced in studies of industrial development, innovation and innovation policy, and has an extensive publication record in international journals. He is also Associate Editor of *European Planning Studies*.

James Karlsen is Associate Professor at the Department of Working Life and Innovation, University of Agder, Norway. His main research interests are regional innovation systems, the role of university in regional development, territorial development, policy learning and action research.

Nina Kyllingstad is PhD candidate at the Department of Working Life and Innovation at the University of Agder, Norway. Her research interests are innovation and regional development.

Santiago M. López is Director of the Master and Doctoral Program in STS (Science and Technology Studies) at the Research Institute of Science and Technology Studies, University of Salamanca, Spain.

Natalia Maehle is Associate Professor at Western Norway University of Applied Sciences, Bergen, Norway. She is conducting research on innovation, digital economy, business models, consumer behavior and branding.

Line Mathisen is Senior Scientist at the Northern Research Institute, Norway. Her research covers innovation, industry and regional development.

Johan Miörner is a PhD candidate in Economic Geography at CIRCLE and the Department of Human Geography, Lund University, Sweden. His main research interests lie in the field of innovation studies, with a focus on regional industrial path development, regional innovation systems and regional innovation policy.

Trond Nilsen is a Senior Research Scientist at the applied research institute Norut, Norway. His research is related to regional path development in thin regions, industrial renewal and innovation.

Rune Njøs is a Researcher at Western Norway University of Applied Sciences, and a PhD candidate at the Department of Geography, University of Bergen, Norway. His research is on regional industry development and restructuring, industry clusters and evolutionary economic geography.

Vigdis Nygaard is a Senior Research Scientist at the Northern Research Institute, Norway. Her research looks at regional development, education and international cooperation in the North.

Inger Beate Pettersen is Associate Professor at the Center for Innovation, Bergen University College, Norway. Her research interests include innovation and entrepreneurship, international strategy and foreign market entry, and open innovation.

Ann Camilla Schulze-Krogh is a PhD candidate at the Department of Working Life and Innovation, University of Adger, Norway. The title of her PhD thesis is 'Regional Policy Learning in times of changing context'.

Bram Timmermans is Associate Professor of Strategy and Management at the Norwegian School of Economics, Norway. His main research interest lies within the field of innovation and entrepreneurship, new venture team development and performance, labor mobility, team mobility, strategic human resource development, employee diversity, organization theory, relatedness and related variety, and industrial dynamics.

Michaela Trippl is Full Professor of Economic Geography at the Department of Geography and Regional Research at the University of Vienna, Austria. Her research interests include regional innovation dynamics, regional structural change and new path development and new forms of regional innovation policies.

Jesus M. Valdaliso is Professor of Economic History and Institutions at the University of the Basque Country in Bilbao, Spain. He is an economic historian interested in cluster life cycles, territorial strategies and regional innovation systems, topics on which he has published several books and articles focused on the Basque Country.

Kristin Wallevik is Dean at the University of Agder, Norway.

New path development between innovation systems and individual actors

Arne Isaksen and Stig-Erik Jakobsen

ABSTRACT

This special issue is devoted to studying mechanisms that may stimulate or hamper the renewal of existing industry paths and the growth of new paths. In this guest editorial, we look closely at the role of policy instruments in situations where the majority of regional industries are embedded in strong regional and/or national innovation systems. This theme is currently very relevant in (parts of) Norway, where the dominant oil sector is downsizing and new growth paths are required to maintain employment and welfare. The guest editorial presents a theoretical framework for new regional industrial path development, followed by a discussion on how two Norwegian policy tools contribute to new path development. The 10 articles of the special issue study different aspects of new regional industrial path development based on cases in Norway, Sweden and Spain. Some papers also discuss the role of policy in new path development. Based on the findings from these articles, we believe that new path development is fostered by policies that incorporate both actor-based and system-based elements. Such policy mix could provide a vital push towards new path development.

Introduction

Recent years have witnessed a growing interest in, and need for, the modernization of existing industry paths, and in particular the development of new industrial paths at the regional and national levels. Industry and innovation systems need to develop activities that go beyond path extension. Thus, the ways in which regions and nations are able to achieve path renewal and path creation are high on the research agenda in disciplines such as evolutionary economic geography (EEG) (Fløysand & Jakobsen, 2016; Isaksen, 2015; Martin & Sunley, 2006; Neffke, Henning, & Boschma, 2011). The EEG approach emphasizes that path renewal and creation are strongly rooted in the existing economic structure of regions and nations. 'The local inherited knowledge and skill base of an industry can form the basis of the rise of related new local paths of industrial and technological activity' (Martin, 2010, p. 19). This focus on historically developed skills and industrial structure is a reminder that regions cannot develop any kind of new industries and growth paths easily, or perhaps at all; for example, most regions cannot replicate initiatives and

1

growth in dynamic high-tech clusters. However, historically developed structures can function as a double-edged sword; they can both hamper and stimulate new industrial growth paths.

On the one hand, functioning innovation systems that industries and their knowledge and support structures have jointly adapted over time strengthen firms' innovation capabilities and competitiveness. This viewpoint is highlighted by Niosi (2010, p. 43), who argues that 'countries possessing national and regional innovation systems in specific sectors will become wealthier'. Innovation systems provide firms with access to relevant competence and other resources, and include institutional frameworks that support their innovation activities.

On the other hand, strong innovation systems may have a weakness that becomes especially evident when the industry has to renew itself quickly. This weakness lies in the fact that innovation systems are mostly geared to support already strong industries. This is particularly apparent in small countries with limited human resources. Thus, innovation systems support path extension in particular, through continual improvements of already strong industries. This is the case when study programmes, R&D activity and policy tools are directed at supporting existing strong regional and national industries. The knowledge infrastructure, such as universities and R&D institutes, may initiate new growth paths, but there is still a significant risk that strong innovation systems will hamper rapid restructuring when the industry is well integrated into such systems.

This special issue is devoted to studying mechanisms that may stimulate or hamper the renewal of existing industry paths and the growth of new paths. The articles use Norwegian cases as their empirical test beds, in addition to two articles that build on cases from Sweden and Spain. In this guest editorial, we look closely at the role of policy instruments in situations where the majority of regional industry is embedded in strong regional and/or national innovation systems. This theme is currently very relevant in (parts of) Norway, where the dominant oil sector is downsizing and new growth paths are required to maintain employment and welfare. We start by providing a theoretical framework for new regional industrial path development. Thereafter, we refer to this framework in a discussion of how two Norwegian policy tools contribute to new path development. Finally, the editorial presents the major findings of the other articles in the issue and considers how these fit into the overall framework discussed in the editorial.

New path development

New regional industrial path development includes path renewal and path creation (Isaksen, 2015). Path renewal involves the growth of new activities and new industries via regional branching; existing knowledge and skills in a region are combined in new ways and may be linked to relevant, extra-regional knowledge to provide new knowledge for a region that enables innovations and entrepreneurship (Boschma & Frenken, 2011). Path creation represents the growth of entirely new industries for a region or nation. These are often created from scratch based on results from R&D activities or imported knowledge.

New regional industrial paths develop through two micro-level processes: (1) formation of new 'local' firms or transplantation of firms from other places in new industries in the region or (2) commencement of new activities by existing local firms in new industries in the region. Both processes highlight the importance of actors such as entrepreneurs, firms and other organizations. The latter group includes for instance venture capitalists, incubator staff and support organizations who facilitate the transplantation of firms from outside the region. However, start-up and renewal of existing firms in new fields in the region will not necessarily lead to new path development. A new industrial growth path emerges in a region (1) when several functionally related firms are established, (2) when the firms face existing or potential demand and a market or (3) when the firms find input factors in a regional innovation system (RIS) and/or gain access to production and knowledge networks outside the region (cf. Binz, Truffer, & Coenen, 2016, p. 177). Firms are functionally related when they use corresponding knowledge and technology, or belong to the same value chain. This interpretation implies that the emergence of new growth paths demands more than just entrepreneurship and innovation activity; it demands the emergence of several related firms linked to supportive actors and institutions.

To simplify somewhat, the innovation system approach has been quite static and has not emphasized the importance of actors in system changes. Approaches that focus on individual actors such as entrepreneurs, on the other hand, have put little emphasis on the fact that actors often need support from those in the 'environment' to contribute to a robust renewal of a regional industry. This guest editorial discusses the 'pure' actor and innovation system approaches to new path development. We argue that a framework that combines the two approaches is the most appropriate for analysing new path development and the most relevant basis for designing policy to support new regional industrial paths. The editorial analyses the extent to which important actor-based and system-based policy programmes in Norway combine the two approaches and the extent to which they (can) lead to new path development.

Actor-based approaches

Entrepreneurs and firm leaders are certainly of vital importance for the renewal of regional industry. However, human agency is also central for the development of supporting institutional frameworks for new path development. For example, policy-makers, university representatives and other actors contribute to the creation of functioning RISs, in which global knowledge links are also often highly important (Saxenian, 2006).

A discussion of the role of human agency in new path development may begin with different conceptualizations of agents – from those embedded in social structures (Uzzi, 1997) to knowledgeable actors that are able to deviate mindfully from existing structures (Garud & Karnøe, 2001). The concept of embedded agents is similar to that in the path-dependent approach, which in some interpretations allows little room for human agency. The approach focuses on technological relatedness, knowledge combinations and branching out of new activities and firms from the existing industrial structure and competences in a region (Boschma & Frenken, 2011). Such an interpretation 'downplays the influence of non-firm actors, institutions and public policy in creating and/or renewing industrial development paths in a region' (Binz et al., 2016, p. 173). Rather, human agency has 'to go with a flow of events that actors have little power to influence in real time' (Garud & Karnøe, 2001, p. 2). As a result, actors mostly extend existing development paths, while 'the emergence of novelty is serendipitous' (Garud & Karnøe, 2001, p. 7).

At the other end of the spectrum, actors are believed to be capable of making 'free' decisions based on their own motivations and priorities. Alsos, Carter, and Ljunggren (2014, p. 97), for example, maintain that 'entrepreneurship research traditionally views both the individual and the firm as decontextualized entities'. Approaches that focus on intentional and purposive action by individual agents consider that new pathways and the renewing of regional industry 'require social action by knowledgeable pioneering individuals, universities, companies and/or governments' (Simmie, 2012, p. 769). In a similar way, mindful deviation from existing structures by entrepreneurs is believed to constitute the heart of path creation (Garud & Karnøe, 2001, p. 6). The 'mindful deviating entrepreneurs' are still affected by social structures in several ways. First, new pathways may result from joint contributions by a number of actors, such as economic agents, policy-makers and potential customers (Simmie, 2012). Second, relevant actors can create favourable framework conditions and resources – for example, through policy actions – and can initiate new economic activity by mobilizing necessary resources. Third, the extent and importance of mindfulness by actors may differ from case to case and over time. Simmie (2012) describes how wind power industry entrepreneurs in Denmark employed and gradually developed local knowledge to supply local markets in rural areas and probably did not deviate from existing knowledge or business models. Later, the emerging cluster of wind power firms was supported strategically by government subsidies and tax relief.

Based on this short review of various approaches, we consider that human agency lies somewhere between 'dependent' actors that are strongly influenced in their decision-making by opportunities and restrictions set by regional and social structures, and actors that make 'free' decisions based on their own motivations and priorities. This interpretation corresponds with a view of entrepreneurship as 'the result of the interaction between individual actors and the surrounding environment' (Bosma, Schutjens, & Stam, 2011, p. 484). Actors 'identify, evaluate and exploit entrepreneurial opportunities within certain structures, while at the same time influencing these structures' (Bosma et al., 2011, p. 482).

Such considerations lead us to consider new regional industrial growth paths initiated by actors that can both utilize pre-existing regional capabilities and develop or mobilize completely new knowledge and skills in a region. A new path also induces 'changes to the relevant institutional contexts of the emerging industry' (Binz et al., 2016, p. 179). Binz et al. (2016) describe steps in the development of an OST (on-site water recycling technology) industry in Beijing, including initiatives by various actors and 'system development'. First, foreign companies entered Beijing to utilize a small niche market created by regional actors. This motivated 'highly skilled returnee entrepreneurs to found de novo start-ups and local actors to start spin-offs from related sectors and local universities' (Binz et al., 2016, p. 191). Thereafter, the imported technology led to a learning-by-doing process, and the development of an RIS with international links formed around the OSTs.

System approach

A system approach to path development departs from the fact that renewal, innovation and new firm formations rely on not only the internal competence of entrepreneurs, firms and organizations, but also networks and systemic configurations that stimulate co-operation and provide actors with new competences and critical resources. There are two main schools of thought concerning regional path development as a systemic phenomenon: RIS theory and cluster theory.

The concept of an RIS was developed during the 1990s and is linked to a broader line of literature on innovation systems that also includes studies of national systems of innovation and sectoral systems of innovation (Asheim & Isaksen, 1997; Cooke, 1992; Edquist, 1997; Jakobsen et al., 2012; Lundvall, 1992). The importance of geography and the regional level in the RIS literature is based on the observation that knowledge spillovers, which are essential in processes of interactive learning and innovation, tend to be spatially bounded and to decrease with distance. It is also true that regions differ with respect to industrial specialization, institutional architecture and patterns of innovation (Isaksen & Trippl, 2016; Tödtling & Trippl, 2005). Thus, different types of RIS need different policies to stimulate upgrading and renewal of the industry.

An RIS can be seen ' ... as a specific framework in which close inter-firm interaction, knowledge and policy support infrastructure, and socio-cultural and institutional environments serve to stimulate collective learning, continuous innovation and entrepreneurial activity' (Isaksen & Trippl, 2016, p. 70). However, RISs differ in many aspects, for instance, in knowledge foundation, type of firms and type of institutions. Asheim and Gertler (2005) distinguish between a broad understanding of RISs that covers all aspects of the (regional) economic structure and institutional set-up (i.e. all firms and the wider system of organizations supporting learning and innovation) and a narrow understanding that considers RISs to be interactions between knowledge organizations (such as universities, colleges or research institutions), knowledge-intensive firms, technology transfer organizations and other supporting organizations. Furthermore, we can differentiate between organizationally thin RISs and organizationally thick RISs (Tödtling & Trippl, 2005). The former type has a low number of firms and organizations in knowledge generation and diffusion, while the latter has a large number of firms and knowledge organizations.

The challenge for achieving new path development varies between types of RISs. In organizationally thin RISs, renewal and new firm formation often presuppose the establishment of links to external expert milieus and the import of new ideas and technology. This can provide existing firms with new competences and new solutions, while a new industry path can be created by importing products and technological solutions developed in other regional settings. In organizationally thick RISs, new path development to a larger extent is stimulated through spin-offs from knowledge institutions, by intensifying cooperation between knowledge organizations (such as universities, colleges and research institutions) and the industry and by the branching of existing industries into new and related industries (Boschma & Frenken, 2011; Isaksen, 2015).

Cluster theory departs from Porter's (1998, 2000) seminal work on industry clusters. He defined a cluster as a geographical concentration of interconnected and related companies and supporting organizations. Thus, a cluster system is narrower than an RIS, which can include several clusters. The basic idea of cluster theory is that geographical concentrations of similar and related firms and organizations stimulate competitiveness and innovation capabilities, and make firms that are part of a cluster more competitive than those that are not. The rationale for this is the presence of an 'upgrading mechanism' within a cluster, with knowledge spillovers, trust, complementarity, collective learning and rivalry as the most important components (Fløysand, Jakobsen, & Bjarnar, 2012).

The evolution of clusters as a systemic configuration is linked to processes of scale and scope. The issue of cluster scale has been thoroughly debated in recent literature. The literature agrees that external links are crucial for the renewal of mature clusters. To be innovative, strong clusters are dependent on access to new knowledge, information and networks (Bathelt, Malmberg, & Maskell, 2004; Nadvi & Halder, 2005). It has been widely acknowledged that knowledge links need to be balanced between the local and the global; the embeddedness of both clusters and their firms has been extensively investigated (e.g. Fornahl & Tran, 2010; Kramer & Diez, 2011; Montagnana, 2010). For instance, Bathelt et al. (2004) argue that the coexistence of intense local networking and a high number of external linkages facilitate collective learning processes that trigger innovation in a cluster.

The scope of a cluster concerns the type of industry actors and associated institutions that should constitute it. As with the debate over scale, there is widespread discussion about how specialized or diverse a cluster should be. Porter (2000) originally argued that a cluster should include firms and institutions in related industries, while others have argued that more narrowly defined and specialized clusters are beneficial for development (Reve & Sasson, 2012; Sölvell, Lindqvist, & Ketels, 2003). New lines of research have been more sceptical (Cooke, 2012), as in fact, specialization can hamper innovation. It is widely understood that innovations are stimulated by new combinations of dissimilar knowledge types. In this context, related variety is a useful concept (Boschma & Frenken, 2011). Aarstad, Kvitastein, and Jakobsen (2016) found that related industry variety promotes both innovation and productivity in clusters.

Traditionally, public cluster programmes in Norway and other Western countries have emphasized that clusters should be regional and specialized (Fløysand et al., 2012; Isaksen, 2009; Njøs, Jakobsen, Aslesen, & Fløysand, 2016; Sölvell et al., 2003). In addition, there has been a strong focus on strengthening external cluster linkages, and a consensus that external links are crucial for cluster evolution and growth. However, it can be argued that cluster policy is often 'more of the same'. It concerns strengthening the development of already strong industrial milieus, so it is closer to path extension than to new path development (Njøs & Jakobsen, 2016).

Two main policy approaches

Based on the above distinction between actor-based and system-based interpretations of regional industrial development, we distinguish between two main types of innovation policy approaches: those that primarily target individual actors and those mainly intended

Table 1. Characteristics of actor-based and system-based regional innovation policy.

Policy approaches	Characteristics	Strength with regard to stimulating new path development	Weakness with regard to stimulating new path development
Actor-based	Support entrepreneurs and firms' innovation projects	May identify and support actors with innovation activities that are new to a region	Little backing of actors with new ideas and projects from the existing clusters and RISs
System-based	Improve the functioning of clusters and RISs; fix system failures	Restructure and further develop clusters and RISs to provide better support for innovation activity in new industries in a region	Actors with relevant competence to initiate new growth path may not be present, that is, 'cathedral in the desert syndrome'

to improve the way in which 'systems' support the innovation capabilities of industry. Here, as in Nauwelaers and Wintjes (2003), we explicitly refer to regional systems and clusters while being well aware that national and international systems and knowledge links are also important for the innovation activities of most firms. Based on the above discussion, Table 1 proposes key strengths and weaknesses of the two types of innovation policy strategies with regard to the development of new regional industrial growth paths. Actor-based policy tools may support the innovation activity of individual entrepreneurs and firms. However, innovation activities risk receiving little support from existing RISs and clusters that are mostly geared towards currently strong industries. System-based policies, on the other hand, may assist in the restructuring of innovation systems and clusters so that education programmes, R&D activities and policy instruments stimulate new growth paths more efficiently. However, if regional industry and entrepreneurs have limited absorptive capacity for new knowledge, few effects are expected, which indicates that knowledge organizations act as 'cathedrals in the desert' (Hansen, 1992).

In the following section, we present two important Norwegian policy tools – one actor-based and the other system-based – and discuss the extent to which the framework in Table 1 characterizes the strong and weak parts of these tools.

Commercializing R&D results – an actor-based policy tool

Research-based innovation is a key concept in Norwegian innovation policy. In its strategy document for 2015–2020, the Research Council of Norway maintains that 'research-based innovation is central for the development and restructuring of Norwegian industry. Therefore, the Research Council has a role to play in industrial politics'.[1]

The FORNY (commercializing R&D results) programme began in 1995 and since then has been the central policy tool for stimulating commercialization of publicly funded research in Norway. From the start, the aim of this policy tool was to improve the ability to commercialize research-based business ideas at universities and research institutes. The main instrument was the establishment of so-called commercialization units to help researchers to manage different parts of the commercialization process. The work is now performed by seven Technology Transfer Offices (TTOs) run by universities or by other actors in which the universities have shares. The TTOs help with patenting, licensing and start-ups, but their activities are seldom linked to other activities at the universities (Spilling, Borlaug, Iversen, Rasmussen, & Solberg, 2015).

An evaluation of the FORNY programme in 2009 criticized its relatively limited achievements (Borlaug et al., 2009). From 1996 to 2009, the programme supported about 300 start-ups, with a total of approximately 700 employees and a turnover of 900 million NOK (ca. 100 million euros) in 2009. The 13 TTOs involved in the FORNY programme at that time employed staff equivalent to 100 man-years. Most of the supported firms survived but on a small scale with turnovers of up to one million NOK (ca. 110,000 euros) and with entrepreneurs as sole employees. Only three or four firms could be characterized as successful and accounted for a large proportion of the total number of jobs and turnover.

The next evaluation in 2015 (Spilling et al., 2015) did not make any similar assessment of results. The evaluation considered the organization of the commercialization support system. It found that the system functioned quite well at the universities and at some of the research institutes and that it was regarded as more focused and targeted than that described in the 2009 evaluation report. The 2015 evaluation found a marked increase in patenting with researcher participation, a clearly more positive attitude towards commercialization among researchers and a steady growth in technology sales and licence agreements from 2011 to 2014. However, no significant change in the number of start-ups was found. An analysis in 2013 (described in Spilling et al., 2015) of the portfolio of 474 firms and 424 agreements of technology sales and licence agreements in the FORNY programme found a number of promising projects. However, commercialization of research results takes time, and the 2013 analysis also found that the programme mainly produced small firms. This suggests that the results of the FORNY programme in terms of the number of jobs generated remain modest, despite the fact that the organization and implementation of commercialization activities are described as good.

The FORNY programme may contribute to new path development, and in particular to path creation. The policy tool helps to commercialize results from research milieus, so it may give rise to innovations and industrial activity that are new to a region. The new innovative firms are mainly spin-offs from universities and research institutes; therefore, they should benefit from ongoing R&D activities at their 'mother organizations'. The programme could also lead to reconfigurations of the R&D system with new and stronger research groups and possibly new education programmes. On the other hand, the evaluation document indicates fairly modest results. It may be pertinent to question whether modest results reflect the linear view of innovation in the programme, whereby research results are 'pushed onto' the market. A system approach entails putting market potential and contributions from potential customers as well as possible technology suppliers and producers higher on the agenda early in the innovation process. A broader set of actors is then brought into the innovation and commercialization process, which can ensure that products based on research target the market and can be produced efficiently. However, this demands a broader view of innovation than the linear approach that seems to dominate the programme and the activities of the TTOs.

The Norwegian Centre of Expertise programme – a system-based policy tool

Our example of a system-based approach is a cluster programme. Promoting the development of clusters has a strong foothold in the innovation policy of Norway. The main scheme is the Norwegian Innovation Clusters programme, run by Innovation Norway. There are three subprogrammes under this scheme. The most important of these is the Norwegian Centre of Expertise (NCE) programme, initiated in 2006 and designed for mature clusters with a strong international position. Financing for projects is granted for up to 10 years. The intention of the programme is to 'enhance sustainable innovation and internationalization processes in the most dynamic and growth-oriented Norwegian clusters' (nce.no). In October 2016, there were 14 NCE cluster projects in operation. In addition, the ARENA programme is aimed at emerging and immature clusters. Cluster projects can receive ARENA status and financing for 3–5 years. At present, 20 ARENA cluster projects are in operation. The public funding for these clusters is substantially smaller than that for the NCE projects. A third cluster level has recently been initiated in Norway: Global Centres of Expertise (GCE). Three GCE projects are running, all of which were previously NCE projects. Status and financing are granted for up to 10 years.

If we examine more closely the most important part of the Norwegian Innovation Clusters scheme – the NCE programme – the description states that NCE clusters should encompass a clear concentration of firms, both small and medium sized enterprises and large specialized suppliers, and many of these should also be globally oriented firms (2014). Furthermore, they must represent a 'specialized, attractive labour market in the cluster's regional area of impact' (p. 2; our translation). Thus, the aims of the programme are to improve the conditions for value creation and to strengthen the position of the cluster firms in national and global value chains. Furthermore, it is especially emphasized that 'connections between different suppliers and connections to buyers and users are crucial for well-functioning systems and solutions' (p. 21). The programme highlights the importance of co-ordinating and strengthening vertical linkages in value chains as a key characteristic of dynamic clusters. Hence, it can be claimed that the NCE programme emphasizes 'value chain thinking' (Njøs & Jakobsen, 2016).

The findings from evaluations and analyses of the NCE programmes reveal that the projects have mainly nurtured the existing value chains in which the firms operate (Econ Pöyry, 2009; Jakobsen et al., 2012). It has also been pointed out that new cluster members have been recruited from existing niches (Oxford Research, 2013, p. 29). In general, this observation supports our initial assumption that system-oriented policy tools contribute to the further development and strengthening of existing structures and networks. By nurturing already strong clusters, the NCE programme mainly contributes to path extension.

However, when we investigate the programme more closely, there are several indications that it can also contribute to path renewal and even path creation. In the 2015 programme description of the NCE initiative, 'cluster-to-cluster co-operation' is listed as one of four priority areas, and all of the NCE projects are expected to use resources to stimulate such co-operation (Norwegian Centre of Expertise, 2015). In some cases, this co-operation can occur between clusters in the same branch or sector, but there are also several examples of co-operation between clusters in different sectors. For instance, NCE Subsea (now a GCE) and NCE Seafood, both located in the Western part of Norway, have launched several 'crossover initiatives' together. As one example, they have supported projects where competences and technology from the oil and gas industry have been used to solve challenges in the aquaculture industry. Such cross-industry innovation practices have the potential to renew existing industry paths (www.gcesubsea.no/). Innovation Norway, which is running the NCE programme, has also recently launched an initiative called 'the cluster as a restructuring engine'. Three NCE cluster projects have been granted funding, and they will use well-known and proven competences and technology from their cluster firms to promote innovation and growth in other sectors. This also demonstrates how system-based tools can stimulate path renewal and path creation[2].

The content of the special issue

The 10 papers that follow study different aspects of new regional industrial path development based on cases in Norway, Sweden and Spain. Some papers also discuss the role of policy in new path development. The article by Doloreux and Porto Gomez includes a comprehensive assessment of the literature on RISs between 1998 and 2015, and discusses how this field of study should move forward. Supporters of the RIS approach aim for policy relevance and particularly stress the importance of building and upgrading regions' knowledge bases and of the interaction and knowledge flow between private and public actors. Nevertheless, Doloreux and Porto Gomez argue that policy-makers find only limited guidance in the RIS literature, as it has not developed any 'standard model' for the development of RISs. Instead, they argue that there is no one-size-fits-all policy, calling for analytical and policy development competence at the regional level rather than blind replication of so-called best-practice policy prescriptions. However, according to Doloreux and Porto Gomez, RIS research should develop a 'true' evolutionary dimension that considers how new actors can emerge and existing actors can alter their roles in RISs. The authors call for more research on the link between firm innovations, regional economic growth and the transformation of RISs.

Several articles address this challenge. The paper by Mæhle, Hauge, Kyllingstad and Schulze-Krogh investigates cross-industry innovation capability (CIIC) building in firms and discusses how conditions for innovation and learning in regions drive this process. CIIC is the firm's ability to transform knowledge and ideas from different industries into new products, processes and systems, and/or its ability to adapt existing products, processes and systems to new industries. The authors predict that if a substantial number of firms in a region possess high CIIC, path renewal will take place. Their study of CIIC building draws on case studies of firms in western and southern Norway, an area highly dependent on oil. The authors observe that firms that institutionalize cross-industry innovation thinking in their strategy are better off developing CIIC. They also find that some regional characteristics favour the development of CIIC, while others do not. They conclude that successful policies cannot focus solely on pushing technology and R&D investment to promote innovation, but should also be concerned with learning processes and the development of a strategic mindset at the firm level.

Gjelsvik and Aarstad analyse the role of entrepreneurship and financial institutions in regional development in south-western Norway. Regions evolve in path-dependent ways, but the degree of dependence or novelty may vary over time and between regions. Using register data, they investigate whether new firm formations reproduce the regional industry structure. They observe a steady decline in new firm formation in both related and unrelated industries after 1998, indicating a pattern of path extension but not diversification. This trajectory coincides with a steady and substantial boost in the oil price. This trend of path extension is stronger for south-western Norway than for the rest of the country. Furthermore, qualitative and quantitative data from financial institutions in the regions indicate that these institutions have contributed more to path extension than to path renewal or path creation. Regarding the policy implications of their study, the authors stress that there is no quick fix to the problem of strong entrepreneurial path dependence. However, policy-makers should be aware of the challenge and should elaborate potential strategies to stimulate sectoral diversification in new firm formation.

The article by Billington, Karlsen, Mathisen and Pettersen also explores the relationship between firm development and the regional environment. Their approach focuses on four firms that have demonstrated resilience by surviving over a long period and through times of external turbulence. The authors argue that the firms have built organizational resilience. The development of resilience is seen not only as the result of long-term investment in competence and workplace culture, but it also reflects values, resources and networks embedded in the region. The regional milieu supports the firms' resilience, and the firms contribute to the development of regional resilience. This conclusion also underlines the need to analyse both the actions of individual firms or entrepreneurs and the characteristics of a region or locality to understand the long-term resilience and innovation capability of regional industry.

One potentially important group of actors in new regional growth paths is multinational companies (MNCs). Aslesen, Hydle and Wallevik explore how MNCs can act as extra-regional sources of new path development in two Norwegian regions with thick RISs and industrial specialization in the oil and gas sector. Based on investigations of 15 MNCs, the authors find that the local units of these companies are highly dependent on acquiring competence from the MNCs' networks and RISs. Although some signs of path renewal are found, path extension through incremental innovations dominates. One reason is that many innovation activities in the local units of MNCs depend on approvals from the MNCs. Another reason is that the RISs are geared to supporting their existing specializations. Thus, path renewal may be difficult to achieve because of the organizational structure of the MNCs and the lock-in tendencies of the RISs. One way to achieve new growth may be to develop the RISs further; for example, through new educational programmes and policies that can spur investment by the MNCs in new areas.

Fløysand, Njøs, Nilsen and Nygård analyse a similar topic. Their article investigates the linkages between foreign direct investment (FDI) and the renewal of industries through case studies of the development of four regional industry paths. They argue for a perspective where the reciprocity between FDI and renewal of industries is the outcome of both material and discursive processes. Hence, they show how interdependence between materiality and discourse has different effects upon industry development. Path exhaustion and path extension are observed when FDIs are capital dominated and contain limited spillover effects, and when anti-FDI narratives and discourses dominate, while path renewal and path creation occur when FDI arrives as a capital–network–knowledge package and there are substantial regional spillovers and pro-FDI narratives and discourses. Policy initiatives are observed to be important for the development of two of the selected industry cases. Here 'local content policy' encourages MNCs, the key actors in FDI, to engage in projects that result in regional spillovers. Furthermore, the article indicates how directed policy action can influence the reciprocity between discourse and materiality. Consequently, the authors argue that policy should be considered as crucial in directing the interplay between FDI and the renewal of industries in a way that enriches both the MNC and regional industry as such.

Several other articles focus more specifically on the role of innovation policy in new regional industrial pathways. Miöner and Trippl focus on how a regional environment that constrains the development of new development paths can be transformed into an enabling environment. Such transformations include changes in the policy support structure, which can take three main forms. Layering consists of gradually adding new elements (such as policies and other institutions) to the support structure. Adaptation includes changes in, or reorientation of, existing institutions and organizations, for example, tailoring education programmes and incubation activities to emerging industries. A novel application is the utilization of existing policy instruments and organizations for new purposes, such as using existing policy tools in new industries. Miöner and Trippl study the emergence of the digital games industry in the Scania region of Sweden. They find that the growth of this industry results from combinations of three types of change in the policy support structure described above and that the changes were implemented by a few key individuals operating in the newly emerging paths. The case illustrates the importance of changes in the RIS for new growth paths to emerge as well as the role of key actors in undertaking new initiatives.

Holmen and Fosse come to a similar conclusion through a somewhat different approach. These authors analyse the role of regional agency in the early phase of path creation. Their study investigates the constitution of two new industry paths in the western part of Norway, a region highly dependent on the oil and gas sector. The study shows that two types of agency are vital in the processes of path creation. First, there is the regional policy agency that contributes to the creation of regional frames for new industry paths. Second, there is a need for a strong entrepreneurial agency that can push the process forward. Such agents can be a person, a firm or a network. In their investigation, Holmen and Fosse found that cluster projects, as a collective organization, created a common arena in which to exercise this type of entrepreneurial agency. Policy lessons from their study are that policy and entrepreneurial agency are interdependent in constitution processes, and policy initiatives need to gain strong support from firms or network organizations to be successful.

Fitjar and Timmermans emphasize the need for context-specific policy approaches. They employ a new method to study related variety in regional industrial structures. The authors develop a regional skill-relatedness measure that builds on labour mobility flows across Norwegian industries, and they identify the regional industries to which each industry in a region is related. Their analyses of Norwegian regions demonstrate a highly differentiated pattern with regard to how many and which industries are related through labour mobility flows, and this applies even to regions of similar size. They find more clearly related industries in urban regions than in small peripheral ones, but the data also reveal large differences within each category of region. This finding causes the authors to warn against policies such as treating all rural or peripheral regions in the same way or dishing out the same policy solutions to all large urban regions. Rather, policies must depart from specific analyses of regional contexts in individual regions.

The article by Elola, Valdaliso, Lôpez and Franco also puts policy at the forefront of analyses, and they investigate the role of public policies in the origin and evolution of six industry clusters in the Basque Country (Spain). Not surprisingly, they observe that industrial dynamics and market conditions have been the most influential factors in the development of the clusters. Public policy has also been important in the emergence and development of the clusters, but in general, public policy has played a secondary role. They also find that a broad-based general policy rather than a specific cluster policy has had the greatest influence on the emergence and development of these clusters. This can partly be explained by the fact that they have conducted historical studies tracing the development of the clusters back to the nineteenth and early twentieth centuries. Cluster policy as a distinct policy field was not introduced until the 1990s. Furthermore, they argue that there is a need for a more specific focus on the linkages between broad-based general policies and cluster policies. In general, cluster policies need to be better co-ordinated with wider policy to be more effective.

Summary

Several articles in this Special Issue indicate that many Norwegian regions are dominated by path extensions. Empirical studies demonstrate a steady decline in new firm formations in both related and unrelated industries over the past 20 years. RISs are mostly geared to supporting existing specializations. The activities of MNCs also frequently strengthen path extension. Local units of MNCs must often stick to the product and market niches appointed by higher levels, and many innovation activities in the local units are quite dependent on approval by the MNCs.

Policy recommendations drawn from the articles suggest that path renewal and path creation require co-ordinated activities by several actors. These demand learning processes at the entrepreneur and firm levels, and the development of a strategic mindset by these actors. MNCs can also stimulate path renewal and path creation when they act as techno-logical gatekeepers and engage in substantial regional spillovers. Moreover, it is illustrated that formalized networks can provide arenas for collective entrepreneurship. However, there is also a need to develop RISs further, for example, with new educational pro-grammes, new R&D activities, new initiatives for co-ordination between subsystems and new proactive policy tools. Policies to develop RISs should also be better co-ordinated with wider policy to be effective.

Based on the findings from the articles, we believe that new path development is fos-tered by policies that incorporate both actor-based and system-based elements. Such an approach is not really seen in the current discussion about policy to create new growth in the wake of the reductions in the numbers of jobs and activities in the oil and gas sector in Norway. Two main strategies are most often proposed by the government, min-istries and other key stakeholders, which are to increase the number of entrepreneurs by providing better access to capital and competence, and to support high-quality basic research that will lead to new research results that can be commercialized. These are mostly actor-based strategies targeting entrepreneurs and research centres and teams of high quality. Thus, we have advocated more emphasis on system-based initiatives. Such a broad innovation policy, consisting of a mix of complementary actor-based and system-based tools, could provide a vital push towards new path development.

Notes

1. Quoted from the *Strategy of the Research Council of Norway*, pp. 7–8. Authors' translation.
2. http://www.nceraufoss.no/startside/aktuelt/item/779-klynger-som-omstillingsmotor

Disclosure statement

No potential conflict of interest was reported by the authors.

Funding

This work was supported by the Research Council of Norway (P233737/o50).

References

Aarstad, J., Kvitastein, O., & Jakobsen, S.-E. (2016). Related and unrelated variety as regional drivers of enterprise productivity and innovation: A multilevel study. *Research Policy, 45*, 844–856. doi:10.1016/j.respol.2016.01.013

Alsos, G. A., Carter, S., & Ljunggren, E. (2014). Kinship and business: How entrepreneurial households facilitate business growth. *Entrepreneurship & Regional Development, 26*, 97–122. doi:10.1080/08985626.2013.870235

Asheim, B. T., & Gertler, M. (2005). The geography of innovation: Regional innovation systems. In J. Fagerberg, D. Mowery, & R. Nelson (Eds.), *The Oxford handbook of innovation.* (pp. 291–317). Oxford: Oxford University Press.

Asheim, B. T., & Isaksen, A. (1997). Location, agglomeration and innovation: Towards regional innovation systems in Norway? *European Planning Studies, 5*, 299–330. doi:10.1080/09654319708720402

Bathelt, H., Malmberg, A., & Maskell, P. (2004). Clusters and knowledge: Local buzz, global pipelines and the process of knowledge creation. *Progress in Human Geography, 28*, 31–56. doi:10.1191/0309132504ph469oa

Binz, C., Truffer, L., & Coenen, L. (2016). Path creation as a process of resource alignment and anchoring: Industry formation for on-site water recycling in Beijing. *Economic Geography, 92* (2), 172–200. doi:10.1080/00130095.2015.1103177

Borlaug, S. B., Grünfeld, L., Gulbrandsen, M., Rasmussen, E., Rønning, L. S., & Vinogradov, E. (2009). *Between entrepreneurship and technology transfer. Evaluation of the FORNY programme* (Report 19, 2009). Oslo: NIFU STEP.

Boschma, R., & Frenken, K. (2011). Technological relatedness and regional branching. In H. Bathelt, M. P. Feldman, & D. F. Kogler (Eds.), *Beyond territory. Dynamic geographies of knowledge creation, diffusion, and innovation* (pp. 64–81). London: Routledge.

Bosma, N., Schutjens, V., & Stam, E. (2011). Regional entrepreneurship. In P. Cooke, B. Asheim, R. Boschma, R. Martin, D. Schwartz, & F. Tödtling (Eds.), *Handbook of regional innovation and growth* (pp. 482–494). Cheltenham: Edward Elgar.

Cooke, P. (1992). Regional innovation systems: Competitive regulation in the new Europe. *Geoforum, 23*, 365–382. doi:10.1016/0016-7185(92)90048-9

Cooke, P. (2012). Knowledge economy spillovers, proximity, and specialization. In B. T. Asheim & M. D. Parrilli (Eds.), *Interactive learning for innovation: A key driver within clusters and innovation systems* (pp. 100–114). Basingstoke: Palgrave Macmillan.

Econ Pöyry. (2009). *Evaluering av seks NCE-prosjekter* [Evaluation of six NCE projects] (Econ-report nr. 2009-045). Oslo: Author.

Edquist, C. (1997). Systems of innovation approaches: Their emergence and characteristics. In C. Edquist (Ed.), *Systems of innovation: Technologies, institutions and organisation* (pp. 1–35). London: Pinter.

Fløysand, A., & Jakobsen, S.-E. (2016). In the footprints of evolutionary economic geography. *Norwegian Journal of Geography, 70*, 137–139. doi:10.1080/00291951.2016.1176073.

Fløysand, A., Jakobsen, S.-E., & Bjarnar, O. (2012). The dynamism of clustering: Interweaving material and discursive processes. *Geoforum, 43*, 948–958. doi:10.1016/j.geoforum.2012.05.002

Fornahl, D., & Tran, A. C. (2010). The development of local–global linkages in the biotech districts in Germany: Local embeddedness or distance learning? In F. Belussi & A. Sammarra (Eds.), *Business networks in clusters and industrial districts* (pp. 332–356). London: Routledge.

Garud, R., & Karnøe, P. (2001). Path creation as a process of mindful deviation. In R. Garud & P. Karnøe (Eds.), *Path dependence and creation* (pp. 1–38). London: Lawrence Erlbaum.

Hansen, N. (1992). Competition, trust, and reciprocity in the development of innovative regional milieux. *Paper in Regional Science, 71*(2), 95–105. doi:10.1007/BF01434257

Isaksen, A. (2009). Innovation dynamics of global competitive regional clusters: The case of the Norwegian centres of expertise. *Regional Studies, 43,* 1155–1166. doi:10.1080/00343400802094969

Isaksen, A. (2015). Industrial development in thin regions: Trapped in path extension? *Journal of Economic Geography, 15*(3), 585–600. doi:10.1093/jeg/lbu026

Isaksen, A., & Trippl, M. (2016). Path development in different regional innovation systems: A conceptual analysis. In M. D. Parrilli, R. D. Fitjar, & A. Rodriguez-Pose (Eds.), *Innovation drivers and regional innovation strategies* (pp. 66–84). London: Routledge.

Jakobsen, S.-E., Byrkjeland, M., Båtevik, F. O., Pettersen, I. B., Skogseid, I., & Yttredal, E. R. (2012). Continuity and change in path dependent regional policy development: The regional implementation of the Norwegian VRI programme. *Norwegian Journal of Geography, 66,* 133–143. doi:10.1080/00291951.2012.681686

Kramer, J.-P., & Diez, J. R. (2011). Catching the local buzz by embedding? Empirical insights on the regional embeddedness of multinational enterprises in Germany and the UK. *Regional Studies, 46,* 1303–1317. doi:10.1080/00343404.2011.571240

Lundvall, B.-Å. (1992). *National systems of innovations – towards a theory of innovation and interactive learning.* London: Pinter.

Martin, R. (2010). Roepke lecture in economic geography – rethinking regional path dependence: Beyond lock-in to evolution. *Economic Geography, 86*(1), 1–27. doi:10.1111/j.1944-8287.2009.01056.x

Martin, R., & Sunley, P. (2006). Path dependence and regional economic evolution. *Journal of Economic Geography, 6*(4), 395–437. doi:10.1093/jeg/lbl012

Montagnana, S. (2010). The internationalisation of the 'footwear agglomeration' of Timisoara: How deeply embedded are local firms? In F. Belussi & A. Sammarra (Eds.), *Business networks in clusters and industrial districts* (pp. 186–213). London: Routledge.

Nadvi, K., & Halder, G. (2005). Local clusters in global value chains: Exploring dynamic linkages between Germany and Pakistan. *Entrepreneurship & Regional Development, 17,* 339–363. doi:10.1080/08985620500247785

Nauwelaers, C., & Wintjes, R. (2003). Towards a new paradigm for innovation policy? In B. T. Asheim, A. Isaksen, C. Nauwelaers, & F. Tödtling (Eds.), *Regional innovation policy for small–medium enterprises* (pp. 193–219). Cheltenham: Edward Elgar.

Neffke, F., Henning, M., & Boschma, R. (2011). How do regions diversify over time? Industry relatedness and the development of new growth paths in regions. *Economic Geography, 87*(3), 237–265. doi:10.1111/j.1944-8287.2011.01121.x

Niosi, J. (2010). *Building national and regional innovation systems. Institutions for economic development.* Cheltenham: Edward Elgar.

Njøs, R., & Jakobsen, S.-E. (2016). Cluster policy and regional development: Scale, scope and renewal. *Regional Studies. Regional Science, 3,* 146–169. doi:10.1080/21681376.2015.1138094

Njøs, R., Jakobsen, S.-E., Aslesen, H. W., & Fløysand, A. (2016). Encounters between cluster theory, policy and practice in Norway: Hubbing, blending and conceptual stretching. *European Urban and Regional Studies, 23.* doi:10.1177/0969776416655586

Norwegian Centre of Expertise. (2015). *Selection criteria for NCE, 2015.* Retrieved from http://www.innovasjonnorge.no/PageFiles/344932/Utvelgelseskriterier2020152028NO29.pdf

Norwegian Innovation Clusters. (2014, December 18). *Programbeskrivelse Norwegian Innovation Clusters* [Programme description Norwegian Innovation Clusters]. Innovation Norway, The Research Council of Norway, SIVA. Retrieved from http://www.innovasjonnorge.no/PageFiles/345849/Programbeskrivelse%2018.12.14.pdf

Oxford Research. (2013). *Evaluering av NCE-prosjekter etter seks år. Evaluering av tre NCE-prosjekter – hovedrapport* [Evaluation of NCE projects after six years. Evaluation of three NCE projects – main report]. Kristiansand: Oxford Research.

Porter, M. E. (1998). Clusters and the new economics of competition. *Harvard Business Review, 76,* 77–99.

Porter, M. E. (2000). Location, competition and economic development: Local clusters in a global economy. *Economic Development Quarterly, 14,* 15–34. doi:10.1177/089124240001400105

Reve, T., & Sasson, A. (2012). *Et kunnskapsbasert Norge* [A knowledge based Norway]. Oslo: Universitetsforlaget.

Saxenian, A. (2006). *The new argonauts. Regional advantage in a global economy.* Cambridge, MA: Harvard University Press.

Simmie, J. (2012). Path dependence and new technological path creation in the Danish wind power industry. *European Planning Studies, 20*(5), 753–772. doi:10.1080/09654313.2012.667924

Sölvell, Ö, Lindqvist, G., & Ketels, C. (2003). *The cluster initiative greenbook.* Stockholm: Ivory Tower.

Spilling, O. R., Borlaug, S. B., Iversen, E., Rasmussen, E., & Solberg, E. (2015). *Virkemiddelapparatet for kommersialisering av forskning – status og utfordringer. Rapport 18/2015.* Oslo: NIFU.

Tödtling, F., & Trippl, M. (2005). One size fits all? Towards a differentiated regional innovation policy approach. *Research Policy, 34,* 1203–1219. doi:10.1016/j.respol.2005.01.018

Uzzi, B. (1997). Social structure and competition in interfirm networks: The paradox of embeddedness. *Administrative Science Quarterly, 42*(1), 35–67. doi:10.2307/2393808

A review of (almost) 20 years of regional innovation systems research

David Doloreux and Igone Porto Gomez ⓘ

ABSTRACT

The literature on regional innovation systems (RISs) has grown impressively in the last two decades. The objective of this study is to provide a comprehensive assessment of all RIS articles published in scholarly journals between 1998 and 2015. It aims to inform researchers of the empirical results obtained so far and highlight areas that need further work. This review describes how the RIS field has developed, charts the current body of RIS research and discusses recommendations for moving the RIS field forward.

1. Introduction

The literature on regional innovation systems (RISs) has grown impressively in the last two decades (Asheim & Gertler, 2005; Asheim, Grillitsch, & Trippl, 2017; Cooke, Heidenreich, & Braczyk, 2004; Doloreux, 2002; Isaksen & Trippl, 2016; Tödtling & Trippl, 2005). RIS research has developed around the ideas that innovation is a systemic process (Edquist, 2005; Lundvall, 2007) and that it benefits from the concentration of economic activities and geographical proximity (Asheim & Gertler, 2005; Boschma, 2005; Carrincazeaux & Gaschet, 2015; Cooke et al., 2004; Torre & Rallet, 2005). The central idea behind this approach is that innovative performance depends on not only the knowledge banked by firms and public-sector organizations, but also the way these different kinds of organizations interact with each other and their environment in regard to production and the dissemination of knowledge.

A RIS is 'a set of interacting private and public interests, formal institutions, and other organizations that function according to organizational and institutional arrangements and relationships conducive to the generation, use, and dissemination of knowledge' (Doloreux & Parto, 2005, pp. 134–135). In this conception, a firm's innovation system consists of a multitude of actors who are involved in the innovation process and interact with each other. These actors include other firms, research institutes, education and training organizations, policy-makers, financial institutions, regulatory authorities and intermediary organizations. Moreover, this environment also includes an innovation-supportive culture and policies that enable both firms and systems to evolve over time (Uyarra, 2010).

In line with RIS research, a significant number of public policies have been developed to promote regional economic growth by stimulating innovation processes and networks (McCann & Ortega-Argilés, 2013) between businesses; knowledge organizations such as universities, laboratories and institutes and technology transfer units; business associations; and financial agencies. Consequently, regions' economic agendas tend to take into account the impact of the region in question on its formal and informal activities, transactions and capacity to produce and share knowledge (Shearmur, 2015).

The purpose of this study is to provide a comprehensive assessment of RIS articles published in scholarly journals between 1998 and 2015. In particular, this study (i) describes the sources and nature of the RIS articles published; (ii) depicts the origin of the authors of these articles; (iii) examines the research adopted by the empirical studies in the RIS articles; (iv) describes the scope of the research conducted in these articles; (v) depicts the specific methodologies adopted and (vi) identifies the structure of the RIS research. This review describes how the RIS field has developed, charts the current body of RIS research and discusses recommendations for moving the RIS field forward.

2. Research method

This article follows a systematic literature review process (Boell & Cecez-Kecmanovic, 2015). The main purpose of a systematic review is to address a specific question for which evidence in the literature is sought. Traditional literature reviews assess the state of knowledge in a problem domain and identify weaknesses and areas for further research. In contrast, a systematic literature review follows a rigorous, replicable and transparent scheme in order to identify key scientific contributions to a research field or a question and provide a conclusive assessment regarding a research question (Amrollahi, Ghapanchi, & Talaei-Khoei, 2013; Boell & Cecez-Kecmanovic, 2015).

The study consists of a systematic review of empirical RIS articles published in scholarly journals between 1998 and 2015. This time frame is sufficiently large to incorporate the vast majority of such articles, as the first writings on the subject only made their appearance in the early 1990s (Cooke, 1992) and the output was small before 1998. The choice of 1998 as the lower limit of the temporal horizon is justified by Braczyk, Cooke, and Heidenteich's (1998) publication that year of the first edition of Regional innovation systems: The role of governance in a globalised world. This book was a first attempt to introduce the concept of RIS, and in particularly the introduction of the book which provides the foundations in defining, justifying and exemplifying the concept of RISs (Cooke in Cooke et al., 1998).

Three considerations are particularly important when doing a systematic review: (1) establishing the inclusion criteria; (2) identifying and selecting the potential articles and (3) classifying the selected articles.

With respect to the inclusion criteria, three criteria had to be met for a study to be eligible for inclusion here. First, RIS must be the core analytical concept under which the empirical investigation was carried out. Empirical studies dedicated to other types of territorial innovation models (regional clusters, industrial districts, innovative milieu, learning regions, local production systems and so on) were not retained. Second, the article had to be published between 1998 and 2015 in a peer-reviewed journal. Other publications' forms (conference proceedings, books, chapters, working papers, etc.) were not considered. And finally, the article must be an empirical study.

With respect to the identification and selection of the articles, the sampling frame consisted of empirical articles published in leading scholarly journals between 1998 and 2015. To identify articles that focus specifically on RISs rather than other territorial innovation models, a three-step process was employed. First, keyword searches using the terms 'regional innovation system' and 'regional systems of innovation' were used to identify the universe of potentially relevant articles. As in other studies, we chose Scopus for this research. The search returned 529 articles published in scholarly journals and containing one or both of these terms in their title, abstract and/or keywords: 'regional innovation system' (494 articles) and 'regional systems of innovation' (35 articles). Second, each of the two authors formed an initial selection of potentially relevant articles addressing the focal topic. We identified the articles that focus explicitly on RISs and excluded those that do not. This review process led to the exclusion of 188 articles that are unrelated to the RIS field, which left us with 341 articles. Finally, of these 341 articles, we identified 292 that are empirical studies and 49 that are theoretical works.[1]

With respect to the classification of the articles, we used the coding framework proposed by Gomes, Barnes, and Mahmood (2016) and Leonidou, Barnes, Spyropoulou, and Katsikeas (2010), who developed a coding schedule for the purpose of 'undertaking a systematic and replicable investigation of text and documents with the objectives of quantifying content using preset categories' (Gomes et al., 2016, p. 3). Content analysis was used 'to apply an objective coding scheme that allowed us to systematically compare the data, utilising classifications, levels and units of analysis' (Berg, 2004, p. 265). The purpose of the analysis was to assess the development and patterns of scholarly RIS research, and we used a number of classification variables. In line with the valuable procedure undertaken by Gomes et al. (2016) and Leonidou et al. (2010), we replicate the procedure and each article was coded and analysed according the following dimensions:

(1) Source of article: Journal name and publication year;
(2) Authorship characteristics: Number of authors, number of countries, location of countries, number of institutions and academic disciplines;
(3) Research design: Problem crystallization, variable association, research environment, communication mode, topical scope and time dimension);
(4) Scope of research:Number of regions analysed, location of region, country of region, nature of the region and types of regions);
(5) Research methodology: Sampling design, data collection, data analysis and analytical technique);
(6) Structure of the RIS research:[2] (1) stakeholders; (2) relationships; (3) trust and informal relationship; (4) innovation process; (5) intermediaries; (6) research topics).

Both empirical and theoretical studies were retained for the analysis of the sources of articles and authorship characteristics (341 articles). For the analysis of the other dimensions, however, only the empirical studies were retained (292 articles). We split the articles into three time periods in order to reflect the stages of development of the RIS research field: 1998–2004 ('early works'), 2005–2010 ('advancing the literature') and 2011–2015 ('recent works').

3. Study findings

3.1. Sources and nature of articles

The 341 theoretical and empirical articles were published in 137 journals. The distribution of the articles shows that the rate of publication has increased remarkably, from eight articles per year for the 1998–2004 period to over 33 articles per year for the 2011–2015 period.

The assessment of the journals in Table 1 reveals that *European Planning Studies* is the main source of RIS articles (15.2%). The journals that followed were *Regional Studies* (7%), *Research Policy* (4.4%) and *European Urban and Regional Studies* (2.9%). The technological dimension surrounding RIS research might explain the level of engagement by *Technology Analysis and Strategic Management* (2.6%), *Industry and Innovation* (2%), *Journal of Technology Management and Innovation* (2%), *Journal of Technology Transfer* (2%), *Journal of the Knowledge Economy* (2%) and *Technovation* (2%). The policy dimension might also explain the engagement of *Environment & Planning C* (2%) and *Science and Public Policy* (2%).

One hundred and seven journals each published fewer than two articles on RIS, while another 15 published between three and five articles (up to 1.5%) each.

Most articles published in the RIS research field were empirical (85.4%), while theoretical and methodological papers accounted for 15.6% of the total. The top three sources for empirical articles were *European Planning Studies* (16.4%), *Regional Studies* (7.5%) and *Research Policy* (4.5%). The journals with the greatest number of theoretical and methodological papers were *European Planning Studies* (7.8%) and *Technology in Society* (5.9%).

3.2. Authorship characteristics

The distribution of the articles by authorship (Table 2) shows that 'single authorship' is the least typical, comprising 30.9%t of the total. 'Two authors' wrote about 36.4% of the articles, while 32.7% were written by 'three or more authors'. There has been a decrease in the number of articles written by one author and a steady increase in articles written by 'three or more authors' since the first period. Articles written by authors from a 'single country' clearly outnumber those written by authors situated in 'two or more countries' (79.6% vs. 19% and 1.5%, respectively). Authors located in 'European countries' produced about 80% of the RIS articles. This publication trend might be a result of the numerous research projects funded by the European Commission on RISs and the series of Community Innovation Surveys carried out in Europe during the last two decades. Authors from the 'same institution' produced more than half of the articles, but over time there was an upward trend in articles written by authors from 'two or more institutions'. RIS research was conducted by authors in various disciplines. Thirty per cent of the authors were located in 'Business/Management' faculties, and this trend has increased over time. The disciplines that follow are 'Technology/Engineering' (18.6%), 'Economics' (12.8%) and 'Human Geography' (12.2%).

Table 1. Journals publishing RIS research[a].

Journals	Total (n = 341) %	Time period			Article type	
		1998–2004 (n = 55) %	2005–2010 (n = 119) %	2011–2015 (n = 167) %	Theoretical (n = 49) %	Empirical (n = 292) %
Annals of Regional Science	0.9	0.0	1.7	0.6	0.0	1.0
Cambridge Journal of Economics	0.9	1.8	0.8	0.6	0.0	1.0
Energy Policy	0.9	0.0	0.8	1.2	0.0	1.0
Entrepreneurship and Regional Development	0.9	0.0	1.7	0.6	0.0	1.0
Environment and Planning A	1.2	1.8	0.8	1.2	2.0	1.0
Environment and Planning C	2.0	0.0	2.5	2.4	0.0	2.4
European Planning Studies	15.2	23.6	16.5	11.4	7.8	16.4
European Urban and Regional Studies	2.9	5.5	1.7	3.0	2.0	3.1
Growth and Change	0.9	0.0	2.5	0.0	0.0	1.0
Industry and Innovation	2.0	3.6	1.7	1.8	2.0	2.1
Innovation	0.9	0.0	2.5	0.0	2.0	0.7
Innovation: Management, Policy and Practice	0.9	0.0	1.7	0.6	0.0	1.0
International Journal of Technology Management	1.2	0.0	2.5	0.6	0.0	1.4
Journal of Technology Management and Innovation	2.0	0.0	0.0	4.2	2.0	2.1
Journal of Technology Transfer	2.0	7.3	2.5	0.0	2.0	2.1
Journal of the Knowledge Economy	2.0	0.0	0.0	4.2	3.9	1.7
Mediterranean Journal of Social Sciences	0.9	0.0	0.0	1.8	2.0	0.7
Norsk Geografisk Tidsskrift	1.5	0.0	0.8	2.4	2.0	1.4
Papers in Regional Science	1.2	1.8	0.0	1.8	2.0	1.0
Regional Studies	7.0	9.1	6.6	6.6	3.9	7.5
Research Policy	4.4	7.3	6.6	1.8	3.9	4.5
Science and Public Policy	2.0	1.8	2.5	1.8	3.9	1.7
Science, Technology and Society	0.9	0.0	1.7	0.6	0.0	1.0
Scientometrics	1.2	1.8	1.7	0.6	0.0	1.4
Technological Forecasting and Social Change	2.6	0.0	0.0	5.4	0.0	3.1
Technology Analysis and Strategic Management	0.9	0.0	2.5	0.0	0.0	1.0
Technology in Society	1.2	3.6	0.8	0.6	5.9	0.3
Technovation	2.0	3.6	2.5	1.2	0.0	2.4
Tijdschrift voor Economische en Sociale Geografie	0.9	1.8	1.7	0.0	3.9	0.3
Urban Studies	0.9	3.6	0.8	0.0	2.0	0.7

[a]We include only journals that have published three or more articles on RIS. There are 91 journals that have published only one paper on RIS and 16 journals that have published two articles. The sum of the percentage of each column therefore is not 100%.

3.3. Research design

The design and structure of the empirical articles analysed are shown in Table 3. Considering now only the 292 empirical articles, 81.1% of the total are exploratory studies and contain 'no predetermined hypotheses'. Articles which are formalized in nature – 'hypotheses' – account for a smaller percentage of the total, but this type of research is slowly but consistently increasing over time. Over half of the articles

Table 2. Key researchers publishing RIS Research.

Authorship characteristics	Total (n = 341) %	Time period 1998–2004 (n = 55) %	2005–2010 (n = 119) %	2011–2015 (n = 167) %	Trend direction[a]
Number of authors					
One	30.9	49.1	35.0	22.0	↓
Two	36.4	38.2	35.8	36.3	∨
Three or more	32.7	12.7	29.2	41.7	↑
Number of countries					
One	79.6	83.6	83.3	75.6	↓
Two	19.0	16.4	15.8	22.0	∨
Three or more	1.5	–	0.8	2.4	↑
Location of countries					
North America	6.1	7.3	9.2	3.6	∧
Europe	70.6	70.9	75.8	66.7	∧
Asia	12.5	14.5	7.5	15.5	∨
South America	2.9	–	0.8	5.4	↑
Others	7.9	7.3	6.7	8.8	∨
Number of institutions					
One	55.7	72.7	55.0	50.6	↓
Two	28.3	14.5	29.2	32.1	↑
Three or more	16.0	12.7	15.8	17.3	↑
Academic disciplines					
Business/Management	30.0	20.0	26.7	35.7	↑
Economics	12.8	14.5	14.2	11.3	↓
Geography	12.2	12.7	15.0	10.1	∨
Technology/Engineering	18.6	14.5	25.0	15.5	∧
Others	18.1	27.3	13.3	18.5	∨
Not mentioned	8.2	10.9	5.8	8.9	∨

[a](↑) Increasing; (↓) decreasing; (∧) increasing and then decreasing; (∨) decreasing and then increasing.

(57.8%) are descriptive, whereas causal studies – 'understanding cause-effect relationships' – account for 41.4% of the total. Over time, both exploratory and articles which are formalized in nature have fluctuated in terms of their frequency, with a decline in the 2005–2010 period, followed by an increase in the 2011–2015 period for the exploratory articles and a decrease for the articles which had hypotheses developed from the literature. In terms of variable association, 'descriptive' articles account for 57.8% of the studies, and for approximately two-thirds (66%) in the 2005–2010 period. 'Causal' articles were published most often in the 2011–2015 period and fluctuated in their numbers, but they remain less important than 'descriptive' articles.

In terms of field research, more than half of the articles (52.7%) required 'fieldwork' in order to collect the data. Articles that did not require fieldwork – 'laboratory work' – are common due to the use of existing databases that require statistical procedures. 'Others' consists of articles that combine field research and laboratory work. The only clear trend is the decrease in this last category. Articles are increasingly based exclusively on either researchers' own data or pre-existing data.

In terms of communication mode, less than two-thirds of RIS articles use 'observational studies'[3] (61.3%), while 'survey studies' account for 34.9% of the total. For both, the trend remains static over the three periods.

In terms of topical scope, case studies appear in 61.3% of all empirical articles, while statistical studies account for 34.9%. Despite a decline in statistical articles in the 2005–2010 period, there was a significant fluctuation in the number of this type of articles for the 2011–2015 period (38.6%).

Table 3. Research design of RIS articles.

Research design	Total (*n* = 292) %	Time period			Trend direction[a]
		1998–2004 (*n* = 44) %	2005–2010 (*n* = 103) %	2011–2015 (*n* = 145) %	
Problem crystallization					
Exploratory	81.1	88.6	87.3	74.4	↓
Formalized	18.8	11.3	12.6	25.5	↑
Variable association					
Descriptive	57.8	50.0	66.0	54.4	∧
Causal	41.4	50.0	33.9	44.1	∨
Other	0.6	–	–	1.3	↑
Research environment					
Field	52.7	45.4	58.2	51.0	∧
Laboratory	43.1	40.9	37.8	47.5	∨
Others	4.1	13.6	3.8	1.3	↓
Communication mode					
Survey	34.9	36.3	33.0	35.8	∨
Observational	64.3	63.6	66.9	62.7	∧
Others	0.6	–	–	1.3	↑
Topical scope					
Statistical study	34.9	36.3	29.1	38.6	∨
Case study	61.3	54.5	66.9	59.3	∧
Others	3.7	9.0	3.8	2.0	↓
Time dimension					
Cross-sectional	81.8	81.8	82.5	81.3	∧
Longitudinal	17.1	18.1	16.5	17.2	∨
Others	1.0	0.0	0.9	1.3	↑

[a](↑) Increasing; (↓) decreasing; (∧) increasing and then decreasing; (∨) decreasing and then increasing.

In terms of time dimension, about 81.8% of the RIS studies examine cross-sectional data, and about 17.1% present longitudinal data. Although slight fluctuations are discernible over time, cross-sectional studies remain the main type of RIS research published.

3.4. Scope of research

Table 4 depicts the results for the scope of RIS research. With respect to the regions analysed, an important tendency is for the research to focus on a 'single specific region' (45.5%). The number of articles focusing on one region has increased over time. Comparative studies dealing with 'four or more regions' account for 38% of all the articles published, but the percentage of this type of article has decreased over time. Articles focusing on 'two or three' regions account for less than 16.4% of all RIS articles.

Looking to the location of those regions, around two-thirds of the articles focus on regions in 'Europe'. However, there has been a slight but continuous decrease in articles focusing on European regions, from 70.4% of the total in the first period to 62.7% in the third. This downward trend is largely a result of the increase in articles focused on regions in 'Asia', from 13.6% in the first period to 24.8% in the third. Comparisons of regions located in different continents and studies focusing on regions in Africa or South America are small in number and have been labelled Others. If we disaggregate the information to the country level, we find 38 different countries. Regions in 'China' are the most frequently studied (10.9%), followed by regions in 'Spain' (7.5%), 'Germany' (6.1%), 'Finland' (5.4%) and the 'UK' (4.7%). Over time, the number of articles on regions in China, 'Sweden', 'Australia', the 'Czech Republic' and 'Brazil' has increased.

Table 4. Scope of research for RIS articles.

		Time period			
Scope of research	Total (n = 292) %	1998–2004 (n = 44) %	2005–2010 (n = 103) %	2011–2015 (n = 145) %	Trend direction[a]
N° Regions analysed					
1	45.5	29.5	45.6	50.3	↑
2	10.6	15.9	8.7	10.3	∨
3	5.8	9.0	7.7	3.4	↓
4 or more	38.0	45.4	37.8	35.8	↓
Location of the region					
North America	6.1	13.6	7.7	2.7	↓
Europe	65.7	70.4	67.9	62.7	↓
Asia	20.2	13.6	16.7	24.8	↑
Others	7.8	2.2	7.7	9.6	↑
Country of the region					
China	10.9	2.2	6.8	16.5	↑
Spain	7.5	6.2	8.7	6.9	∧
Germany	6.1	9.0	6.8	4.8	↓
Finland	5.4	–	7.7	5.5	∧
UK	4.7	6.8	4.8	4.1	↓
Italy	3.4	2.2	5.8	2.0	∧
Russia	3.4	2.2	–	5.5	∨
Austria	3.0	4.5	1.9	4.1	∨
Sweden	3.0	2.2	2.9	3.4	↑
US	3.0	6.8	2.9	2.0	↓
Canada	2.7	6.8	3.8	0.6	↓
Norway	2.7	2.2	1.9	3.4	∨
Australia	2.0	–	1.9	2.7	↑
Korea	2.0	6.8	0.9	1.3	∨
Czech Republic	1.7	–	1.9	2.0	↑
Portugal	1.7	4.5	0.9	1.3	∨
Brazil	1.0	–	0.9	1.3	↑
Denmark	1.0	–	2.9	–	∧
Japan	1.0	2.2	1.9	–	↓
The Netherlands	1.0	6.8	–	–	↓
Others	9.9	6.8	5.8	13.7	↑
Comparison of Countries	21.9	20.4	28.1	17.9	∧
Nature of the region					
Developed	78.7	95.4	82.5	71.0	↓
Newly Industrialized	13.0	2.2	10.6	17.9	↑
Developing	5.4	2.2	1.9	8.9	↑
Others	2.7	0.0	4.8	2.0	∧
Types of regions					
Metropolitan regions	46.9	27.2	42.7	55.8	↑
Peripheral/rural regions	30.1	25.0	35.9	27.5	∧
Multiples types of regions	22.9	47.7	21.3	16.5	↓

[a](↑) Increasing; (↓) decreasing; (∧) increasing and then decreasing; (∨) decreasing and then increasing.

In contrast, the number of articles on regions in Germany, the UK, the 'US', 'Canada', 'Japan' and the 'Netherlands' has decreased.

With respect to the nature of the region studied, more than three-quarters (78.7%) of the articles focus on 'developed regions': Europe, Canada, the US and Australia. While 'newly industrialized' (13%) and 'developing' (5.4%) regions do not even constitute one-fifth of the published works, there is an important trend to focus on countries such as China, India, Thailand, Malaysia and Brazil, which can explain the increase in the percentage of articles focused on these types of regions. For the first period, articles about newly industrialized and developing regions constitute no more than 4.4% of the total, while for the 2011–2015 period they constitute more than a quarter (26.8%). The number of articles focused on developed regions has decreased from 95.4% in the 1998–2004 period to 71% in the 2011–2015 period.

Also interesting is the type of region analysed. 'Metropolitan regions' (46.9%) account for nearly half of the studies, and they have increased to 55.8% for the 2011–2015 period. There has been an increase in the analysis of capital cities in particular, from 8.3% in the first period to 37.8 in the third. Around one-third of the empirical articles analyse 'peripheral and rural regions' (30.1%), but the percentage of research focused on this area fluctuated in the 2005–2010 period and then decreased in the last period.

3.5. Methods of investigation

Another way to assess the body of knowledge about RIS research is according to the methods of investigation employed (Table 5). Each article is classified according to the sampling design, the channel employed to collect data, the type of analysis conducted and the analytical procedures performed with the data. While many RIS studies use mix methods, in order to classify the articles we have taken into consideration only the main method employed and registered in each one.

Considering the sampling methods, we identify two main types of design: 'non-probability sampling' and 'probability sampling'. Articles with non-probability designs include those in which the sampling does not include random selection. In contrast, articles with sampling designs infer the results obtained for a subset analysed to the whole population. The aim of probability sampling is to calculate the chance of obtaining a particular effect in the studied group. More than half of the articles (53.4%) have a non-probability sampling design. The number of articles with a non-probability sampling design increased in the second period but declined in the 2011–2015 period. About one-third of the articles reviewed adopt probability sampling in their research

Table 5. Study methodology of RIS research.

Study methodology	Total (n = 292) %	Time period			Trend direction[a]
		1998–2004 (n = 44) %	2005–2010 (n = 103) %	2011–2015 (n = 145) %	
Sampling design					
Probability	33.5	36.3	33.0	33.1	V
Non-probability	53.4	59.0	66.9	42.0	ʌ
Not available	13.0	4.5	–	24.8	V
Data collection					
Secondary information	31.5	40.9	41.7	21.3	ʌ
Existing databases	32.5	29.5	26.2	37.9	V
Mail survey	8.2	15.9	5.8	7.5	V
Telephone survey	2.4	2.2	0.9	3.4	V
Personal interviews	22.2	11.3	22.3	25.5	↑
Other	3.0	–	2.9	4.1	↑
Data analysis					
Qualitative	47.6	45.4	54.3	43.4	ʌ
Quantitative	33.5	40.9	31.0	33.1	V
Modelling (formula)	18.8	13.6	14.5	23.4	↑
Analytical technique					
Descriptive	58.9	59.0	62.1	56.5	ʌ
Uni-/bivariate	2.4	4.5	1.9	2.0	V
Multivariate	38.0	34.0	35.9	40.6	↑
Other	0.6	2.2	–	0.6	V

[a](↑) Increasing; (↓) decreasing; (ʌ) increasing and then decreasing; (V) decreasing and then increasing.

design (33.5%) and their number has slightly decreased over the different periods investigated.

With respect to data collection, about one-third of the articles rely on 'secondary information' (31.5%), another third use 'existing databases' (32.5%) to obtain data that are usually analysed statistically. 'Personal interviews' account for 22.2% of the articles reviewed, but the percentage of this type of article has increased over time. Of the remainder, 8.2% used 'mail surveys' and 2.4% 'telephone surveys' to collect data.

'Qualitative' analysis is used in a large proportion of studies (47.6%). The number of articles employing 'qualitative' analysis increased in the 2005–2010 period and declined in the last period. Quantitative analysis accounts for one-third of the articles (33.5%), followed by 'formula modelling' (18.8%), with the number of articles using the latter increasing over time.

Finally, considering the analytical techniques used, 'descriptive' studies are used in a large proportion of RIS studies (58.9%), followed by 'multivariate analyses', which have increased over time.

3.6. Structure of the RIS research

We now consider the content dimension of the RIS literature, which we classified as falling into six areas: (1) stakeholders involved, (2) trust and informal relationship, (3) type of relationships, (4) innovation process, (5) intermediaries and (6) research topics investigated.

3.6.1. Stakeholders

One-fifth of the articles focus on 'triple-helix' relationships between firms, universities or other knowledge organizations and public institutions (22.6%). The number of articles in this category has increased over time. Articles that deal only with 'firms' account for 11.3%, with a peak in the 1998–2004 period, since when they have decreased remarkably. A reason for this decrease may be that there is now a better understanding of the logic of regional innovation systems and the three subsystems – productive, knowledge generator and institutional – of which they are composed. A large proportion of articles deal with regions in which 'only firms and knowledge stakeholders' participate (54.1%). Those knowledge centres can be not only universities, but also research centres and vocational training centres. The proportion or articles dealing with this type of stakeholder is decreasing as a result of the increasing trend in the number of articles dealing with triple-helix relationships which mainly focus on knowledge exchange, without mentioning the role of policy-making.

3.6.2. Relationships

We establish four different categories of relationships. Articles whose focus is on 'value chain relationships'[4] (35.6%) concentrate mainly on client–supplier connections. This focus is most common among articles dealing with firms in the first period (1998–2004). In contrast, hardly any articles deal with 'competition' and 'coopetition' within RISs. Those dealing with competition (4.4%) have decreased over time, while those dealing with coopetition only appear in the third period. Finally, two-fifths (41.7%) of the articles deal with 'cooperative' relationships between all the stakeholders.

3.6.3. Trust and informal relationships

An interesting dimension in the RIS field is informal relationships, social capital, values and trust. Although comparative and statistical articles (68.4%) do not focus on this issue, the individual case studies (31.5%) do explicitly mention the 'importance of trust' in shaping territorial cohesion, and the trend has increased over time, from 22.7% of the articles discussing this issue in the 1998–2004 period to 34.4% for the 2011–2015 period.

3.6.4. Innovation process

Articles discussing innovation processes focus on three themes: 'R&D', 'technological innovation' and 'non-technological innovation'.[5] Most studies focus on R&D (50.3%) and technological innovation (29.4%). Interest in non-technological innovation is marginal, with only 2% of the articles focusing on it. There is very little variation in these trends over time.

3.6.5. Intermediaries

Intermediaries constitute another aspect of interest in the RIS literature. About 13.7% of RIS articles examine 'knowledge support organizations' – knowledge brokers, gatekeepers, etc. – and 9.9% examine 'knowledge-intensive business services (KIBS)'. The number of articles that examine these two types of organizations has grown gradually over time. A small number of articles focus on 'financial services', including venture capital organizations (4.1%).

3.6.6. Research topics

We have identified eight different research topics in the RIS articles based on the authors' knowledge of the research field as well as other reviews on RIS. Although articles may deal with more than one topic, we have classified and registered each article attending to the principal issue discussed by the authors. A quarter of the articles offer a case study of an RIS in a given context ('RIS examples', 26%). This focus seems to be decreasing over time, from nearly two-fifths (38.6%) in the first period to less than a quarter (22.7%) in the third. The same trend is observed in articles focused on 'networks and cooperation' (9.5%). This group includes articles whose focus is on cooperative relationships between different organizations inside and organizations outside the RIS under investigation. Articles that focus on policies to strengthen ties between stakeholders are included in this section. Nevertheless, the majority of articles dealing with the role of 'governance and policies' (16.7%) in promoting RIS are included in the same category. These articles deal with decentralized political systems and the ways in which regional governments or public development support regional innovation. The number of articles focused on this topic has remained static over the years. We also include two topics linked to knowledge and spillovers. The first, involving 'higher education institutions (HEI) and knowledge' (13.3%), includes works describing the participation of universities, research centres and vocational training centres in the knowledge generation of the RIS. It also includes the participation of KIBS, which also contribute to the generation of new knowledge. The number of articles on this topic has increased remarkably, from 6.8% in the first period to 15.8% in the third. The second group of articles deals with knowledge bases and 'knowledge spillovers' (6.8%). Studies on this topic have increased over time, but they do not represent a significant percentage of RIS research for the 2011–2015 period.

Another important category is the 'evaluation of RIS' (10.2%), with its prevalence increasing over time, nearly doubling from 6.82% in the first period to 11.7% in the third. Some articles describe the importance and problems that geographical as well as technological proximity may have, including the possible creation of lock-in effects. These publications are grouped under 'proximity and related variety' (9.5%). Within this group, the number of articles discussing the evolution of RIS has increased. Although there were only 2 articles on this issue for each of the first and second periods, there were 12 in the third. Finally, 7.5% of the articles deal with 'innovation intermediaries', with an increase in the third period in particular (9.6%), due to the appearance of a new trend linked to innovation intermediaries, gatekeepers and other types of mediators (Table 6).

4. Discussion

Based on the six key dimensions analysed, several interesting findings have emerged. First, although the number of RIS publications has increased over time, RIS research has not

Table 6. Structure of the RIS research.

Thematic areas	Total (n = 292) %	Time period 1998–2004 (n = 44) %	2005–2010 (n = 103) %	2010–2015 (n = 145) %	Trend direction[a]
Stakeholders					
Firms	11.3	22.7	8.7	9.6	∨
Firms + knowledge organization	54.1	65.9	54.3	50.3	↓
Firms + knowledge organization + public administration	22.6	11.3	24.2	24.8	↑
Not mentioned	11.9	–	12.6	15.1	↑
Relationships					
Value chain	35.6	27.2	41.7	33.7	∧
Cooperation	41.7	40.9	39.8	43.4	∨
Competition	4.4	13.6	3.8	2.07	↓
Coopetition	0.6	–	–	1.3	↑
Not mentioned	17.4	18.1	14.5	19.3	∨
Trust and informal relationships					
Important feature	31.5	22.7	31.0	34.4	↑
Not important feature	68.4	77.2	68.9	65.5	↓
Innovation process					
R&D	50.3	43.1	54.3	49.6	∧
Tech. innovation	29.4	36.3	28.1	28.2	∨
Non-tech. innovation	2.1	2.2	3.8	0.7	∧
Not mentioned	18.1	18.1	13.5	21.3	∨
Intermediaries					
KIBS	9.9	4.5	8.7	12.4	↑
Knowledge support org.	13.7	9.0	13.5	15.1	↑
Financial services	4.1	4.5	3.8	4.1	∨
Others	5.1	2.2	5.8	5.5	∧
Not mentioned	67.1	79.5	67.9	62.7	↓
Research topics					
Governance & policy	16.7	18.1	16.5	16.5	∨
HEI & knowledge	13.3	6.8	12.6	15.8	↑
Innovation intermediaries	7.5	4.5	5.8	9.6	↑
Knowledge spillovers	6.8	2.2	7.7	7.5	∧
Networks & cooperation	9.5	15.9	9.7	7.5	↓
Proximity & related variety	9.5	6.8	12.6	8.2	∧
RIS evaluation	10.2	6.8	9.7	11.7	↑
RIS examples	26.0	38.6	25.2	22.7	↓

[a](↑) Increasing; (↓) decreasing; (∧) increasing and then decreasing; (∨) decreasing and then increasing.

received much exposure, and its impact on the academic community has remained limited. Only a small number of journals have been instrumental in generating and disseminating knowledge on RIS. In particular, two journals – 'European Planning Studies' and 'Regional Studies' – have published about 22.5% of all empirical RIS research.[6] There are also very few articles that have been published in highly ranked journals. The journal with the highest impact factor that has published RIS research is 'Research Policy'.[7] A high number of empirical articles have been published in journals that are not indexed (i.e. in the Social Science Citation Index). Finally, the lack of exposure and impact of RIS research can also be related to the absence of research networks and of a cohesive group of RIS scholars who drive the field. Leading scholars in the RIS field in the early period have retired or moved to other fields, while new scholars entering the field have proposed new approaches and studies on the ways geography can explain (or not) innovation, criticizing the early literature for relying too much – and often exclusively – on regional factors when explaining the success of innovation and economic development.

Second, while Europe still dominates the production of RIS research, it lost ground during 2011–2015 to Asia, which has become an important focus of empirical studies. The results reveal not only a major acceleration in publications from the Business/Management discipline, but also that this discipline dominates the production of RIS research. This result might be intriguing but it is not. It reveals in fact the importance in Business/Management contribution to the RIS field in investigating the theoretical, managerial and political implications of entrepreneurial innovation in different social, economic and institutional contexts. RIS research taps into other academic disciplines as well.

Third, the design of RIS research is mainly exploratory, although formalized research is gaining in popularity, as is evident in the increasing number of RIS papers that have predetermined hypotheses. RIS research continues to oscillate between descriptive and causal variable association. It also relies heavily on cross-sectional studies and rarely employs longitudinal designs. Observational study is the most commonly used data-collection method, and there is a strong emphasis on case studies.

Fourth, RIS research focuses largely on single-region studies. Consequently, this focus limits the transferability of the observations made in the literature and reveals the difficulty involved in producing studies that are strictly comparable across different national contexts, as well as the need for such studies. The predominant geographical focus of the studies has been regions in Europe, although the scope has been broadened to regions in Asia, and particularly in China. This result is in line with the fact that the RIS field has been shaped by a few research networks, mainly in Europe, consisting of connected researchers whose focus has been on 'successful' regions. A large majority of articles focus on regions in industrialized countries, although the number of articles on regions in newly industrialized and, to a lesser extent, developing countries has increased over time. Although there is no consensus on the types of regions most conducive to innovation, RIS research shows a greater interest in metropolitan than in peripheral/rural regions. This may partly reflect the view that metropolitan regions provide the most propitious environment for innovation systems to develop and grow.

Fifth, the methodologies employed in RIS research are quite diverse. A large percentage of RIS research uses non-probability sampling. Data collection oscillates between secondary information and existing databases – like the Community Innovation Surveys – but remains consistent over time. The use of personal interviews has increased over time, which could be a result of researchers' desire to gain in-depth knowledge of the conditions and mechanisms that are conducive to innovation at the regional level. Qualitative methods and descriptive analysis are used in a large proportion of RIS studies, while the use of more sophisticated statistical methods (modelling) and advanced techniques of analysis (multivariate analysis) continues to grow.

Sixth, the analysis of the thematic areas investigated in empirical RIS studies paints a picture from which, on its own, it is difficult to draw a clear conclusion about the state of RIS research. The review has identified several differences relating to the RIS research topics. Some of the topics are gaining in popularity (HEI; innovation and knowledge intermediaries; RIS evaluation), while others are declining (RIS examples; networks and collaborations). RIS research investigating regional actors focuses on the whole range of stakeholders involved in innovation in a region, with a particular emphasis on firms and knowledge organizations. The RIS research field is still dominated by a focus on two major issues – the role of different organizations in producing and disseminating knowledge and the way those organizations interact with each other, and R&D and technological innovation. Interest in trust and informal relationships appears to be increasing, but the number of articles dealing with these topics remains marginal. The same holds true for interest in some aspects related to intermediaries, including knowledge support organizations and KIBS. For example, although RIS research emphasizes the key components in RIS (firms, universities), the characteristics common to RIS (knowledge, innovation, networks) and the factors conducive to their development and growth (proximity, culture, trust), there is still room for further development in the RIS research field, for instance on the understanding of the role and impact of service industries and non-technological forms of innovation. And while KIBS have been conceptualized as an important key component in RIS, their role and contribution in RIS remains largely unexamined. Similarly, despite the documented diversity of sectors and regions, RIS research strongly favours the productive system (firms and industry), and studies that focus on other components typically neglect to investigate the contribution and impact of intermediaries as key actors within the RIS.

5. Conclusions

This review has examined an extensive body of research that attempts to explain the uneven geography of innovation and the factors that shape the innovation capacities of regions, but it also reveals major gaps that can be viewed as future research opportunities. The first is that an accepted model of RIS and the different processes that lead to its development and growth must be developed. The extant literature is quick to indicate the difficulties involved in creating such a model, since there is a large variety of regional landscapes, resulting from, among other things, their different national and local histories, political logics and functions. One must recognize the differences that exist within the various types of organizations (firms, knowledge-creation and knowledge-diffusion organizations), the variety of knowledge links and interactive learning within these organizations and the significant differences between the institutional and social contexts in different regions. One key ambiguity is that RIS research has been problematized and theorized around stylized facts and the general belief that RIS can develop more easily in (metropolitan) regions that have built their competitive advantage from particular kinds of localized learning, which are functionally integrated in Marshallian agglomeration economies. This belief has led RIS research to fail to take into account newer approaches that acknowledge the diversity of pathways that can be adopted by non-metropolitan regions, and in particular approaches that seek to make sense of growth paths in peripheral and rural regions.

Another ambiguity relates to practical advice and the way RIS research can serve as a foundation to help and guide policymakers. Research on RIS is strongly linked to the policy mission to build and upgrade the knowledge base of a region and the interactions among different private and public stakeholders. This puts the development and implementation of policy tools at the forefront of much RIS research. Nonetheless, policy-makers who want to start or improve their strategic priorities and programmes to better support an innovative environment will find only limited help from the available RIS literature. This situation may be a result of the fact that most RIS researchers show that there is no one-size-fits-all policy that can be applied to any region. The basic argument is that regions differ, and that policies therefore need to be adjusted to the specificities of the industrial context, innovation culture and governance structure of the region. The key question that cannot be avoided is: 'how can RIS research handle the challenge of both developing coherent theoretical categories and developing policy strategies for building RIS?' One can certainly speculate that this 'all-embracing' mission is another reason that we lack a good definition on what an RIS actually is, let alone a 'standard' model for the main mechanism for RIS development. We do not have a response to this question, but the discussion here on RIS shares affinities with the discussion on the related concept of industry cluster, whose 'elasticity', as Njøs, Jakobsen, Aslesen, and Fløysand (2016) have argued, makes it difficult to develop a common definition of what a cluster is and how policies can be used to promote it.

The second research gap is the 'true' evolutionary dimension of RIS and the factors that can influence and impact the transformation of RIS. Most of the literature adopts static and comparative static models to explain the elements and conditions that trigger knowledge-generation processes and innovation capabilities. RIS research would benefit from adopting a more dynamic approach that would consider RIS as real, complex evolutionary systems wherein new actors can emerge and/or the roles of 'traditional' actors can mutate, thereby affecting the production, commercialization and business models that can considered appropriate for a given region. In particular, one key dimension that deserves attention is the extent to which wider structures in a given RIS (organizations, networks and knowledge) influence and impact on the RIS itself, but also on its future development.

Last but not least, RIS research has primarily explored how regions generate the conditions conducive to innovation. Most RIS research has focused on how regional dynamics foster firm-level innovation, but it has not systematically explored the benefits of innovation at the regional level. As a result, the RIS literature is nearly silent on the conditions that enable growth to accrue in regions where innovation occurs, often assuming that the conditions conducive to innovation will automatically lead to growth. RIS research would benefit from a better understanding of the extent to which local innovation is associated with regional economic growth and the transformation and mutations of RISs.

To conclude, these propositions should deepen and broaden our theoretical understanding of the development and application of RISs and provide direction in attempting to respond to these important questions.

Notes

1. The complete list of articles, both theoretical and empirical, used to conduct the review are available on request.
2. The rationale for defining six different thematic areas is based on the authors' knowledge of the RIS field and previous review papers on the topics, which proved useful in identifying the various strands in this research field.
3. Observational studies analyse the behaviour of a sample, whereas surveys are used to collect larger amounts of data.
4. Articles concerned with value chain relationships mainly discuss relationships between the firms of the productive subsystems in the RIS; those concerned with competition deal with competitors inside RIS; and those concerned with coopetition discuss the cooperative relationship between direct competitors.
5. Nearly 20 per cent of the articles do not specify the type of innovation involved.
6. For the 1998–2004 period, about one-third of all RIS empirical research was published in *European Planning Studies* and *Regional Studies*, a period when two leading scholars in the RIS field (B.T. Asheim and P. Cooke) were acting as journal editors.
7. Impact factor of 3.117 (Journal Citation Index, 2015).

Acknowledgements

The usual disclaimers apply. Additionally, we would like to acknowledge the valuable comments provided the two reviewers. Finally, we are also most thankful to Arne Isaksen and Stig-Erik Jakobsen for inviting us to contribute this special issue on a research project financed by the Research Council of Norway on path dependence and regional renewal.

Disclosure statement

No potential conflict of interest was reported by the authors.

Funding

The authors acknowledge financial support from the Social Sciences and Humanities Research Council of Canada [grant number SSHRC 410-2011-0108].

ORCiD

Igone Porto Gomez ⓘ http://orcid.org/0000-0003-2865-4818

References

Amrollahi, A., Ghapanchi, A. H., & Talaei-Khoei, A. (2013). A systematic literature review on strategic information systems planning: Insights from the past decade. *Pacific Asia Journal of the Association for Information Systems, 5*(2), 39–66. Retrieved from http://aisel.aisnet.org/pajais/vol5/iss2/4

Asheim, B. T., & Gertler, M. S. (2005). The geography of innovation: Regional innovation systems. In J. Fagerberg, D. Mowery, & R. Nelson (Eds.), *The Oxford handbook of innovation* (pp. 291–317). Oxford: Oxford University Press.

Asheim, B. T., Grillitsch, M., & Trippl, M. (2017). Regional innovation systems: Past - present – future. In R. Shearmur, C. Carrincazeaux, & D. Doloreux (Eds.), *Handbook on the geographies of innovations*. Cheltenham: Edward Elgar.

Berg, B. L. (2004). *Qualitative research methods for the social sciences* (4th ed.). Boston: Allyn and Bacon.

Boell, S. K., & Cecez-Kecmanovic, D. (2015). On being 'systematic'in literature reviews in IS. *Journal of Information Technology, 30*(2), 161–173. doi:10.1057/jit.2014.26

Boschma, R. (2005). Proximity and innovation: A critical assessment. *Regional Studies, 39*(1), 61–74. doi:10.1080/0034340052000320887

Braczyk, H. J., Cooke, P., & Heidenreich, M. (Eds.). (1998). *Regional innovation systems: The role of governance in a globalised world* (1st ed.). London: UCL Press.

Carrincazeaux, C., & Gaschet, F. (2015). Regional innovation systems and economic performance: Between regions and nations. *European Planning Studies, 23*(2), 262–291. doi:10.1080/09654313.2013.861809

Cooke, P. (1992). Regional innovation systems: Competitive regulation in the new Europe. *Geoforum, 23*(3), 365–382. doi:10.1016/0016-7185(92)90048-9

Cooke, P., Heidenreich, M., & H. J. Braczyk (Eds.). (2004). *Regional innovation systems* (2nd ed.). London: Routledge.

Cooke, P., Uranga, M. G., & Etxebarria, G. (1998). Regional systems of innovation: An evolutionary perspective. *Environment and Planning A, 30*(9), 1563–1584. doi:10.1068/a301563

Doloreux, D. (2002). What we should know about regional systems of innovation. *Technology in Society, 24*(3), 243–263. doi:10.1016/S0160-791X(02)00007-6

Doloreux, D., & Parto, S. (2005).Regional innovation systems: Current discourse and unresolved issues. *Technology in Society, 27*(2), 133–153. doi:10.1016/j.techsoc.2005.01.002

Edquist, C. (2005). Systems of innovation: Perspectives and challenges. In J. Fagerberg, D. Mowery, & R. Nelson (Eds.), *Oxford handbook of innovation* (pp. 181–208). Oxford: Oxford University Press.

Gomes, E., Barnes, B. R., & Mahmood, T. (2016). A 22 year review of strategic alliance research in the leading management journals. *International Business Review, 25*(1), 15–27. doi:10.1016/j.ibusrev.2014.03.005

Isaksen, A., & Trippl, M. (2016). Exogenously led and policy-supported new path development in peripheral regions: Analytical and synthetic routes. *Economic Geography*, 1–22. doi:10.1080/00130095.2016.1154443

Leonidou, L. C., Barnes, B. R., Spyropoulou, S., & Katsikeas, C. S. (2010). Assessing the contribution of leading mainstream marketing journals to the international marketing discipline. *International Marketing Review, 27*(5), 491–518. doi:10.1108/02651331011076563

Lundvall, B. Å. (2007). National innovation systems—analytical concept and development tool. *Industry and innovation, 14*(1), 95–119. doi:10.1080/13662710601130863

McCann, P., & Ortega-Argilés, R. (2013). Modern regional innovation policy. *Cambridge Journal of Regions, Economy and Society, 6*(2), 187–216. doi:10.1093/cjres/rst007

Njøs, R., Jakobsen, S. E., Aslesen, H. W., & Fløysand, A. (2016). Encounters between cluster theory, policy and practice in Norway: Hubbing, blending and conceptual stretching. *European Urban and Regional Studies, 6*, 1–16. doi:10.1177/0969776416655860

Shearmur, R. (2015). Far from the madding crowd: Slow innovators, information value, and the geography of innovation. *Growth and Change, 46*(3), 424–442. doi:10.1111/grow.12097

Torre, A., & Rallet, A. (2005). Proximity and localization. *Regional Studies, 39*(1), 47–59. doi:10.1080/0034340052000320842

Tödtling, F., & Trippl, M. (2005). One size fits all? Towards a differentiated regional innovation policy approach. *Research policy, 34*(8), 1203–1219. doi:10.1016/j.respol.2005.01.018

Uyarra, E. (2010). What is evolutionary about 'regional systems of innovation'? Implications for regional policy. *Journal of Evolutionary Economics, 20*(1), 115–137. doi:10.1007/s00191-009-0135-y

Developing cross-industry innovation capability: regional drivers and indicators within firms

Elisabet S. Hauge, Nina Kyllingstad, Natalia Maehle and Ann Camilla Schulze-Krogh

ABSTRACT

The role of firms in the process of regional renewal and path development is a somewhat neglected area in the existing literature. With few exceptions, the literature is mainly concerned with aggregated development paths. To cover this gap, the current study turns its attention to cross-industry innovation capability (CIIC) building in firms and discusses how conditions for innovation and learning in a region drive this process. We introduce a new concept of CIIC – that is, the firm's ability to transform knowledge and ideas from different industries into new products, processes and systems and/or its ability to adapt existing products, processes and systems to new industries – and identify its drivers and indicators. The discussion is supported by empirical studies of firms in three Norwegian case regions that undergo the restructuring process due to the recent severe decrease in oil prices. Our empirical data demonstrate that organizationally thick and diversified regions are more favourable for firms' abilities to develop CIIC and cross-industry innovation activity. As a result, we emphasize that future regional policies should have a stronger focus on the linkages between internal firm characteristics and regional innovation systems to contribute to the firms' absorptive capacity for developing cross-industry innovation.

1. Introduction

The 2008 global financial and economic crisis slowed the European economy and the following recession has negatively influenced the development of many European regions. Highly specialized regions dependent on a single industry can be particularly vulnerable to economic disruptions, as a more diverse economic structure often provides greater regional resistance to shocks (Martin, 2012, 2013). Therefore, cross-industry innovation – the process where ' … existing solutions from other industries are creatively imitated and retranslated to meet the need of the company's current market and products' (Enkel & Gassmann, 2010, p. 256) – becomes an important mechanism for regional renewal. Despite the fact that variety is recognized as an important driver for regional growth and renewal, some degree of cognitive proximity (i.e. the extent to which firms share a knowledge base (Boschma, 2005)) between the industries is necessary for effective learning and knowledge spillover. A number of studies show that related variety (several related industries) positively affects regional renewal (Frenken, Van Oort, & Verburg, 2007) and innovation (Aarstad, Kvitastein, & Jakobsen, 2016). However, most of the evolutionary and systemic literature on innovation and regional renewal ignores the heterogeneity of firm practice and firms' capabilities (Boschma & Martin, 2007; Christiansen & Jakobsen, 2012; Maskell, 2001). With few exceptions (Garud, Kumaraswamy, & Karnøe, 2010; Sydow, Schreyögg, & Koch, 2009), the existing literature is mainly concerned with aggregated development paths, and there is limited knowledge about the role of firms in the process of regional renewal and path development.

To cover this gap, the current study turns its attention to cross-industry innovation capability building in firms and discusses how conditions for innovation and learning in a region drive this process. We introduce a new concept of cross-industry innovation capability (CIIC) by extending Lawson and Samson's (2001) notion of innovation capability into cross-industry settings and identify its drivers and indicators. CIIC is the firm's ability to transform knowledge and ideas from different industries into new products, processes and systems and/or its ability to adapt existing products, processes and systems to new industries. We expect that if a considerable number of firms in a region possess high CIIC, this will result in path renewal. For example, if firms in the oil-related industries diversify into new but related activities – such as shipping, aquaculture and maritime industries – that allow them to exploit existing capabilities, regional path renewal will be established. However, effective cross-industry innovation is difficult to achieve. Therefore, to enhance our understanding of what stimulates and influences cross-industry innovation, this paper addresses the following research question: What are the indicators of CIIC in firms and how is CIIC influenced by regional conditions?

Our study is based on empirical data from three Norwegian regions: Hordaland, Rogaland and Agder. Over the past 10 years, the firms in these regions have increased their investments in the oil and gas industry, becoming gradually more oil-dependent. The recent severe decrease in oil prices has had a negative impact on their industrial development and economy and led to downsizing of many firms and rising unemployment numbers (Statistics Norway, 2016a). Some policy initiatives have already tried to reduce the economic effect of the oil crisis, and the ongoing restructuring process represents an interesting case for studying cross-industry innovation. By conducting in-depth interviews with firms related to the oil and gas industry, we try to understand why they demonstrate different degrees of cross-industry innovation ability.

Based on the observations of the challenges in the oil and gas industry and the important role of firms' CIIC in the process of regional renewal, we suggest the following analytical model to emphasize our argument in this paper (see Figure 1).

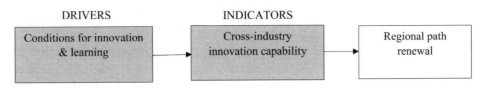

Figure 1. Analytical model.

We argue that the degree of a firm's CIIC is influenced by regional conditions for innovation and learning, which are as such the independent variable. The CIIC indicators in firms – that is, practices and processes within the firm that stimulate and reinforce cross-industry innovation (see Section 2.1) – represent the dependent variable. Arguably, there is a conditioned relationship between the drivers and the indicators. The discussion in this paper is focused on the left-hand side of the model (highlighted in grey). However, we encourage future studies to explore the right-hand side and look at the relationship between the degree of CIIC and regional path renewal. We expect that a higher degree of CIIC in firms will lead to a greater potential for regional path renewal.

This paper is structured as follows. Section 2 describes the theoretical framework. Section 3 addresses our methodological approach and research design, while we discuss the results in Section 4. Finally, we present concluding remarks, suggestions for future research and policy implications in Section 5.

2. Theoretical framework

We draw on the discussion on firms' capabilities within the business literature and the efforts within the field of evolutionary economic geography to lay the foundation of our theoretical framework. These are conditions for innovation and learning and how these influence the CIIC building in firms (see Figure 1). The current section starts with an elaboration of CIIC followed by the drivers of CIIC, which are the innovative firm and the regional context.

2.1. Cross-industry innovation capability

CIIC is defined as (1) the firm's ability to continuously transform knowledge and ideas from different industries into new products, processes and systems and/or (2) the ability to adapt existing products, processes and systems to new industries. This definition builds upon the theory of dynamic capabilities (Teece & Pisano, 1994) and the notion of innovation capability proposed by Lawson and Samson (2001). The dynamic capabilities approach focuses on how firms achieve new and innovative forms of competitive advantage and is, therefore, especially relevant for studying innovation, in particular cross-industry innovation. The main idea is that developing competitive advantage requires not only the exploitation of existing firm-specific capabilities, but also renewing them and developing new ones where cross-industry inputs might be valuable (Teece, Pisano, & Shuen, 1997).

Aligned with the dynamic capability concept, Lawson and Samson's (2001) concept of innovation capability represents a higher order integration capability, allowing the combination and management of multiple capabilities (Fuchs, Mifflin, Miller, & Whitney, 2000). We use this concept as our point of departure and adjust it to the case of cross-industry innovation where firms can either use cross-industry knowledge in the development of new products or extend to new industries with existing products. Innovation capability is defined as '(...) the ability to continuously transform knowledge and ideas into new products, processes and systems for the benefit of the firm and its stakeholders' (Lawson & Samson, 2001, p. 384). The idea is that firms with strong innovation capability achieve more effective innovation performance. Lawson and Samson (2001) argue that innovation capability is not a separately identifiable construct, but rather is composed of practices and processes within the firm that stimulate and reinforce innovation. Based on the literature on the management of innovation and best practice models, they suggest a theoretical framework, which defines the elements of innovation capability. These elements are grouped into the following seven major groups:

- Vision and strategy: Institutionalizing innovation.
- Harnessing the competence base: The ability to correctly and effectively direct resources to where they are required.
- Organizational intelligence: The capability to process, interpret, encode, manipulate and access information in a purposeful, goal-directed manner.
- Creativity and idea management: Encouraging creativity and divergent thinking at all levels.
- Structures and systems: Optimal overall formal business structure (organizational structure, reward systems, etc.).
- Culture and climate: Tolerance of ambiguity, empowered employees and creative time.
- Management of technology: Linking core technology strategies with innovation strategy and business strategy.

By understanding these innovation capabilities through the lens of cross-industry challenges and by adding the dimension of cross-industry experience, we have developed an analytical framework used to detect CIIC in firms. These indicators are shown in Table 1.

Firms' cross-industry experience is added as an eighth CIIC indicator since the literature highlights the importance of a firm's history for its performance and development (Rathe & Witt, 2001; Teece et al., 1997). In this analytical framework, the CIIC is influenced by both the modes of innovation in firms and the regional context in which they operate.

2.2. The innovative firm

Developing CIIC in firms is about combining different knowledge types and different modes of learning (Isaksen & Karlsen, 2010; Jensen, Johnson, Lorenz, & Lundvall, 2007). The logic of CIIC can be linked to core concepts within the field of economic geography and innovation research, such as STI (Science, Technology and Innovation) and DUI (Doing, Using and Interaction). Some scholars argue that the dichotomous distinction between STI and DUI, as well as between tacit and codified knowledge, is an oversimplification (e.g. Tödtling & Grillitsch, 2014). Although the concepts are useful for anticipating innovation, learning and capability building, the process of innovation and learning is far more complex. Approaches using the typology of knowledge bases have, to some extent, contributed to clarify our understanding of this complexity (Tödtling & Grillitsch, 2014).

Building upon different rationales for knowledge creation, dominance of tacit and codified knowledge, and different modes of learning and innovation (Martin, 2013), a distinction is made between three types of knowledge base. These are analytical (mainly STI based, know-what and codified knowledge), synthetic (mainly DUI, know-how and tacit knowledge) and symbolic (mainly DUI, know-who and tacit knowledge) (Asheim

Table 1. Indicators of CIIC.

Innovation capability	CIIC	Description
Vision and strategy	CIIC1: Institutionalizing cross-industry innovation as a part of a firm's strategy	• The firm has consciously chosen to focus on cross-industry innovation and states it in the strategy. • Cross-industry innovation is discussed in the firm's strategy documents and during strategy meetings.
Harnessing the competence base	CIIC2: Effective resource management combining different types of competences	• The firm is able to combine and recombine knowledge and resources from different industries, for example, develop products based on 'across-industries' knowledge and resources. • The firm combines several knowledge bases. • The firm hires employees with various professional backgrounds.
Organizational intelligence	CIIC3: Learning from different industries and modes of innovation	• Employees are encouraged to gain extra education (e.g. courses) and acquire knowledge from different related industries. • Employees are moved between departments inside the firm to learn new skills and are involved in cross-industry projects. • Combination of STI and DUI learning modes.
Creativity and idea management	CIIC4: Encouraging divergent 'across-borders' thinking	• Employees are encouraged to think 'across industries', for example, to develop products which can be sold to customers in different industries, to combine different kinds of knowledge in one product.
Structures and systems	CIIC5: Organic organizational structure breaking down barriers between different functions and product groups	• Firm's structure is very flexible and can be easily modified if necessary. • Employees are easily moved between different departments and different projects. • Employees know each other very well and can easily communicate across departments.
Culture and climate	CIIC6: Open and tolerant culture	• The firm's culture is open and everyone is motivated to suggest innovative solutions. • The firm's manager effectively facilitates communication between employees in different departments (e.g. organizes common meetings).
Management of technology	CIIC7: Management of related technologies	• The manager has 'across-industries' experience or has some knowledge of different technologies; therefore, he understands his employees in different departments and can manage related technologies successfully.
	CIIC8: Cross-industry experience	• The firm has historically been involved in cross-industry activities and/or has a cross-industry origin.

& Gertler, 2005; Asheim, Boschma, & Cooke, 2011; Cooke & Leydesdorff, 2006). Related to their structural, relational and geographical dimensions, knowledge base characteristics are used to explain how different firms innovate, as well as the nature of the different innovation networks involved (Martin, 2012). Much research seems to focus on firms with a dominant synthetic knowledge base, which frequently include engineering firms such as the ones in this study. Many of these firms are characterized by the DUI mode of innovation and user–producer interaction. In line with cross-industry innovation, more recent approaches have stressed the need for combining different knowledge bases to increase firms' innovation performance (Tödtling & Grillitsch, 2014). A study by Grillitsch et al. (2014) provides evidence that firms perform better and are more innovative if they combine different types of knowledge and that '(...) firm-internal competencies related to symbolic knowledge (design competencies) and analytical or synthetic knowledge (product and process development competencies) have a significant positive effect on the innovativeness of firms' (as cited in Tödtling & Grillitsch, 2014, p. 1743).

2.3. Regional context

Firms that operate in a regional context are often referred to as the regional innovation system (RIS) in the literature. Isaksen and Trippl (2014, p. 5) describe a RIS as '(...) a specific framework in which close inter-firm interactions, knowledge and policy support infrastructure and socio-cultural and institutional environments serve to stimulate collective learning, continuous innovation and entrepreneurial activity'. Moreover, Isaksen and Nilsson (2013) conceptualize RISs in terms of (a) the production structure, (b) the knowledge infrastructure and (c) the support structure. The theoretical construct of a RIS has been further elaborated by adding dimensions of specialization and dominating modes of innovation, the latter referring to either STI or DUI (Isaksen & Trippl, 2014).

Isaksen and Trippl (2014) have developed a typology of different RISs characterized as (1) organizationally thick and diversified RIS, (2) organizationally thick and specialized RIS and (3) organizationally thin RIS. This typology explains different paths to regional development (Isaksen & Trippl, 2014). The first type of RIS (1) includes well-performing regions, with a relatively large number of different industries and a high density of R&D institutions and support organizations. The second type of RIS (2) has a highly specialized support infrastructure and a more narrow industry structure with a small number of dominant industries. The final type of RIS (3) has less developed support and knowledge infrastructure, including no or weakly developed industrial clusters. The latter RIS is often dominated by traditional industries with a DUI mode of innovation (Isaksen & Trippl, 2014).

The different types of RISs relate to different regional industrial development in terms of the production system, knowledge infrastructure and support structure. In thick and diverse RISs, the knowledge infrastructure is well developed and supported by a diverse support structure. We thereby assume that the conditions for stimulating CIIC development in firms are better in such RISs compared to that in more thick and specialized RISs. The existence of a variety of firms within different sectors increases the opportunity for cross-industry collaboration. In addition, a rich knowledge infrastructure is assumed to stimulate a varied knowledge base among regional actors, compared to thinner RISs.

Table 2. Comparison of the case regions.

	Hordaland	Rogaland	Agder
Production system	Diversified production system	Specialized production system	Specialized production system
Knowledge infrastructure	5 educational institutions and 22 R&D institutes	4 educational institutions and 7 R&D institutes	1 educational institution and 5 R&D institutes
Support structure	15 RCN[a] supported programmes/projects	Five RCN supported programmes/projects	Four RCN supported programmes/projects
RIS classification	Thick and diversified RIS	Thick and specialized RIS	Thick and specialized RIS

[a]The Research Council of Norway.

Based on the RIS theory (Isaksen & Nilsson, 2013; Isaksen & Trippl, 2014), we compare firms in three regions according to the following characteristics: production system, knowledge infrastructure and support structure (see Table 2). The production system is evaluated in terms of percentage distribution of established companies within selected European industrial activity classification codes (NACE 02) (see Appendix 1). The knowledge infrastructure is a frequency count of educational institutions and R&D institutes established within the region, and the support structure is evaluated in terms of funding from the Research Council of Norway's main programmes for enhancing innovation activity. The following programmes are included: Centres for Research-based Innovation (SFI), Norwegian Centre of Excellence (SFF), Centres for Environment-friendly Energy Research (FME), National centres of expertise (NCE), Global centres of expertise (GCE) and the Arena programme. As a result, we regard Hordaland as a thicker and more diversified region compared to Rogaland and Agder, which are regarded as thick and specialized RISs. The significant difference in knowledge infrastructure, support structure and industry structure in Hordaland, compared to Rogaland and Agder, is one of the main explanations for why Hordaland is regarded as a diversified RIS.

Table 2 illustrates the regional context in which the firms operate. This context, together with different modes of innovation in firms, is argued to influence firms' innovation possibility space and, therefore, be the driver for developing CIIC. We also assume that firms developing CIIC are beneficial for path renewal and path creation (Frenken & Boschma, 2007; Isaksen & Trippl, 2014; Martin & Sunley, 2006). The theory of path dependency emphasizes that the decisions business actors face at any given circumstance are limited by the decisions one has made in the past, even though past circumstances may no longer be relevant (Praeger, 2007); that is, choices made in the past influence subsequent choices (Schienstock, 2007). Therefore, firms making decisions to improve CIIC are better equipped to contribute to new path development, and avoid the fallacy of organizational lock-in.

3. Research design

The regional context for the current study is three Norwegian regions, namely, Hordaland, Rogaland and Agder. The rationale behind the choice of firms in these specific regions is that they act as representatives of firms and regions that were greatly influenced by the reduction in oil prices in Norway at the end of 2014. Thus, they are in need of organizational restructuring and look for opportunities to extend into other industries. This makes these firms interesting to study from the cross-industry perspective.

Hordaland is located on the western coast of Norway and has 516,497 inhabitants (Statistics Norway, 2016b). It has multiple industries and many small and medium-sized companies with long traditions of doing business internationally and a vibrant research and educational environment. Rogaland is located on the south-west coast of Norway and has 470,175 inhabitants. The industry in Rogaland is specialized, with both primary industries such as agriculture and fishing and the mining and petroleum industries playing an important role on a national scale. The research and educational environment is less developed than in Hordaland. Agder is located on the southern coast of Norway and has 298,486 inhabitants (Statistics Norway, 2016b). As a region with a long history of traditional industries, Agder is highly dependent on the oil industry and is referred to as the 'drilling bay' because of its many sub-suppliers to the drilling division of the oil industry. The region has the least developed research and educational environment of the case regions. The different regional characteristics may indicate different reactions to the current decline, and as such represent interesting cases to study.

Studying CIIC assumes a research strategy that 'follows the actors' and explores how actions become possible, for example, through common learning processes initiated by both short-term and long-term interaction, cooperation and networking. Such an approach helps explore how actors themselves experience (and enact) complex processes, for example, establishing and developing collaborative relationships. Therefore, the current study is characterized by an explorative design and uses a qualitative research method.

3.1. Data collection: semi-structured interviews

To select the firms for the analysis, we used the following two main criteria: firm's size (small or medium) and connection to the oil and gas industry. These more or less similar firms were chosen to advance our understanding of how prepared they are when faced with changes in the oil and gas industry. As a result, 15 firms (5 from each region) were selected for the analysis.

We chose to use semi-structured interviews to explore our research question, because they enable us to acquire a deep, meaningful understanding of the firms' CIIC construct (McCracken, 1988). The interviews lasted between 50 and 90 minutes, and the interview guide was developed based on the theory of innovation capability (Lawson & Samson, 2001), RISs and modes of innovation, as discussed in Sections 2 and 3. In Hordaland, interview questions were designed to cover all the characteristics of each CIIC indicator (see Table 1). For example, the firms were asked the following questions to evaluate the presence of CIIC1: (1) Is it the firm's deliberate strategy to innovate across industries? (2) Is cross-industry innovation discussed in the corporate strategy documents? (3) Do you discuss cross-industry innovation at strategy meetings? In Rogaland and Agder, the questions were formulated slightly differently, without using the 'cross-industry' label. However, they were also designed to detect different indicators of CIIC.

3.2. Analysis procedure

Data analysis began by identifying the characteristics of the eight indicators of CIIC in the 15 firms. This was done by applying a retroductive strategy where we tried to establish the existence of causal mechanisms and structures (Blaikie, 2009), by linking the evidence (induction) of CIIC to existing theory (deduction) in a dynamic process. Yes/no questions were formulated for each CIIC indicator to ease the process of identifying the characteristics in the interview transcripts (see Appendix 2). Some of the CIIC indicators are more complex than others, and therefore require more than one yes/no question. Then the researchers went through the interview transcripts to determine whether there was any evidence of the characteristics of CIIC indicators in the interviewed firms. A cross in a data-analysis table (see Table 3) signified evidence of a CIIC indicator in the interview transcript.

Table 3. Identifying CIIC (data-analysis table).

Regions	Firms	CIIC1	CIIC2	CIIC3	CIIC4	CIIC5	CIIC6	CIIC7	CIIC8	CIIC classification
HORDALAND	A	X	X	X	X	X	X		X	Strong
	B	X	X	X	X	X	X	X	X	Strong
	C	X	X	X			X		X	Moderate
	D	X	X	X	X	X	X	X	X	Strong
	E	X	X	X		X	X	X	X	Strong
AGDER	A	X		X		X	X			Moderate
	B			X		X				Weak
	C	X	X	X			X		X	Moderate
	D			X				X	X	Weak
	E					X		X	X	Weak
ROGALAND	A		X	X			X	X		Moderate
	B		X	X						Weak
	C	X	X			X		X		Moderate
	D							X		Weak
	E					X	X			Weak

During this identification stage, all authors were involved in cross-checks and discussions to increase the validity and reliability of the data analysis. Firstly, each author independently identified the evidence of a CIIC indicator in each interview transcript, and then all authors jointly discussed this evidence. For example, statements such as[1] 'For us it's important to have versatile (all-round) employees, because dependent upon project, customer or industry, we need to show flexibility' (CEO of firm B in Hordaland) provided the evidence of CIIC5: 'Organic organisational breaking down barriers separating different functions and product groups'. CIIC1 'Institutionalised cross-industry innovation as part of firm's strategy' was identified by statements such as 'Today offshore is 90% of the market strategy, including onshore and subsea. However, we have also done work within shipping and construction. Now we see a potential in mining and nuclear. It's a sea of opportunities' (CEO of firm C in Agder). Any discrepancies in classification were discussed until the authors agreed upon the number of CIIC indicators identified for each firm. Insights provided by such discussions are highly valued in content analysis and qualitative research (Welch, Piekkari, Plakoyiannaki, & Paavilainen-Mäntymäki, 2011). The author team followed these steps systematically for each firm. Finally, the authors performed a 'frequency count'. If a firm possessed one to three CIIC indicators, it was identified as weak on the CIIC classification. Four to five CIIC indicators resulted in a moderate CIIC classification, and finally a firm with six to eight CIIC indicators was identified as strong in CIIC (see Table 3).

4. Results and discussion

Table 3 presents the results of our data analysis. Four of the interviewed firms have high CIIC, five have a moderate level of CIIC and the rest are weak on CIIC.

The data analysis reveals the following regional patterns. Most of the firms in the Hordaland region (four out of five) demonstrate strong CIIC, while the firms in the Agder and Rogaland regions show moderate or weak CIIC. Firms with weak CIIC dominate in both the Agder and Rogaland regions (three out of five firms in each). This finding indicates that regional settings may influence the degree of CIIC among firms. All the regions in our study are organizationally thick. However, the Hordaland region is more diversified, while Rogaland and Agder are more specialized in terms of industrial structure. This may explain our findings and will be further discussed in the following.

4.1. Indicators of CIIC

Regional growth and innovativeness are determined by both systemic factors (e.g. RISs) and internal firm factors (indicators) (Nauwelaers, 2011). The majority of the cases in our study demonstrate some degree of CIIC by combining DUI and STI innovation modes (see Table 3). However, to strengthen firms with a DUI-dominated knowledge base, their access to STI knowledge has to be stimulated. Firms dominated by the STI mode of innovation would benefit from stimulating more DUI-based innovation processes.

The following practices are typical for firms with a high degree of CIIC indicators. For example, firms scoring on CIIC1 highlight the importance of strategic choices: 'It was a conscious choice. We never intended to rely on just the oil and gas industry, even if that is where we started' (firm B, Hordaland). This demonstrates the significance of institutionalizing cross-industry innovation as a part of a firm's strategy. Moreover, hiring employees with different backgrounds leads to more effective resource management due to the combination of different competences. Therefore, it is important for CIIC2: 'We have chemists, opticians, and employees who studied instrumentation. And it is our conscious choice' (firm E, Hordaland). CIIC3 is characterized, among other things, by a combination of different learning modes: 'Subcontractors are important ... If we have an idea we should go to the workshop to see the most reasonable way to produce it ... Collaboration with University of Agder is also important for us ... And to some degree NTNU' (firm A, Agder). As we can see, many firms with a high degree of CIIC focus on building collaborations with other firms and research institutions to learn from different industries and modes of innovation. Encouraging employees to work and think across industries is crucial for developing divergent 'across-borders' thinking which is indicated by CIIC4: 'Employees are motivated to innovate across industries. We are not a kind of company which is locked in a specific industry ... ' (firm B, Hordaland). Moreover, it is important to make employees think and collaborate across functions. Therefore, the easy transfer of employees between departments is a typical example of CIIC5: 'Right now one from the electronics department works in the software department, and a little back and forth' (firm D, Hordaland). Firms having such organic organizational structure with low barriers between different functions and product groups motivate employees to work together across departments. A high level of employee-driven innovation is also essential and indicates the presence of CIIC6: 'In every new project (employees) seek to improve what they have done earlier ... to be better. Find new solutions, cheaper solutions, more lasting solutions ... ' (firm E, Rogaland). It is one of the conditions for having an open and tolerant culture leading to more engaged and innovative employees. Firms with managers with cross-industry background and experience possess high CIIC7: 'I am a civil engineer from Denmark and have MBA from the USA. Before working in the oil and gas industry I worked in Denmark with maritime projects' (CEO, firm A, Rogaland). Having experience with managing related technologies can be an important factor for successful cross-industry activities. Finally, the historical aspect is important, so the firms having cross-industry experience usually possess a higher degree of CIIC. For example, firms' cross-industry background is one of the conditions for CIIC8: 'The idea is coming from the shipyard business ... The purpose was to move from the defence industry to the oil and gas industry ... ' (firm D, Agder). For further examples, see Appendix 3.

There are variations in what kind of CIIC indicators are most common and most rare in firms. Only three of the interviewed firms encourage 'across-border thinking' among their employees. At the same time, most firms (eleven) score on CIIC3: 'Learning from different industries and modes of innovation'. A majority of the firms scored here due to their combined modes of innovation, including both STI and DUI. The rest of the CIIC indicators are represented in eight to nine firms in our study. Our findings also indicate which indicators are the most critical for developing high CIIC. For example, all firms that have cross-industry innovation as an explicit part of their strategy have moderate or high CIIC. This shows that institutionalizing cross-industry innovation in firm strategy helps firms to focus on developing CIIC; it needs to be present to develop a high CIIC level.

Firms' CIICs may stimulate and encourage a more diverse knowledge base. We argue that micro-level perspectives such as CIIC are in fact important for our understanding of the bigger picture of regional industrial growth and resilience.

4.2. CIIC and regional context

The current study indicates that different RISs and conditions for innovation and learning in firms influence firms' absorptive capacity for developing CIIC. In Hordaland, the RIS characteristics in combination with the identified CIIC indicators implicate that these regional firms are better equipped to address economic decline. The reason for this is twofold. Firstly, diversified industrial structures are favourable conditions for knowledge flow and cross-industry collaboration (Asheim et al., 2011). Combinatorial knowledge bases and industry cross-overs are seen as imperative for diversification processes (Trippl, Grillitsch, & Isaksen, 2015). Secondly, self-reinforcing mechanisms in organizations and firms can lead to organizational path dependency (Sydow et al., 2009). Organizational path dependency may lead to lock-in, where inefficiency is characterized by a limited scope of actions and activities (Sydow et al., 2009). Firms inherently focused upon cross-industry innovation are better equipped to avoid organizational path dependency. Examples of how cross-industry innovation is reliant upon the regional context are evident in the interview data. For example, firm A in Hordaland explained that they actively use local clusters (e.g. GCE Subsea) to build their contact network and 'it is all about using the networking opportunities in Bergen to find resources'. Firm B in Hordaland also highlights the importance of local networks and mentions their participation in the 'Climate partners' network, where many firms in Hordaland meet to discuss 'what challenges large companies in Hordaland meet in relation to their carbon footprint and climate impact'. Firm D in Hordaland actively involves the local university by providing student internships and later recruiting them for permanent positions: 'Most of our employees come from University of Bergen'. Firm E in Hordaland also recruits students from various local educational institutions: 'We recruit from both Norwegian School of Economics, University of Bergen and Bergen University College, from different disciplines'. These quotes demonstrate that firms in Hordaland are actively using the available regional infrastructure to build their CIIC and in this way benefit from their location in a more diversified region. For instance, the well-developed support infrastructure in

Hordaland (e.g. industrial clusters and local networks) facilitates more extensive collaboration between firms in the region. This collaboration between diversified firms leads to learning from different industries and modes of innovation, which is an important condition for building CIIC. Moreover, close relationships with various research institutions working within different disciplines encourage learning and creative 'across-borders' thinking that are essential for developing strong CIIC.

Specialized regions, such as Agder and Rogaland, with firms less focused on cross-industry innovation, differ from the more diversified regions. Organizationally thick and specialized RISs lack crucial elements for new path development, for example, diversity of industries, combinatory knowledge bases, and a well-developed support and knowledge infrastructure. A majority of the oil and gas firms, in particular those located in Agder and Rogaland, have a dominant synthetic knowledge base, recombining existing knowledge and engineering skills. Current policy instruments seem to reinforce path extension rather than new path development in the cases of organizationally thick and specialized RISs (Asheim & Grillitsch, 2015). In such RISs, a different approach must be applied to avoid organizational and regional path dependency. For example, Firm A in Agder is hopeful about the future when it comes to the regional cluster (NCE Node): 'I am hoping that Node will be a technology driver and support spin-off firms'. In regard to recruitment in Agder, Firm C sees the regional setting as both an advantage and a disadvantage: 'The obvious disadvantage is the amount of available competence in the region (…) on the other hand, a stable work force with a low turnover is important when building a specific competence'. Rogaland has several actors within the oil and gas industry, and the importance of this localization is explained by the respondent from Firm B in Rogaland:

> This region has become a gigantic power centre for everything that happens in the oil and gas industry in Norway. And it also gives us a contact network because all the major and global oil service companies have established offices in our district.

However, the respondent acknowledges a challenge for other actors in the Rogaland region: 'Everything is very focused towards the oil and gas industry, so I believe people wanting to establish something outside of this industry will meet a huge disadvantage because of the massive establishments within this industry.' Specialized regional structure can, therefore, hinder more cross-industry-oriented development outside of the oil and gas sector.

5. Conclusion and policy implications

In times of economic decline, strategic decisions to innovate or build CIIC may not be the main priority for firms struggling to survive. Policy-makers play a crucial role in times of economic growth, but their role becomes even more imperative in times of decay and economic decline. Policies can either reinforce path extension modes, or stimulate new path development. It is crucial to know firms' strategic mindset (Coenen, Moodysson, & Martin, 2015), such as how and why they make their priorities. Combining the knowledge about CIIC and the knowledge on how to link firms to extra-regional knowledge sources, as suggested by Isaksen and Trippl (2014), makes a solid base for developing regional policies for path renewal. Initiatives that stimulate firms' CIIC may loosen up a negative lock-in situation and contribute to new industrial paths in regional economies. Our study shows that institutionalizing cross-industry innovation in the strategy helps firms to keep a focus on developing CIIC. Thus, a stronger focus on both internal firm characteristics and the role of RISs in contributing to and influencing the firms' absorptive capacity for developing cross-industry innovation seems crucial for future policy development. The role of regional policies is to capitalize on regional strengths, and there is no 'one size fits all' policy (Tödtling & Trippl, 2005). The policies should not only be adapted to the region and the industry they aim to support, but also specifically address and stimulate cross-industry innovation at the firm level. The CIIC approach can contribute to policy-makers' understanding of firm-specific characteristics, and work as a tool in developing innovation policies for path renewal.

The reason for arguing this is twofold. Firstly, in this paper, we develop a theoretical concept of CIIC and suggest a procedure that can be applied to identify different CIIC indicators in firms (see Appendix 2). In combination with the knowledge of different RIS contexts, this is a useful tool to suggest what kind of regional structures are favourable for CIIC as well as how to encourage capability building. In developing adaptive regional innovation policies, we emphasize the importance of establishing joint technology and knowledge platforms and argue for more generic policies going beyond borders of a specific industry. The reason for this is that such initiatives encourage growth in combinatory knowledge bases in firms. Examples of joint technology and knowledge platforms are found in the Centres for Research Based Innovation (the Norwegian SFI schemes) as well as the European initiative of European Technology Platforms (ETPs). ETPs are industry-led platforms focusing on developing research and innovation agendas, as well as roadmaps for action in the EU. The stakeholders are mobilized to deliver on agreed priorities and exchange their knowledge across the EU (European Commission, 2016). Both initiatives make connections between state-of-the-art industrial challenges and related research and would, therefore, benefit firms' absorptive capacity for CIIC by making their knowledge base more diverse.

Secondly, many of the larger funds and instruments available to firms focus on R&D collaborations, networks, mobility and recruitment within one specific sector.

Drawing on a case analysis of a policy programme in Sweden, Coenen et al. (2015) explore how policy programmes can contribute to the renewal of mature industries. They conclude that successful policies cannot focus solely on pushing technology and R&D investments, but should also be concerned with learning processes such as firms' strategic mindsets. The obstacles for renewal are not only specific to the industry (Coenen et al., 2015), but also relate to firms' innovation capability. Accordingly, policy-makers need to extend their focus and include support for innovation within firms (Moodysson & Zukauskaite, 2014), for example, by focusing on CIIC. Because cross-industry innovation is about going beyond the borders of your own industry or sector, most of the current policy initiatives may fail to stimulate cross-industry innovation and, more importantly, path development.

Path development is defined as either path extension, path renewal or path creation. This paper mainly addresses path renewal, which can be the result either of new firms entering the region (through relocation or new firm formation) or of existing firms changing their activities (through CIIC). A strategy to enhance economic growth, in a period of economic decline and recession, is to stimulate path renewal by enhancing firms to constantly revitalize their CIIC. To loosen up a negative lock-in situation, initiatives that stimulate firms' CIIC might encourage new industrial paths in regional economies.

This paper contributes to the ongoing debate on path development by proposing a new theoretical concept of CIIC and exploring its drivers and indicators. The drivers – conditions for innovation and learning that vary according to different regional contexts (RISs) – influence the firms' absorptive capacity for building CIICs that arguably are important for new path development. Our empirical data demonstrate that organizationally thick and diversified regions are more favourable for developing CIIC and cross-industry innovation activity, while specialized regions need to increase their focus on CIIC to avoid organizational and regional path dependency, which can be especially dangerous in times of economic recession. We argue that encouraging CIIC building in firms is an important mechanism for cross-industry innovation and regional renewal. Thus, we cover a gap in the literature implying a rather passive notion of firms in regional renewal (Boschma & Martin, 2007; Christiansen & Jakobsen, 2012; Cooke, 2012).

Our study encourages further examination of how innovation processes on a firm level contribute to regional development. We recommend that future studies continue exploring the concept of CIIC and use the suggested procedure to measure the degree of CIIC in different types of firms (e.g. large firms) located in different regions. It may also be interesting to develop a survey tool based on the CIIC concept, which will make it possible to collect larger amounts of data and compare firms' CIIC across regions. Moreover, there is a need for further investigation of our analytical model. For example, future studies using a larger firm sample may focus on the relationship between CIIC on the firm level and path renewal on the regional level.

Note

1. Authors' own translation.

Disclosure statement

No potential conflict of interest was reported by the authors.

Funding

This work was supported by the Research Council of Norway.

References

Aarstad, J., Kvitastein, O. A., & Jakobsen, S.-E. (2016). Related and unrelated variety as regional drivers of enterprise productivity and innovation: A multilevel study. *Research Policy, 45*(4), 844–856. doi:10.1016/j.respol.2016.01.013

Asheim, B., & Gertler, M. (2005). The geography of innovation. In J. Fagerberg, D. C. Mowery, & R. R. Nelson (Eds.), *The Oxford handbook of innovation* (pp. 291–317). Oxford: Oxford University Press.

Asheim, B., & Grillitsch, M. (2015). *Smart specialisation: Sources for new path development in a peripheral manufacturing region*. Retrieved from https://ideas.repec.org/p/hhs/lucirc/2015_011.html

Asheim, B. T., Boschma, R., & Cooke, P. (2011). Constructing regional advantage: Platform policies based on related variety and differentiated knowledge bases. *Regional Studies*, 45(7), 893–904. doi:10.1080/00343404.2010.543126

Blaikie, N. (2009). *Designing social research*. Cambridge: Polity Press.

Boschma, R. A. (2005). Proximity and innovation: A critical assessment. *Regional Studies*, 39(1), 61–74. doi:10.1080/0034340052000320887

Boschma, R. A., & Martin, R. (2007). Editorial: Constructing an evolutionary economic geography. *Journal of Economic Geography*, 7(5), 537–548. doi:10.1093/jeg/lbm021

Christiansen, E. A. N., & Jakobsen, S.-E. (2012). Embedded and disembedded practice in the firm-place nexus: A study of two world-leading manufacturers of ski equipment in the Lillehammer ski cluster. *Geografiska Annaler: Series B, Human Geography*, 94(2), 177–194. doi:10.1111/j.1468-0467.2012.00403.x

Coenen, L., Moodysson, J., & Martin, H. (2015). Path renewal in old industrial regions: Possibilities and limitations for regional innovation policy. *Regional Studies*, 49(5), 850–865. doi:10.1080/00343404.2014.979321

Cooke, P. (2012). Relatedness, transversality and public policy in innovative regions. *European Planning Studies*, 20(11), 1889–1907. doi:10.1080/09654313.2012.723426

Cooke, P., & Leydesdorff, L. (2006). Regional development in the knowledge-based economy: The construction of advantage. *The Journal of Technology Transfer*, 31(1), 5–15. doi:10.1007/s10961-005-5009-3

Enkel, E., & Gassmann, O. (2010). Creative imitation: Exploring the case of cross-industry innovation. *R&D Management*, 40(3), 256–270. doi:10.1111/j.1467-9310.2010.00591.x

European Commission. (2016). *European technology platform*. Retrieved from http://ec.europa.eu/research/innovation-union/index_en.cfm?pg=etp

Frenken, K., & Boschma, R. A. (2007). A theoretical framework for evolutionary economic geography: Industrial dynamics and urban growth as a branching process. *Journal of Economic Geography*, 7(5), 635–649. doi:10.1093/jeg/lbm018

Frenken, K., Van Oort, F., & Verburg, T. (2007). Related variety, unrelated variety and regional economic growth. *Regional Studies*, 41(5), 685–697. doi:10.1080/00343400601120296

Fuchs, P. H., Mifflin, K. E., Miller, D., & Whitney, J. O. (2000). Strategy integration: Competing in the age of capabilities. *California Management Review*, 42(3), 118–147. doi:10.2307/41166045

Garud, R., Kumaraswamy, A., & Karnøe, P. (2010). Path dependence or path creation? *Journal of Management Studies*, 47(4), 760–774. doi:10.1111/j.1467-6486.2009.00914.x

Isaksen, A., & Karlsen, J. (2010). Different modes of innovation and the challenge of connecting universities and industry: Case studies of two regional industries in Norway. *European Planning Studies*, 18(12), 1993–2008. doi:10.1080/09654313.2010.516523

Isaksen, A., & Nilsson, M. (2013). Combined innovation policy: Linking scientific and practical knowledge in innovation systems. *European Planning Studies*, 21(12), 1919–1936. doi:10.1080/09654313.2012.722966

Isaksen, A., & Trippl, M. (2014). *Regional industrial path development in different regional innovation systems: A conceptual analysis*. Retrieved from https://ideas.repec.org/p/hhs/lucirc/2014_017.html

Jensen, M. B., Johnson, B., Lorenz, E., & Lundvall, B. Å. (2007). Forms of knowledge and modes of innovation. *Research Policy*, 36(5), 680–693. doi:10.1016/j.respol.2007.01.006

Lawson, B., & Samson, D. (2001). Developing innovation capability in organisations: A dynamic capabilities approach. *International Journal of Innovation Management*, 5(3), 377–400. doi:10.1142/S1363919601000427

Martin, R. (2012). *Knowledge bases and the geography of innovation*. Sweden: Media-Tryck, Lund University.

Martin, R. (2013). Differentiated knowledge bases and the nature of innovation networks. *European Planning Studies*, 21(9), 1418–1436. doi:10.1080/09654313.2012.755836

Martin, R., & Sunley, P. (2006). Path dependence and regional economic evolution. *Journal of Economic Geography*, 6, 395–437. doi:10.1093/jeg/lbl012

Maskell, P. (2001). The firm in economic geography. *Economic Geography*, *77*(4), 329–344. doi:10. 2307/3594104

McCracken, G. (1988). *The long interview*. Newbury Park, CA: Sage.

Moodysson, J., & Zukauskaite, E. (2014). Institutional conditions and innovation systems: On the impact of regional policy on firms in different sectors. *Regional Studies*, *48*(1), 127–138. doi:10. 1080/00343404.2011.649004

Nauwelaers, C. (2011). Intermediaries in regional innovation systems: Role and challenges for policy. In P. Cooke (Ed.), *Handbook of regional innovation and growth* (pp. 467–481). Cheltenham, UK: Edward Elgar Publishing Limited.

Praeger, D. (2007). *Our love of sewers: A lesson in path dependence*. Retrieved from https:// progressivehistorians.wordpress.com/2007/10/page/4/

Rathe, K., & Witt, U. (2001). The nature of the firm – static versus developmental interpretations. *Journal of Management and Governance*, *5*, 331–351. doi:10.1023/A:1014051112548

Schienstock, G. (2007). From path dependency to path creation: Finland on its way to the knowledge-based economy. *Current Sociology*, *55*(1), 92–109. doi:10.1177/0011392107070136

Statistics Norway. (2016a). *Greatest rise in unemployment among those with higher education*. Retrieved from https://www.ssb.no/en/arbeid-og-lonn/statistikker/regledig/aar/2016-01-19#content

Statistics Norway. (2016b). *Population and population changes, 1.January 2016*. Retrieved from https://www.ssb.no/en/befolkning/statistikker/folkemengde/aar-per-1-januar/2016-02-19?fane= tabell&sort=nummer&tabell=256010

Sydow, J., Schreyögg, G., & Koch, J. (2009). Organizational path dependence: Opening the black box. *Academy of Management Review*, *34*(4), 689–709. doi:10.5465/AMR.2009.44885978

Teece, D. J., & Pisano, G. (1994). The dynamic capabilities of firms: An introduction. *Industrial and Corporate Change*, *3*(3), 537–556. doi:10.1093/icc/3.3.537-a

Teece, D. J., Pisano, G., & Shuen, A. (1997). Dynamic capabilities and strategic management. *Strategic Management Journal*, *18*(7), 509–533. doi:10.1002/(SICI)1097-0266(199708)18: 7<509::AID-SMJ882>3.0.CO;2-Z

Tödtling, F., & Grillitsch, M. (2014). *Does combinatorial knowledge lead to a better innovation performance of firms?* Retrieved from https://ideas.repec.org/p/wiw/wiwsre/sre-disc-2014_07.html

Tödtling, F., & Trippl, M. (2005). One size fits all?: Towards a differentiated regional innovation policy approach. *Research Policy*, *34*(8), 1203–1219. doi:10.1016/j.respol.2005.01.018

Trippl, M., Grillitsch, M., & Isaksen, A. (2015). *External "energy" for regional industrial change: Attraction and absorption of non-local knowledge for new path development*. Retrieved from https://ideas.repec.org/p/hhs/lucirc/2015_047.html

Welch, C., Piekkari, R., Plakoyiannaki, E., & Paavilainen-Mäntymäki, E. (2011). Theorising from case studies: Towards a pluralist future for international business research. *Journal of International Business Studies*, *42*(5), 740–762. doi:10.1057/jibs.2010.55

Appendix 1. List of firms categorized by NACE 02 in the studied regions and in Norway as a whole, in percentages[a].

Based on data derived from the Dun & Bradstreet data set.

	Norway	Agder	Rogaland	Hordaland
Construction and energy	11.4	12.2	11.2	12.7
Estate and consulting	20.4	17.4	20.7	20
Trade	36.3	38.4	36.3	35.3
Health and social services	2.9	3.2	2.5	2.5
Industry	11.9	14.3	12.8	11.8
ICT/telecom	3.3	1.9	2.9	2.8
Culture and NGO	2.9	2.4	2.4	3.2
Oil, gas and mining	0.1	0.1	0.9	0.2
Primary production	1.7	1.3	1.6	2.1
Shipping	0.7	1	1.2	1.5
Transport and tourism	4.6	4.2	3.5	4.3
Total number of firms	82012	4150	6129	7522

[a]Total number of firms (Norway: 82012 firms; Agder: 4150 firms; Rogaland: 6129 firms and Hordaland: 7522 firms)

Appendix 2. Questions for identifying the presence of CIIC indicators.

CIIC1: Institutionalizing cross-industry innovation as a part of a firm's strategy
Does the firm explicitly state cross-industry innovation as part of its strategy?
CIIC2: Effective resource management combining different types of competences
Does the firm combine knowledge and resources from different industries to develop their products and services?
Does the firm hire employees with different backgrounds?
CIIC3: Learning from different industries
Does the firm encourage employees to learn from different industries?
Does the firm combine DUI and STI modes of learning in innovation processes?
CIIC4: Encouraging divergent 'across-border' thinking
Does the firm encourage creative across-industry thinking?
CIIC5: Organic organizational structure breaking down barriers separating different functions and product groups
Does the firm have a flexible structure?
CIIC6: Open and tolerant culture
Does the firm encourage employee-driven innovation processes?
CIIC7: Management of related technologies
Do the management/manager have cross-industry experience?
CIIC8: Firm's history of cross-industry activities
Does the firm's history include cross-industry innovation?

Appendix 3. Examples of CIIC quotes from the interviews.

Cross-industry innovation capability	Examples of quotes
CIIC1: Institutionalizing cross-industry innovation as a part of the firm's strategy	• Yes, development of our connectors (type of product) for use under water. It is one of our priorities. We try to extend our product assortment ... to work under water ... (Agder, firm C).
CIIC2: Effective resource management combining different types of competences	• Our product idea is actually two-fold. On one side, we perform monitoring of drilling operations. On the other side, through treatment of real-time data ... we make sure that the operation goes within established limits ... It is a lot of instrumentation ... and there is measuring of different values ... We have employees who are engineers in drilling and of course computer programmers (Rogaland, firm B).
CIIC3: Learning from different industries and modes of innovation	• We encourage employees to learn from related knowledge areas. We organise courses ... (Hordaland, firm A).
CIIC4: Encouraging divergent 'across-borders' thinking	• In the departments that work with marine transport and aquaculture they are encouraged to look at different related industries and see if the solutions can be used in several industries (Hordaland, firm A).
CIIC5: Organic organizational structure breaking down barriers separating different functions and product groups	• We have flow between the different departments ... also, employees in the development department may work one year to develop the crane systems and next year to develop an oceanographic system ... those in the software development department work at different places as the project moves through the technology (Hordaland, firm A).
CIIC6: Open and tolerant culture	• The creative ideas come all the time, it is even no need to ask (Hordaland, firm C).
CIIC7: Management of related technologies	• I have been an apprentice and took a certificate and worked for 7 years ... I come from a farm ... I am a farmer ... In the beginning I worked a little bit for farming and a little bit for the oil industry ... (Rogaland, firm D). I am a civil engineer and have a Master's degree in industrial economics (CEO, Hordaland, firm B).
CIIC8: Cross-industry experience	• We worked with sound technology in the Norwegian Armed Forces. When we started our firm in 1999, we worked a little further with it, but we started pretty fast to look at how we could use this technology in the oil and gas industry (Hordaland, firm D).

Entrepreneurial industry structures and financial institutions as agents for path dependence in Southwest Norway: the role of the macroeconomic environment

Martin Gjelsvik and Jarle Aarstad

ABSTRACT
Guided by an evolutionary perspective, we study how macroeconomic shifts as an exogenous factor contribute to the endogenous roles of financial institutions and the entrepreneurial industry structure as indicators for path extension or diversification in Southwest Norway. Path extension implies that new firm formation reproduces itself with limited variation. Path diversification implies a departure from existing paths, in that entrepreneurial activities expand into unrelated or related industries. Between 1992 and 1998, we observe a departure from path extension and an increase in entrepreneurial path diversification into unrelated industries, but this trend declines in the following years. The increase and decline are stronger for Southwest Norway than for the rest of the country. Throughout the whole period of observation (1992–2011), we observe a steady decline in path diversification into related industries. Thus, Southwest Norway, and the country as a whole, experiences an extension of an industry structure that increasingly reproduces itself, which implies stronger path dependence and decreasing diversification of related and unrelated entrepreneurial activity. Financial institutions mostly reinforce path extension, even in periods when abundant capital is available, but to some degree, they also induce related path diversification.

Introduction

Over the past four decades, Norway in general, and the Southwest region of the country in particular, has become more and more dependent on the petroleum sector. During this period, we have observed a strongly path-dependent regional economic development dominated by continuation and path extension. Yet with the recent major drop in the price of oil and stronger environmental concerns, a regional growth strategy dominated by the petroleum sector is risky indeed. Hence, it is critical to gain knowledge about whether the region has been able to develop alternative trajectories of economic activity through firm formation into new industries, and our paper will address this issue. Specifically, we will examine the entrepreneurial industry structure in Southwest Norway between 1992 and 2011. In so doing, we will also assess the role of financial institutions as potential mediators and catalysts for the emerging industry structure.

It is well acknowledged that entrepreneurial start-ups can act as agents spurring innovation and economic growth in the society (Wennekers & Thurik, 1999), and studies have also investigated how entrepreneurship affects regional development (Bosma, 2011; Fritch, 2011). However, we lack systematic knowledge about whether the entrepreneurial industry structure reproduces patterns of path extension or path diversification, respectively. Our paper will address this void in knowledge. Path extension implies that regional start-ups reproduce existing patterns with limited variation (Martin & Sunley, 2006). Path diversification, on the other hand, implies a departure from existing paths in that start-ups expand into dissimilar industries (Coenen, Moodysson, & Martin, 2015).

Financial institutions are a vital element in the ecology of the regional industry structure (Martin, Berndt, Klagge, & Sunley, 2005; Martin, Sunley, & Turner, 2002; Sorensen & Stuart, 2001), but the focus in the literature is often confined to the spatial distribution of venture capital and not to entrepreneurial patterns of path extension or diversification. Recently, another strand of research in economic geography has surfaced to study the geography of finance in itself (Dixon, 2015), but without explicit links to regional development. Our paper addresses the knowledge gap in the research literature by assessing the role of banks, venture and seed capital as potential catalysts or mediators of path development in a regional context.

Analysing start-ups and financial institutions, we will aim to assess the potential impact of macroeconomic shifts. Specifically, we will address how the price of oil and financial crises as exogenous factors have contributed to the endogenous roles of financial institutions and the entrepreneurial industry structure as agents for path extension or diversification in Southwest Norway.

Path dependence can be studied at a firm, industry or regional level of analysis. In this paper, we primarily study the concepts at a regional level; more precisely, we analyse data from the counties of Hordaland, Rogaland and Agder, which constitute the region of Southwest Norway. Largely, this region has been dependent on the oil and gas industry. In itself, this fact makes economic regional development vulnerable. Furthermore, the destiny of this industry is highly dependent on the price of oil and gas, which is set outside the region, adding to the vulnerability of regional trajectories. We argue that new firm formation and financial institutions' approach to support entrepreneurs may mitigate a lock-in into one particular industry.

To strengthen the validity of the study, we make a comparative analysis of similar entrepreneur data at a national level (minus the region of Southwest Norway). Comparative analyses of regional and national data can enable us to scrutinize in what ways patterns and dynamics of path dependence are unfolding as a function of regional or national particularities.

We argue that our study has relevance beyond the regional context of Southwest Norway. Many regions are dominated by one industry, be it petroleum or other industries. Such a situation is always risky, in particular if that industry evolves into decline.

Guided by an evolutionary perspective, we will further elaborate conceptually the dynamics of regional path dependence. The behaviour of entrepreneurs may lead to path extension if new firms reproduce the existing path trajectories, or to path diversification if new firms evolve into dissimilar industries. In the same manner, financial institutions may prioritize technologies and firms related to the present paths, or contribute to the development of new ones.

We are unfamiliar with a unified framework by which regional path dependence has been studied, but we will argue later that the dimensions of unrelated and related industry variety (Frenken, Van Oort, & Verburg, 2007) may serve as potent indicators or proxies of entrepreneurial path extension or diversification. The Dun & Bradstreet industry database was the primary source of raw data for this study. In addition, we have relied upon historical data of the oil price and other macroeconomic shifts. We finally lean upon quantitative analyses and qualitative in-depth interviews with managers in a differentiated set of financial institutions in Southwest Norway. In the methodological section, we elaborate in detail how we operationalized and measured the data for this study. In the final sections, we present the major empirical results and discuss the empirical findings. We will also address the study's limitations and suggest avenues for future research.

Theoretical perspectives

In general, evolutionary perspectives help to explain the movement of something over a time period, or explain how a situation got there at a moment in time. Second, an evolutionary explanation includes both random elements, which may generate variation in the variables under study, and mechanisms that systematically select on extant variation (Dosi & Nelson, 1994). Evolutionary models involve processes of learning and discovery as well as selection mechanisms. This paper discusses the potential for transformations of a region through new firm formation and the selection mechanisms of financial institutions. The region thus represents the aggregate level of analysis. However, regional transformation is a function of the actual behaviour of agents at a micro level. The agents in this particular study are entrepreneurs that we assume will act in response to opportunities and threats in the macroeconomic environment, and in interaction with financial institutions.

Path dependence

In evolutionary theory, history matters, which is expressed through the concept of path dependence (Arthur, 1994). Path dependence is a ubiquitous phenomenon, which pertains to firms and institutions at the micro level, and to regions and nations at the macro level. Path dependence evolves when the current realization of socio-economic processes depends on previous states, even back to the initial conditions (Castaldi & Dosi, 2006). One potential cause for path dependence is the process of learning. When agents learn, their behaviour depends on their memory of the past, that is, on their prior experience. Path-dependent learning is furthermore influenced by the trade-off between 'exploitation' and 'exploration' (March, 1991), that is, whether selection mechanisms favour the refinement and exploitation of what one already knows, or the exploration and search for new potentially valuable knowledge and technologies.

New knowledge accumulates and displays dynamic increasing returns when it cumulatively builds upon existing knowledge, often making present improvements easier (Scott & Storper, 2003). These dynamics are related to technological improvements that are shaped and constrained by particular technological paradigms and proceed along specific technological trajectories (Dosi, 1982). Formal and informal institutions such as conventions and customs influence decisions and selection criteria at the micro level (Scott, 2008). The degree of path dependence may accordingly depend on agents' cognitive 'models' of the world, that is, the very interpretative structures through which they process information from the environment. Information has the property of high upfront cost in its generation, but can be used repeatedly by others afterwards. Furthermore, information is typically non-rival in use, meaning that it can be used indifferently by one or numerous people. A general source of path dependence is accordingly associated with the presence of increasing returns in production or in the adoption of technologies and products (Arthur, 1994).

At the regional level, path dependence may evolve from the so-called agglomeration effects (Krugman, 1991). These include technological spillovers among producers, access to specialized labour in the region and easier interactions with advanced suppliers. As paths evolve, networks emerge of producers, suppliers, universities and support organizations that institutionalize specific patterns of development.

A basic thesis in our study is that dependence on the oil and gas industry is reflected in a path-dependent pattern of the entrepreneurial industry structure. The competence level may be particularly strong in the oil and gas industry, and the prospective income may also be high. The cognitive schema and learning have likewise induced a perception that entrepreneurial opportunities are most likely to be exploited or explored in limited, but seemingly very profitable, businesses. A strong oil and gas industry has probably also created a strong demand for products or services in industries that are related to this particular sector.

Entrepreneurial path dependence can also be a function of the role that financial institutions play in the regional economy. Financial institutions act as a selection mechanism by their allocation of monetary and other resources (Dosi, 1990). In particular, they operate as selection devices among different technologies, thus shaping processes of industrial paths. According to Dosi (1990), in a path-dependent evolutionary system, firms as well and financial institutions have the capacity to search, make mistakes and sometimes obtain unexpected successes, and they try to learn through such processes. The aggregate performance of the system changes over time as self-organizing collective properties of the interactions between the respective industrial agents and financial institutions. The influence of financial institutions on industrial dynamics – potentially shaping path-dependent patterns – turns out to be a query of how the agents learn, and the criteria on which the relevant environments select among firms and technologies. The financial institutions operate as a selection device both as a direct source of financial resources to more or less risky endeavours in firms, and as a 'disciplining' influence on management behaviour as they spell out 'the rules of the game'. It should be noted that the financial institutions are permanently facing the dilemma between a prudent management of their funds (on behalf of their investors and depositors) and their capacity to take risk. Finance constitutes a crucial bridge between the present and the future, between experience on what has proved to work in the past and the exploration of what is possible. Below we will assess whether financial institutions are likely to support entrepreneurs in existing industries, inducing path extension, or support new firm formation in related or unrelated industries, inducing path diversification.

Path extension

Regional development is always path dependent; it evolves from the past. The issue is how much history actually matters, how dependent is the path dependency of the history. David (2001) suggests the following categorization: weak history, moderate history and strong history. The concept of path extension expresses the strongest form of history; in our context it implies that the economic development of the region is strongly path dependent.

Path extension applies to the continuation and extension of an industry through the infusion of incremental innovations in production technologies and business models, or the introduction of product or service enhancements. It entails more incremental innovation than the radical or potentially disruptive innovations related to new path creation. Firms improve what they already know. In our context, path extension implies that entrepreneurial agents behave in accordance with the context of the existing industry structure into which they are embedded. The selection mechanisms in the financial institutions favour the refinement and improvement of existing industries.

Path extension may be positive when an industry is being built up in a region and the firms achieve benefits from increased scale and scope. It may be negative when an existing industry or product portfolio is 'locked-in' to a present (and maybe outdated) trajectory.

Path diversification

Path diversification is a process in which entrepreneurial activities expand into related or unrelated industry structures (Martin & Sunley, 2010; Neffke, Henning, & Boschma, 2011). It can be considered as a 'de-locking' or 'decoupling' process from the established industry pattern in a region, and in which technology and knowledge are being redeployed into new industry paths. In general, path diversification can occur as a result of new combinations enacted by heterogeneous firms in terms of knowledge, behavioural repertoires, strategies and consumer preferences. The heterogeneity stems from managers and firms holding different expectations about the future, and diversified mental models and identities. Path diversification may also evolve from imitation and technology transfer from outside the region, rather than innovation. It requires absorptive capabilities at both the firm and the institutional level (cf. Cohen & Levinthal, 1990). Lester (2005) has coined this transformation path transplantation. An example is the transplantation of the American oil and gas industry into Aberdeen, UK, and Stavanger, Norway (Hatakenaka, Westnes, Gjelsvik, & Lester, 2011).

Path diversification may evolve when an existing industry goes into decline because of shrinking markets or outdated technology or business models. Entrepreneurs that find opportunities in other pastures may reallocate available resources into new industries. In our context, fluctuations of the price of oil constitute both opportunities and threats, and may induce a pattern of path diversification (cf. Gladwell, 2000). Historically, we have observed strong fluctuations in the price of oil. Expectations of a consistently high oil price are assumed to lock the firms and the region into path extension, whereas a low or decreasing oil price may induce slack in resources with a potential decoupling or diversification from a dominant path.

Related and unrelated variety as indicators of path diversification

In the following, we argue that entrepreneurial path diversification can be analysed along a two-dimensional continuum, labelled as related and unrelated industry variety (cf. Frenken et al., 2007). If we theoretically assume that all entrepreneurial firms in a given region over time are established in the same industry, this can be labelled a highly path-dependent pattern. There is no discernible variation and no deviation from the previous industry pattern of entrepreneurial activity. We describe this pattern as a strongly specialized industry structure. Research has shown that a specialized industry structure can be positive by inducing efficiency and productivity in a regional context (Aarstad, Kvitastein, & Jakobsen, 2016; Wixe, 2015). However, a specialized industry structure can be vulnerable if the market on which the highly specialized industry is dependent shrinks, or new technologies or industries arise that outperform the products or the services of the established and highly specialized industry.

Let us now instead assume that entrepreneurial firms in a given region expand into new industries instead of reproducing the pattern of a specialized structure. This implies a departure from the established path into a pattern of path diversification. We furthermore argue that path diversification may imply that the entrepreneurial activity expands into industries that are unrelated to the established industry structure in the region. Alternatively, entrepreneurial path diversification may imply that firms are established in new, but related, industries. Entrepreneurial path diversification (vs. path extension) may thus be assessed along the two dimensions of unrelated path diversification (vs. path-dependent specialization) and related path diversification (vs. path-dependent specialization). We illustrate these dimensions in Figure 1. If we over time observe a consistent

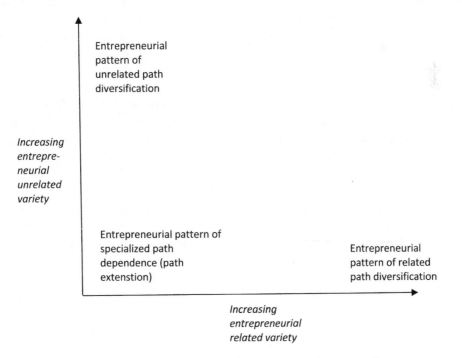

Figure 1. The dimensions of the entrepreneurial industry structures in a regional context.

pattern of entrepreneurial specialization, we argue that the entrepreneurial industry structure will tend to strengthen path extension. On the other hand, an increase in entrepreneurial unrelated or related variety will induce a departure from existing paths into an entrepreneurial industry pattern of either unrelated or related path diversification.

Research has shown that a regional industry structure of related variety can increase innovation (Aarstad, Kvitastein, et al., 2016; Castaldi, Frenken, & Los, 2015; Tavassoli & Carbonara, 2014). Unrelated variety can increase the probability of radical innovations (Castaldi et al., 2015), but decrease productivity (Aarstad, Kvitastein, et al., 2016). Frenken et al. (2007) have also shown that unrelated variety can hamper unemployment growth. In other words, related variety seems to have an overall positive innovation effect, while unrelated variety has shown mixed effects along different dimensions. Analysing innovation and productivity effects from unrelated and related variety, Aarstad, Kvitastein, et al. (2016) find that while related variety increases enterprises' propensities of innovation, it does not preclude or hamper productivity. Thus, we may assume that entrepreneurial path diversification into related industries can increase regional innovation, but not at the expense of loss in productivity. Finally, entrepreneurial diversification into unrelated industries may increase the probability of radical innovation and hamper unemployment growth, but at the same time, it may also hamper regional productivity.

Methodologies

Research context and data

Data on the entrepreneurial industry structure are derived from the Dun & Bradstreet data set. We also used data from Dun & Bradstreet to model the volume of entrepreneurial activity. In addition, we used historical data on the oil price and macroeconomic trends and shifts. Data from financial institutions in Southwest Norway are based on in-depth interviews with 23 managers in banks and in venture and seed funds. These institutions are expected to have different attitudes towards risk and new ventures. The interviews were carried out over a period of half a year, from November 2014 to June 2015. All interviews were taped and transcribed. These interviews offer opportunities to study the micro foundations of regional path development, as they reveal the selection criteria financial institutions use in evaluating firms and their technologies in association with access to financial resources. In addition to in-depth interviews, the banks' annual reports were used to get an overview of how the banks have distributed their resources (loans) across respective industries, and how this distribution has evolved over the past 10 years. The combination of the interviews and the annual reports enables us to study how institutions learn and adopt over time, and how this experience (from both failures and successes) changes their priorities over time.

Triangulating data on entrepreneurial activities with data on oil price and macroeconomic shifts – along with qualitative and quantitative data from financial institutions – offers a rich opportunity to gain a perspective on factors that are likely to influence regional path dependence. Comparing regional data of the entrepreneurial industry structure with that of the rest of the country further enables us to identify potential regional, vs. national, trends.

Modelling unrelated variety, related variety and entrepreneurial volume

The quantitative data from Dun & Bradstreet include the years between 1992 and 2012. For year t_0, we first identified firms that were established in year t_{-1} and had at least one employee in year t_0. In other words, we define a start-up as a firm established in year t_{-1} having at least one employee in year t_0. This implies that we have data for the time-window between 1992 and 2011. To define an industry, we used the Standard Industrial Classification (SIC) codes as of 2002 at level two (the classification of SIC codes was updated in 2007, but for our purpose we had most complete data for the whole time period by using the SIC classification as of 2002). The SIC codes include a hierarchy of five levels to distinguish the 'crudeness' of industrial classes. The SIC code at level two represents a relatively 'crude' distinction. The SIC code at level five represents the finest graded distinction of industrial classes.

To calculate the regional structure of unrelated and related variety, we first identified entrepreneurial firms that were located within the counties of Southwest Norway and the rest of the country, respectively. To model unrelated variety, we used a diversity index, which is based on Shannon's (1948a, 1948b) entropy measure. We used start-ups' SIC codes at level two for each year of observation. Formally, we define start-up diversity as $\sum_{k=1}^{n} s_{k,t}\ln(1/s_{k,t})$, where $s_{k,t}$ is the proportion of start-ups in class k (SIC code at level two) at time period (year) t. If $s_{k,t} = 0$, then $\ln(1/s_{k,t}) = 0$; n is the number of identified SIC codes at level two. To model related variety, we first modelled industry diversity in a similar way as we did when modelling unrelated variety, but we instead used start-ups' SIC codes at level five. This index contains information on total industry variety, both related and unrelated variety. In order to crystallize the related variety construct, we next subtracted unrelated variety from the equation. Similar procedures have been followed in other research (e.g. Frenken et al., 2007).

In addition, we measured the very volume of start-ups over the time window, and the values were standardized and set to one in the first year of observation. This enabled us to compare the very entrepreneurial activity in Southwest Norway with that of the rest of the country over the described time period. The measure also enables us to compare the very entrepreneurial activity with the entrepreneurial industry structure of unrelated and related variety.

Results

Entrepreneurial path dependence and diversification in light of the macroeconomic environment

In Figure 2, we observe an industry pattern of entrepreneurial unrelated variety between 1992 and 2011. For Southwest Norway, there is a strong increase in unrelated variety between 1992 and 1998. For the rest of the country there is also an increase, but less marked. During this period, the financial institutions were in the process of recovering after the financial and banking crisis between 1988 and 1992. The oil price was relatively low during this period, $20–30 a barrel, dipping as low as $10 in 1999. The strong increase in entrepreneurial unrelated variety in general, and in Southwest Norway in particular, indicates an increase in path diversification into unrelated industries. This can be explained as a function of a better functioning financial sector and less dependence on

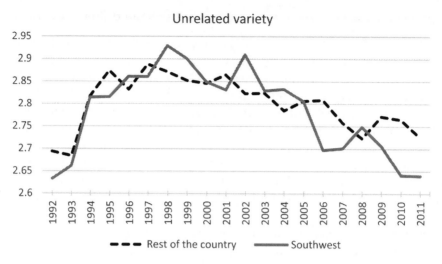

Figure 2. Entrepreneurial industry structure of unrelated variety between 1992 and 2011.

the oil and gas sectors (compared to the period after 2000 with a far higher price of oil and which we discuss shortly).

Comparing the pattern of unrelated variety that we observe between 1992 and 1998 with the very volume of entrepreneurial activity, we observe an increasing trend during the same time period (Figure 3). The increase has been very similar in Southwest Norway and the rest of the country, respectively. Algebraically, an increase in the very number of observations can inflate the diversity index (Aarstad, Kvitastein, et al., 2016). Thus, the increase in unrelated variety can partly be explained as an increase in the very volume of entrepreneurial activity that we have observed between 1992 and 1998. In other words, it appears to have been an expansion in entrepreneurial activity in general, and in Southwest Norway in particular, which largely has expanded into new and unrelated industries.

Returning to Figure 2, we observe that the pattern of unrelated variety has decreased after 1998, and the decrease appears to have been more marked for Southwest Norway than for the rest of the country. During this period, Norway experienced steady economic growth, disrupted only by a short dip as a consequence of the financial crisis in 2008. The oil price also had a substantial and steady increase during this period, apart from a brief dip in 2008. However, the oil price quickly returned to the level before the crisis, reaching $100 in 2011. In this period, the unrelated variety of entrepreneurship decreased both nationally and regionally. This indicates that the region evolved in a trajectory characterized by path extension, as the region became more dependent on the oil and gas industry.

Taking another look at Figure 3, we observe a steep decline in entrepreneurial activity in 1999 and thereafter a pattern of steady activity, except for a small dip in 2009. The dip can be attributed to the financial crisis, and the one in 1999 to the historically low price of oil. From 2001, we observe a relatively stronger tendency of entrepreneurial activity in Southwest Norway than in the rest of the country. This can be attributed to entrepreneurial opportunities in the oil and gas industry (as a result of increasing oil price).

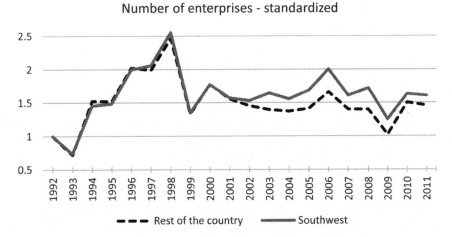

Figure 3. Relative volume of entrepreneurial activity between 1992 and 2011.

Figure 4 illustrates the pattern of related variety between 1992 and 2011. The figure shows a decreasing trend, except for 1998 and 2002 that shows temporary steep increases. The overall score is relatively lower in Southwest Norway.

Taken together, we conclude that between 1992 and 1998, there is a departure from a strong path dependence (path extension) to an increase in entrepreneurial path diversification into unrelated industries, but which declines in the following years (Figure 2). After 1998, the relative volume of entrepreneurial activity is steady (Figure 3). However, entrepreneurial activities seem to strengthen existing paths, since the diversification into related and unrelated industries is limited, and even declining (Figures 2 and 4). For unrelated variety, we observe that the trend particularly declines in Southwest Norway after 2005, the year the oil price peaked $100.

Thus, Southwest Norway in particular, and the country as a whole, appears to experience an entrepreneurial industry structure of increasing path dependence with decreasing

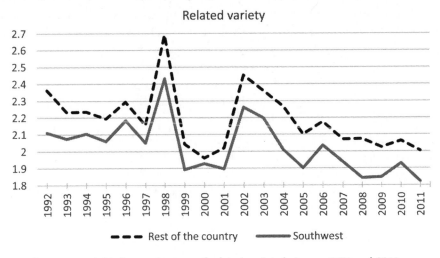

Figure 4. Entrepreneurial industry structure of related variety between 1992 and 2011.

variation of related and unrelated entrepreneurial activity. The behaviour of entrepreneurs seems to aggregate into path extension rather than path diversification.

The role of financial institutions

Banks

In this section, we discuss the role of financial institutions in shaping regional economic paths; more specifically, we assess how their selection mechanisms support path extensions and/or regional transformation through path diversification. We start with the banks.

Both commercial and savings banks are physically present in Southwest Norway.[1] The commercial banks Nordea, Danske Bank and Handelsbanken (all foreign owned) and DNB are present in the region. The region also enjoys the presence of regional savings banks, and hosts their respective headquarters. A number of smaller savings banks are also present, but they have minor interest in this context. DNB, a merger between the former DnC, Bergen Bank, Postbanken and Gjensidige NOR,[2] is the largest financial institution in Norway, in which the state holds a 34% ownership stake. The bank commands a strong international position in shipping, energy, fisheries and fish farming, and has a strong position in the oil and gas sector. Danske Bank, in Norway based on the former Fokus Bank, is headquartered in Copenhagen. Handelsbanken is owned by Svenska Handelsbanken, with its head office in Stockholm. Nordea is a Nordic financial services group, also headquartered in Stockholm. Nordea Norway is headquartered in Oslo, and the Norwegian presence is based on the former Kreditkassen. Nordea and DNB are world leading on syndicating loans to offshore oil and gas and shipping. The major savings banks have also grown through mergers. In other words banks, like regions, evolve in a path-dependent way.

Generally, a bank is a financial intermediary that creates credit by lending money to a borrower based on deposits. If the credit is funded by deposits from the same segment, regional firms in our case, the bank redirects financial resources from firms with surplus money to firms in need of funding. Banks may also create additional credit for regional firms based on external funding such as bonds in international markets. In other words, the banks can fund regional firms beyond the available resources in the region. The overall trend is that both commercial and savings banks increased their lending to the corporate sector relative to their deposits before the financial crisis in 2008, but in its aftermath, this pattern was reversed.

Banks differ in their strategies and attitudes to risks, which may constrain entrepreneurial activities. A conservative commercial bank describes their policies:

> We finance growth in existing firms rather than start-ups, and companies with customers and proven technology. We pass a person with a promising technology, and we are not competent to link him to the public innovation system. When entering new markets or [introducing a] novel technology, the risk exposure increases. Without a large equity base, we don't participate.

Banks are generally reluctant to fund new product and service development in start-ups; but entrepreneurs imitating other firms' products or services are an exception to this rule. Proven technology and existing markets normally reduce the risks involved, most likely supporting path extension. Technologies harboured in spin-offs from existing firms are more readily funded than greenfields: 'An established company with a running cash flow represent a collateral for us; that makes funding easier'. Most interviewees support this view.

The more conservative banks rule out start-ups altogether: 'We prefer grown-ups; they are more attractive for the bank. It is not our role to finance equity in start-ups'. A somewhat more nuanced approach:

> We are ownership focused. A private limited company without backing from the mother company will run into problems at our bank. We are sceptical to single-purpose companies that attempt to isolate the risk in one [single] project. We may finance the project when the mother company backs up.

International standards and requirements have a strong and increasing influence on the behaviour and risk policies in banks. European regulations such as Basel II and Advanced IRB[3] may have hampered banks' willingness to take risk. This may have had a negative influence on entrepreneurs' possibility to obtain funding. Some bank managers are concerned:

> The regulator wants less risk exposure in the banks. What are the consequences for start-ups? Are we developing a less diversified society with less room for innovation? Twenty years ago decisions were taken on a more discretionary individual basis, on intuition and our knowledge of the customer.

Another informant echoes this view: 'Historically, savings banks carried out micro finance, took a social responsibility to get people started. Now they are risk averse'. This scenario implies a greater convergence of banks' strategies and risk attitudes. However, start-ups and innovation are not necessarily synonymous concepts. Innovation takes place in existing firms, and may spin off activities and product portfolios to new firms, sometimes to new owners. Profitable incumbent firms possess the capital and competence base required to extend their business and grow, which is very different from an individual starting from scratch.

The size of the bank matters, too. The largest banks obviously command a more encompassing knowledge base than the smaller ones. Internal specialization enables them to get involved in all industries, including industries that undergo radical changes at high speed, including mergers and acquisitions. As a rule, these transactions take place within a given industry, thus leading to path extension. The volume of assets under management and the qualifications and skills of the bank go hand in hand. Midsized and smaller banks more often decline to participate in emerging or fast-changing industries.

In general, banks are reluctant to fund new product and service development in start-ups, that is, the phase prior to marketing and contracting. The exception from this rule is standard products, in other words when new firms imitate other products rather than to innovate. Proven technology and existing markets normally reduce the risks involved. This behaviour typically ends up in path extension. Start-ups, if financed by banks, are often established in extant industries, thus supporting path extension. If the technologies have a disruptive power, it may lead to path diversification.

Annual reports of the relevant banks offer access to the distribution of corporate loans to the various industries. Loan portfolio is an indicator of how the respective banks are involved with the regional businesses. For all banks, loans to commercial real estate development occupy the largest share of total loans. In the commercial banks, that sector constitutes around 30%. The savings banks display a larger variety, ranging from 30% to 60%. These numbers indicate two features. First, the commercial real estate sector is regarded as relatively less innovative than other industry sectors. A large share of these loans thus indicates a risk-averse bank. Second, the potential risks of these engagements are evaluated by the quality of collateral offered. Other industries are evaluated on the foundation of the expected future cash flow, the so-called turnover-based industries. Evaluating and processing collateral are regarded as a traditional bank craft. Assessing a future cash flow requires knowledge of the industry, the effectiveness of the business model and potential market shares. These assessments are harder to do than collateral evaluations, and even more so in industries that the bank is unfamiliar with. In other words, banks may have to upgrade their skills and knowledge to get involved with firms and industries representing diversifications from existing industries.

The commercial banks supply advisory services and internationally acknowledged economic research and analysis. These functions serve large, capital-intensive start-ups, mergers and acquisitions, or existing companies with extensive projects. The expertise of these functions is mainly located in Oslo, but some of the banks in Southwest Norway also experience a growing demand for both funding and advice in mergers and acquisitions. As a rule, mergers and acquisitions take place within a given industry, thus restraining path diversification.

Some banks offer seminars and advice on how to set up a new company, how to recruit a competent board, how to set up a shareholder agreement template, etc. One bank has introduced the concept of a 'start-up pilot' that guides the entrepreneur through the bureaucracy from an embryonic stage to public funding: 'Our task is not limited to funding; we contribute with knowledge to firms in order for them to access capital from relevant sources'. If a customer approaches the bank with an idea, they usually recommend Innovation Norway, a governmental body, which assists with funding, competence and networks. Some banks also co-fund with Innovation Norway:

> There are projects we would not have participated in without Innovation Norway. It is of mutual interest. Innovation Norway relies on the bank's evaluations. They think that when the bank dares to be involved, we [Innovation Norway] may as well.

For small- and medium-sized enterprises, banks are active advisors: 'Just a handful of our firms have their own finance managers. The bank is financial director for 90% of our customers; both in the nascent and in the mature phases'.

The large commercial banks have centralized specialist departments. As a rule, these specialists are located outside of Southwest Norway. The exception is DNB, which has located their expertise of fish farming in Bergen. Nordea has located their specialists in Stockholm, Copenhagen and Oslo. The interviewees disagree as to whether being headquartered outside the region has implications for the capacity to serve the regional businesses. Some argue, mostly neutral observers, that regional credit policies are defined by a head office that necessarily takes the situation of the entire bank into account. If the bank runs into trouble in other countries than Norway (which has been the case after the financial crisis in 2008), the credit lines to Norwegian customers will suffer. The implication is that foreign-owned banks are less predictable, with reference to enterprise finance, than banks with a regional head office. In general, commercial banks display a higher preference to firms and commercial lending, but in the aftermath of the financial crisis in 2008, the overall trend indicates that they too have diminished their exposure to the business market.[4] For banks headquartered in Norway, the tendency is less pronounced.

We conclude that the behaviour of banks and their general risk aversion, including those imposed by regulations, primarily lead to path extension. To some extent, their behaviour may induce an industry pattern of diversification into related industries.

Seed and venture capital funds

The term 'seed' indicates a very early investment, meant to raise equity to fund a business, typically a technology company, until it can generate cash of its own, or until it is ready for further investments (for a review, see Baron, 2012, Ch. 8). Seed money may be provided by seed funds (formal organizations), but may also be obtained through friends and family funding, angel funding and crowdfunding. The size of the investments tends to be moderate. In many cases, 25–75,000 euro will suffice in the earliest phase, before public funding may be relevant or new investors are invited in.

Seed funds are constantly risk-takers, but have implemented selection mechanisms to take the inherent risk down: 'We prefer ideas that have been evaluated in the 'Innovation Park Incubator' or 'Bergen Technology Office' and [that have] obtained grants from Innovation Norway. We appreciate that others have done the ruminating'. Such screening by competent institutions may inhibit that ideas go further than they should. This behaviour seems to be confirmed by statistics: 'The 'Innovation Park' tells us that 70% of their start-ups are still operating after 5 years. Our experience is that 70% of start-ups generally (without support from the Innovation Park) do not survive the first five years'. Intuitively we may assume that seed capital institutions fund technologies that lead to path renewal, but that is not always the case; start-ups funded by these investors are often established in extant industries, thus supporting path extension.

Investors make their decision whether to fund a project based on the perceived strength of the idea and the capabilities, skills and history of the founders. There are several seed funds in the region, most of them small; consequently, they play minor roles. Some of them have lost money and new investments are hard to find in the aftermath of the financial crisis. Entrepreneurs also express reluctance from the seed funds in the region (Aarstad, Pettersen, & Henriksen, 2016). Due to challenges and risks involved in the funding of start-ups, some seed funds have now transformed into consultancy services.

Because of the high risks involved, the state participates in several seed funds, often on a 50–50 basis with private capital. The banks may invest in the funds, but not in equity investments in the individual firms. Sarsia Seed in Bergen may serve as an example. With a capital base of NOK 333 million (50% state/private), the company invests in start-ups in energy, cleantech and in biotech and life sciences. They have obtained additional NOK 622 million from co-investors such as banks and individual investors. These investment areas are typical for other small seed funds in the region. Energy, cleantech and biotechnology investments are likely to induce entrepreneurial path diversification in the region, but we have yet to see that investments in these sectors have resulted in new and strong industry segments.

Venture capital funds are independently managed pools of capital that focus on equity and equity-linked investments in privately held, high-growth companies (Lerner, 2009). The largest pool of venture capital comes in the form of private limited partnerships (Gladstone & Gladstone, 2002). These partnerships are companies that source their funds from pension funds, insurance companies, large foundations and wealthy individuals. The managers of these partnerships are general partners and the investors are limited partners with a passive role. These managers are professional investors, and identify and select those ventures that have the greatest potential for success, and, second, provide management expertise and access to non-financial resources. They are expected to have better capabilities than banks to select profitable investments, to keenly monitor and follow-up their investments, supply relevant knowledge for increased value creation and manage risks associated with the investments (Manigart & Sapienza, 2000). However, it is important to note that the definition of venture capital differs. The classic definition refers to long-term equity invested in high-risk ventures, especially new companies or new technologies, that offer large potential capital gains to compensate for the high risk involved (Martin et al., 2002). Venture capital associations, such as the Norwegian Venture Capital & Private Equity Association in this case, include relatively short-term investment in business expansions and management buyouts. To illustrate, the employment figures in portfolio firms owned by their members show 552 employees in the seed stage, 9441 in the venture stage and 57,772 in the buyout phase.

The region hosts three venture funds of substantial size. Argentum, located in Bergen, is wholly owned by the state, and specializes in energy-focused private equity funds. The company has NOK 17 billion under management. Stavanger hosts Energy Ventures (NOK 7 billion) and Hitec Vision (NOK 45 billion). Both their annual reports and our interviewees testify to the fact that venture capital firms have become more risk averse, and contribute mostly to restructuring of existing industries. We conclude that neither banks nor venture funds, the two major financial actors, have so far played a noticeable role in new firm formation and diversification of the region into new paths. Seed funds do, but they command modest amounts of capital.

Conclusion

Our focus in this paper has been to study the evolutionary pattern of regional economic development. Regions evolve in path-dependent ways, but the degree of dependency or novelty may vary over time and between regions. Path extension involves incremental product and process innovation in existing industries, leading not only to continuation, but also to the danger of path exhaustion. We have focused on two groups of actors believed to have substantial influence on economic development: entrepreneurs and financial institutions. These actors are part of the regional innovation system. Their behaviour is furthermore assumed to be influenced by major external factors: financial crises and the price of oil. Analysing data from Dun & Bradstreet, we observed a departure from existing paths and an increase in entrepreneurial path diversification into unrelated industries between 1992 and 1998, but the trend declined in the following years. The increase and decline were stronger for Southwest Norway than for the rest of the country, due to the region's sensitivity to changes in the price of oil. Unrelated variety, and thus a diversification of the regional industries, coincides with a modest price of oil and peaks the years prior to the dot.com bubble. In the subsequent period, we observed a steady decline of entrepreneurial activity into both related and unrelated industries, which indicates that a pattern of path extension, and not diversification, emerges. This trajectory coincides with a steady and substantial boost in the price of oil. Qualitative and quantitative data from financial institutions in the region furthermore indicate that they have contributed more to entrepreneurial path extension than to renewal, even in periods when abundant capital was available. The selection mechanisms in banks and venture capital firms seem to have favoured path extension, and the availability of seed funds has been too moderate as to make a difference.

Theoretical and practical implications

To our knowledge, this is the first study that has analysed how entrepreneurial industry patterns influence economic paths at a regional and a national level. The paper has further contributed to the scholarly literature by using a longitudinal research design to illustrate how entrepreneurial activities may contribute to regional development through path extension or related or unrelated path diversification. We have also illustrated the differentiated roles of financial institutions in regional development, a role often left out in the discussion of regional innovation systems.

Largely, this paper has shown that Southwest Norway, and the country as a whole, has experienced an entrepreneurial industry structure of path extension due to an increasing dependence on the oil and gas sector. In our opinion, this is a highly risky trend, potentially prohibiting a broader industrial diversity that may mitigate the effects of external economic shocks. Since July 2014, the price of oil has declined by more than 50% and we have yet to see emerging industries that can represent the 'new oil' in the Norwegian economy. There is of course no quick fix to remedy the strong entrepreneurial path dependence, but policy-makers, in concert with financial institutions, should, at the very least, be aware of and elaborate potential strategies to face the challenges uncovered in this study.

Limitations and avenues for future research

Our major aim in this study has been to examine the role of entrepreneurs and financial institutions in differentiated regional trajectories. A limitation is the assumed relationships between these two important actors, rather than explicitly linking them together. Future studies should aim to address these issues, for instance, by analysing financial institutions' de facto role as financiers of entrepreneurial activity in different industries. Preferably, this should be done by econometric modelling of entrepreneurial industry structures in a longitudinal research design. It would also be advantageous to develop more indicators of the role of banks and other financial institutions than those used here. Another limitation is that we have assumed, rather than explicitly investigated, the potential link between macroeconomic shifts and the development of the entrepreneurial industry structure in a regional and national context. Future studies should aim to study this potential relationship more explicitly. Finally, 2011 is the last year of observation in our data. Since then, Norway, and the Southwest region in particular, has been strongly affected by a steep decline in the price of oil. This situation actualizes a potential path barely mentioned in this paper, path exhaustion. Being dependent on a single industry is risky indeed, and may lead to the decline and exhaustion of that path.

Notes

1. As a result of the liberalization of the financial markets in the 1980s, savings banks and commercial banks operate very similarly. Norwegian savings banks play a major role in the economy, as in Germany and Austria.
2. Gjensidige NOR was a financial corporation formed by the merger between Sparebanken NOR (savings bank) and the insurance company Gjensidige in 1999. This entity ended when in 2003 the savings bank division of Gjensidige NOR merged with Den norske Bank to establish DnB NOR (which was renamed DNB).
3. The term 'Advanced IRB' is an abbreviation of advanced internal ratings-based approach and refers to a set of credit risk measurement techniques proposed under Basel II capital adequacy rules for banking institutions. Under this approach, the banks develop their own empirical model to quantify required capital for credit risk. Banks can use this approach only subject to approval from their national regulators. Some commercial banks and smaller savings banks are exempt from these specific regulations.
4. The data to which we refer in this subsection can be accessed by contacting the authors of this paper.

Disclosure statement

No potential conflict of interest was reported by the authors.

Funding

This work was supported by the Research Council of Norway.

References

Aarstad, J., Kvitastein, O. A., & Jakobsen, S.-E. (2016). Related and unrelated variety as regional drivers of enterprise productivity and innovation: A multilevel study. *Research Policy*, 45(4), 844–856. doi:10.1016/j.respol.2016.01.013

Aarstad, J., Pettersen, I. B., & Henriksen, K.-E. (2016). Entrepreneurial experience and access to critical resources: A learning perspective. *Baltic Journal of Management*, 11(1), 89–107. doi:10.1108/BJM-09-2014-0141

Arthur, W. B. (1994). *Increasing returns and path dependence in the economy*. Ann Arbor: The University of Michigan Press.

Baron, R. A. (2012). *Entrepreneurship: An evidence-based guide*. Cheltenham: Edward Elgar.

Bosma, N. (2011). Entrepreneurship, urbanization economies, and productivity of European regions. In M. Fritch (Ed.), *Handbook of research on entrepreneurship and regional development: National and regional perspectives* (pp. 107–132). Cheltenham: Edward Elgar.

Castaldi, C., & Dosi, G. (2006). The grip of history and the scope for novelty: Some results and open questions on path dependence in economic processes. In A. Wimmer & R. Kössler (Eds.), *Understanding change: Models, methodologies and metaphors* (pp. 99–128). London: Palgrave Macmillan UK.

Castaldi, C., Frenken, K., & Los, B. (2015). Related variety, unrelated variety and technological breakthroughs: An analysis of US state-level patenting. *Regional Studies*, 49(5), 767–781. doi:10.1080/00343404.2014.940305

Coenen, L., Moodysson, J., & Martin, H. (2015). Path renewal in old industrial regions: Possibilities and limitations for regional innovation policy. *Regional Studies, 49*(5), 850–865. doi:10.1080/00343404.2014.979321

Cohen, W. M., & Levinthal, D. A. (1990). Absorptive capacity: A new perspective on learning and innovation. *Administrative Science Quarterly, 35*(1), 128–152. doi:10.2307/2393553

David, P. A. (2001). *Path dependence, its critics and the quest for 'historical economics'*. Cheltenham: Edward Elgar.

Dixon, A. D. (2015). *The new geography of capitalism*. Oxford: Oxford University Press.

Dosi, G. (1982). Technological paradigms and technological trajectories. *Research Policy, 11*(3), 147–162. doi:10.1016/0048-7333(82)90016-6

Dosi, G. (1990). Finance, innovation and industrial change. *Journal of Economic Behavior & Organization, 13*(3), 299–319. doi:10.1016/0167-2681(90)90003-V

Dosi, G., & Nelson, R. R. (1994). An introduction to evolutionary theories in economics. *Journal of Evolutionary Economics, 4*(3), 153–172. doi:10.1007/bf01236366

Frenken, K., Van Oort, F., & Verburg, T. (2007). Related variety, unrelated variety and regional economic growth. *Regional Studies, 41*(5), 685–697. doi:10.1080/00343400601120296

Fritch, M. (2011). The effect of new business formation on regional development: Empirical evidence, interpretation, and avenues for future research. In M. Fritch (Ed.), *Handbook of research on entrepreneurship and regional development: National and regional perspectives* (pp. 58–106). Cheltenham: Edward Elgar.

Gladstone, D., & Gladstone, L. (2002). *Venture capital handbook*. London: Financial Times Prentice Hall.

Gladwell, M. (2000). *The tipping point: How little things can make a big difference*. New York, NY: Little, Brown and Company.

Hatakenaka, S., Westnes, P., Gjelsvik, M., & Lester, R. K. (2011). The regional dynamics of innovation: A comparative study of oil and gas industry development in Stavanger and Aberdeen. *International Journal of Innovation and Regional Development, 3*(3–4), 305–323. doi:10.1504/IJIRD.2011.040528

Krugman, P. (1991). Increasing returns and economic geography. *Journal of Political Economy, 99*(3), 483–499. doi:10.2307/2937739

Lerner, J. (2009). *Boulevard of broken dreams: Why public efforts to boost entrepreneurship and venture capital has failed - and what to do about it*. Princeton, NJ: Princeton University Press.

Lester, R. K. (2005). *Universities, innovation, and the competitiveness of local economies: A summary report from the local innovation Systems Project-Phase1* (Local Innovation Systems Working Paper 05-005). Cambridge, MA: MIT-IPC.

Manigart, S., & Sapienza, H. J. (2000). Venture capital and growth. In D. Sexton & H. Landstrom (Eds.), *The Blackwell handbook of entrepreneurship* (pp. 240–258). Cambridge: Blackwell.

March, J. G. (1991). Exploration and exploitation in organizational learning. *Organization Science, 2*(1), 71–87. doi:10.1287/orsc.2.1.71

Martin, R., Berndt, C., Klagge, B., & Sunley, P. (2005). Spatial proximity effects and regional equity gaps in the venture capital market: Evidence from Germany and the United Kingdom. *Environment and Planning A, 37*, 1207–1231. doi:10.1068/a3714

Martin, R., & Sunley, P. (2006). Path dependence and regional economic evolution. *Journal of Economic Geography, 6*(4), 395–437. doi:10.1093/jeg/lbl012

Martin, R., & Sunley, P. (2010). The place of path dependence in an evolutionary perspective on the economic landscape. In R. Boschma & R. Martin (Eds.), *The handbook of evolutionary economic geography* (pp. 62–92). Cheltenham: Edward Elgar.

Martin, R., Sunley, P., & Turner, D. (2002). Taking risks in regions: The geographical anatomy of Europe's emerging venture capital market. *Journal of Economic Geography, 2*(2), 121–150. doi:10.1093/jeg/2.2.121

Neffke, F., Henning, M., & Boschma, R. (2011). How do regions diversify over time? Industry relatedness and the development of new growth paths in regions. *Economic Geography, 87*(3), 237–265. doi:10.1111/j.1944-8287.2011.01121.x

Scott, A., & Storper, M. (2003). Regions, globalization, development. *Regional Studies, 37*(6–7), 579–593. doi:10.1080/0034340032000108697a

Scott, W. R. (2008). *Institutions and organizations: Ideas and interests* (3rd ed.). Thousand Oaks, CA: Sage.

Shannon, C. E. (1948a). A mathematical theory of communication. *The Bell System Technical Journal, 27*, 379–423. doi:10.1002/j.1538-7305.1948.tb01338.x

Shannon, C. E. (1948b). A mathematical theory of communication. *The Bell System Technical Journal, 27*, 623–656. doi:10.1002/j.1538-7305.1948.tb00917.x

Sorensen, o., & Stuart, T. (2001). Syndication networks and the spatial distribution of venture capital investments. *American Journal of Sociology, 106*, 1546–1588. doi:10.1086/321301

Tavassoli, S., & Carbonara, N. (2014). The role of knowledge variety and intensity for regional innovation. *Small Business Economics, 43*(2), 493–509. doi:10.1007/s11187-014-9547-7

Wennekers, S., & Thurik, R. (1999). Linking entrepreneurship and economic growth. *Small Business Economics, 13*(1), 27–56. doi:10.1023/a:1008063200484

Wixe, S. (2015). The impact of spatial externalities: Skills, education and plant productivity. *Regional Studies, 49*(12), 2053–2069. doi:10.1080/00343404.2014.891729

Unfolding the relationship between resilient firms and the region

Mary Genevieve Billington, James Karlsen, Line Mathisen and Inger Beate Pettersen

ABSTRACT

This research explores organizational resilience in four manufacturing firms in four different regions of Norway. While regional resilience has gained attention in research, there have been few studies with a micro-level focus, investigating firms and their distinctive features of resilience. We chose a qualitative multiple-case study approach and employed a critical incident technique to study resilience in selected firms that had experienced external shocks and shifts in regard to changing markets, globalization and advances in technology. Each, however, had managed to continually develop resilience capacity over time. Our framework considered three dimensions of organizational resilience: the cognitive, the behavioural and the contextual. We address how resilience is sustained over time, the evolutionary nature of organizational resilience in firms and how resilient firms relate to the region. We found that all three dimensions of resilience capacity were evident in each firm, but appeared as a complex and unique blend. Furthermore, each dimension was supported by regional ties and affiliations. The findings suggest that organizational resilience is a dynamic capability conditioned by firm–region interactions, which are cultural, social and economic. Regional resilience is built through the contribution of the firm to the economic and social systems of the region.

Introduction

The concept of resilience, stemming originally from the natural sciences, has recently gained popularity within the field of economic geography. In the Natural Sciences, resilience refers to the ability of a mechanical, biological or ecological organism or system to regain equilibrium or an enhanced state after a shock or shift in the external environment. The transposition of the concept to the field of economic geography is perhaps an acknowledgement of an increasing complexity and turbulence in the economic and political environments (Christopherson, Michie, & Tyler, 2010; Teixeira & Werther, 2013). Davoudi and Porter (2012) challenge the equilibrium, bounce back, survival, discourse on resilience, advocating instead the notion of evolutionary resilience where resilience is not conceived of as a return to normality, but rather as the ability of complex socio-eco-logical systems to change, adapt and, crucially, transform in response to stresses and strains. These stresses and strains may be immediate or slow developing (Hassink, 2010). This approach highlights the importance of developing a capacity to exploit the opportunities that arise during crisis and 'bouncing forwards' by innovation and reinvention (Shaw, 2012).

For most studies within economic geography, employing the resilience concept, the unit of analysis is larger systems, such as cities, regions or nations (Doran & Fingleton, 2016). Resilience is considered as a useful notion in describing regions that manage to transit successfully short- and long-term economic shocks and challenges. Regional resilience is principally understood in relation to a systems structure, performance and overall functioning (Bristow & Healy, 2014, p. 924). It should be noted that the concept presents as somewhat malleable and disputed (Balland, Rigby, & Boschma, 2015; Boschma, 2015; Christopherson et al., 2010; Davoudi & Porter, 2012; Hassink, 2010).

Though it is acknowledged that larger systems are driven by the interactions between the diverse range of constituents and their environments, there has been relatively little analysis of regional resilience with a micro-level focus (Bristow & Healy, 2014, p. 925). Swanstrom (2008) suggests that understanding regional resilience and path development implies understanding the ability of the individual economic actors to adapt and reconfigure their industrial, technological, network and institutional structures within an economic system that is in constant motion (based on Boschma, 2015). Indeed, Boschma (2015) argues that it is crucial to relate resilience to the different agents in regions, that is, individuals, organizations, industries and so on, as each may present distinctive features of resilience.

Both Bristow and Healy (2014) and Doran and Fingleton (2016) consider the role of human agency, at the individual and collective levels, in regional resilience. We turn our attention to firms, small economic units, studying four firms that each have demonstrated a remarkable ability in their host regions to engage continually in both path extension and path renewal over time. To understand resilient firms and their ability to survive may give a better understanding of regional resilience and the conditions for path renewal and path creation (Isaksen, 2015). We address the following questions:

> How does organizational resilience unfold/materialize in firms in response to periods with shocks and shifts?
>
> How do firms develop and sustain resilience capacity over time?
>
> How do resilient firms relate and connect with the region?

We address three issues not commonly addressed in the literature: firstly, the issue of sustainability – how resilience is sustained in a firm over time; secondly, the dynamic and evolutionary rather than static nature of organizational resilience and, thirdly, the relationship of resilient firms to the region. In addressing the first and second issues, we consider the roles of history and context. Boschma (2015) claims that these are important elements in understanding regional resilience. 'History' is a combination of different layers of activity that consist of economic, cultural, political and ideological strata, and the layers reflect the position of a region's industry within the broader geographical division of labour at different times (Massey, 1984, p. 118). The concept of context we will return to later in the article in connection with the presentation and discussion of organizational resilience. The third issue implies an exploration of the relations resilient firms may have with the region.

Theoretical considerations and framework

About organizational resilience

As our empirical data are at the firm level, the theoretical framework for analysis is therefore drawn principally from theories of organizational resilience. Reviewing current research, Annarelli and Nonino (2016, p. 10) claim that academics have reached a shared consensus on the definition, foundations and characteristics of organizational resilience and that future research needs to investigate how organizations achieve resilience, and to investigate more fully the dynamic capabilities of resilience.

The definition of organizational resilience given by Annarelli and Nonino (2016, p. 3) stresses the capacity of the organization for two types of response: anticipatory, which is termed static, and strategic, which is termed dynamic. Anticipatory response minimizes the impact of environmental turbulence, while strategic response maximizes recovery or renewal when faced with crisis or disruption. To some extent, these notions parallel the notions of adaption and adaptability found in the literature on regional resilience. Adaption refers to the specialization of resources to fit the environment, while adaptability depends on the availability of unspecific and uncommitted capacities that can be put to a variety of unforeseeable uses (Grabher, 1993, p. 265). Adaptability is contingent on the ways in which existing assets are utilized for new purposes (Martin & Sunley, 2015). Organizations that survive and prosper over time display the ability for dual responses. While material, financial and social resources necessarily play a role in supporting resilience (Pal, Torstensson, & Mattila, 2014), research suggests that resilience stems from the internal working of the organization (Sheffi & Rice, 2005; Teixeira & Werther, 2013). Each organization is said to be unique but changes through time, thus implying that leaders can reshape the traditions and customs of the organization, leading to a more resilient organization (Sheffi & Rice, 2005; Teixeira & Werther, 2013). The characteristics of resilient organizations include distributed leadership and decision-making, and encouraging their employees to be passionate about the company's mission (Sheffi & Rice, 2005).

Our theoretical framework

In structuring and analysing our data, we adopt a framework developed by Lengnick-Hall and Beck (2005) and Lengnick-Hall, Beck, and Lengnick-Hall (2011). Though this framework stems from an earlier date, we argue that it encompasses both the dimensions proposed by Teixeira and Werther (2013) and the resource categories of Pal et al. (2014).

In their framework, Pal et al. (2014) detail five categories of resources that support resilience: (1) material, (2) financial, (3) human resources and teamwork, (4) network resources, that is, collaborative inter-organizational resources, and (5) the intangible resources of the social fabric of good will. Teixeira and Werther (2013) relate continuous innovation to an underlying culture of resilience, defined by four dimensions: (1) leadership's forward-looking dialogue with the organization, (2) an open and trusting environment, (3) strategic planning that is anticipatory in nature and (4) a culture that promotes innovation. Each of these resources and dimensions may be categorized into the components in our research.

Lengnick-Hall and Beck (2005) and Lengnick-Hall et al. (2011) see resilience capacity as constituted of three components: cognitive, behavioural and contextual. 'Cognitive resilience' is a conceptual orientation that allows a firm to respond to events in a nuanced and creative fashion, looking beyond mere survival and seeing opportunities in adversity. It is a shared mindset characterized by expertise, opportunism, creativity and decisiveness despite uncertainty. 'Behavioural resilience' is the ability of the firm to follow different and often counter-intuitive courses of action. Internally, it is characterized by routines of collaboration, flexibility and habits of continuous dialogue. 'Contextual resilience' provides the setting for integrating and using both cognitive and behavioural resilience. It is about building social capital by forming and strengthening trusting relationships between people both within and without the organization. Internally, it is characterized by a climate of psychological safety that supports risk-taking, experimenting and admitting mistakes. Externally, it is characterized by a broad resource network that provides an operational platform for the firm.

Of the three mentioned components, contextual resilience is perhaps the one least tangible. Context is a many faceted concept and may be interpreted in different ways (Karlsen & Larrea, 2016). Firstly, it may be something that surrounds an organization, something external to the organization. Secondly, context may also be a part of the actors' cognitive frameworks and their interpretation of that which surrounds them. In this case, the actors see themselves as a part of the context; that is, that they are not spectators to the context, but participants in it (Karlsen & Larrea, 2016). This implies that the region where an organization is located is a context for the organization. A resilient organization behaves dynamically and actively, constantly transforming. In so doing, the organization influences the region and contributes to change the context of which it is a part. By implication therefore, organizational resilience is a necessary condition for regional resilience.

Akgün and Keskin (2014) have criticized Lengnick-Hall and Beck (2005) and Lengnick-Hall, Beck, and Lengnick-Hall (2011) model as abstract, implicit and not operationalized. We challenge this criticism. Building on the work of Dewald and Bowen (2010), we see cognitive resilience as a decision-making intention based on the ability to notice, interpret, analyse and formulate responses to pending and actual environmental change. Behavioural resilience represents the action of implementing the response developed through cognitive resilience. As such, behavioural resilience is observable in the actions and organization of the firm. Cognitive resilience, on the other hand, must be inferred from analysis of observed patterns of interaction and of analysis of dialogue as recorded in interviews and expressed in documents. Contextual resilience can be both observed and inferred. Operationalized, cognitive – how do organizations think strategically, behavioural – how do they act, and contextual – where are they located and how do they interact with the region.

Context and method

The empirical study is a multiple-case study (Piekkari, Plakoyiannaki, & Welch, 2010; Yin, 2013) that focuses on four firms in four industries in different regions (overview of cases in Table 1). Cooke (1998) defines a region in a rather broad and vague manner, as a unit between a nation and the local.

Table 1. Overview of the cases.

Firm	Case 1 Arges	Case 2 Bjølvefossen	Case 3 Nøsted	Case 4 Tranberg
Location and population	Alta, 20 000	Ålvik, 491	Mandal, 15,000	Stavanger, 132,000
L&R (residential and labour market regions) region	Small city region	Rural region	Small city region	Populous city region
Core activity	Production of specially designed plastic pipe	Production of master ferroalloys for international iron and steel industry	Production of chains	Production of lighting, heating systems & casings for extreme conditions
Product characteristics	High-quality, new to market, system solutions	High-quality, customer-tailored products and solutions	High-quality, flexible production tailored to customers' specifications	High-quality, durability, system solutions, specification design to production
Recruitment	Local	Mainly local	Local	Prefer local
No. employees	20	160	350 (75 in Mandal)	70
Established	2013	1905	1939	1901
Ownership – present	Employees and local investors	Elkem, China National Bluestar	Family owned, local in Mandal	R. Stahl Technology Group
Turnover 2014	NOK 30 mill	NOK 480 mill	NOK 400 mill	NOK 160 mill
Export	Not revealed	90 %	90 %	50 % (2015)
Competence	Certified tradesmen, engineers, business and marketing professionals	Process operators, certified tradesmen, mechanics, electro-operators, engineers and civil engineers	Certified tradesmen, engineers, business and marketing professionals	Certified tradesmen, engineers, business and marketing professionals, experience and adaptability
Employee turnover	Stable	Low – stable	Low – stable	Low – stable
Organization		Team based, Lean inspired, flat structure	Team, flexible, rotation in production,	Team, rotation in production, sharing of knowledge
Customer relationships	Close	Close	Close	Close

The study traces the significant incidents in the four firms, highlighting the role of the relation between the firms and their region in cultivating and maintaining organizational resilience. The firms selected have been exposed to different forms of shocks and shifts, and exhibit adaptability in response to changes in the external environment (Flyvbjerg, 2006). Their adaptability makes them interesting cases for testing assumptions about the dimensions of organizational resilience underlying this study. In addition, by choosing four different firms located in four regions, we may be able to draw out salient features, which can contribute to expand the knowledge of resilient firms and their relationship with the region.

As the research focuses on experienced crises and shifts, the interviews were inspired by the critical incident technique (CIT). CIT originates from the work of Flanagan (1954), and has been used in a number of studies (e.g. Coetzer, Redmond, & Sharafizad, 2012; Cope & Watts, 2000; Kraaijenbrink, 2012). The CIT is a qualitative interview procedure that permits an understanding from the individual firm's perspective (Coetzer et al., 2012). A majority of CIT studies have adopted a retrospective approach, even though a general limitation of such studies is that they rely on the respondent's ability to provide correctly a detailed description of a past event. Yet, despite this drawback, the CIT is recognized amongst academics to be a suitable technique for gathering rich data on significant events (Coetzer et al., 2012; Kraaijenbrink, 2012) as it focuses on events that have actually happened, rather than on generalizations or opinions.

Table 2. Overview of data-collection and methods.

Method	Arges	Bjølvefossen	Nøsted	Tranberg
Semi-structured interviews	Seven in-depth interviews	Two in-depth interviews one focus group interview with five to seven workers	One focus group interview with three informants, one in-depth interview and 11 shorter interviews	Three in-depth interviews, two shorter interviews
Observation	Guided tour	Two days in the firm, data collection/chatting observation	Guided tour	Two days in the firm, data collection/ chatting observation
Document analysis	Articles, brochures, website, social media	History book, PhD on organ, team-based change, newspaper articles, web articles, website	Master thesis, brochures, online newsletters and news clippings	Published history, newspaper articles, brochures, website, registers

Data collection

We collected the data through semi-structured individual and focus group interviews. Further, to elicit and trace information linked to the critical incidents, we asked the informants to tell us about the firm and its history with a particular focus on the critical incidents. The interviews were based on an interview guide, audio recorded and later transcribed. The transcripts facilitated the identification of issues that enabled each case firm to respond to the critical incidents. In addition to the interviews, the researchers participated in meetings, guided tours in the firms and collected secondary data on the firms from other sources (see Table 2 for an overview of the data collection process).

We analysed the data in two phases, a within-case analysis followed by a cross-case analysis (Yin, 2013). Firstly, based on the information and transcriptions, issues linked to the critical incidents/periods for each case were formulated and discussed in relation to our theoretical framework. The case findings were then compared across the cases; salient features were identified, discussed and integrated into the case descriptions. The case stories differed somewhat in how the firms experienced the shocks and shifts. Two of the firms, Arges and Bjølvefossen, recently experienced profound crisis within a specific period and the analyses, therefore, concentrate on these periods. With respect to Tranberg and Nøsted, these firms refer more to a continuous handling of shocks and shifts in the external environment during their lifespan, and report on anticipation rather than concrete handling of specific crises. The narratives of the four firms, therefore, unfold differently.

The research emphasizes triangulation of methods, the use of multiple informants across levels and functions. In addition, careful connection of interview questions to research questions and the theoretical foundation enhances the study's reliability and validity (Stake, 2013; Yin, 2013). The research team comprised four researchers, one from each region, who met regularly. This contributed to strengthen the reliability in the data collection and analysis.

Analysis of the four firms

Arges

About the firm

Arges, formerly known as Polyfemos, was founded in Alta in 1992, by a local entrepreneur, Arnstein Johansen. Alta, situated in the far north of Norway, is a small but growing city characterized by a strong entrepreneurial culture, visible in the large private sector with its variety of locally owned private firms (Isaksen, 2005; Selstad & Onsager, 2004). Since initialization, the firm Arges has been successful in producing tailor-made solutions in high-density polyethylene (HDPE) plastic for contracting firms and the telecommunication market. The firm was sold to the Norwegian Wavin group in 2007. Despite initial success and high turnovers – the firm was the most profitable in the Wavin concern – the firm was dissolved in 2012, when Wavin AS decided to consolidate their production in the south of Norway. Wavin AS is part of the Wavin Group based in the Netherlands, which is the leading supplier of plastic pipe systems in the sewage, water and plumbing sector in Europe. Local employees, including the original founder, supported by local investors, restarted the firm in 2013. Today the firm has approximately 20 local employees and a yearly turnover of around 30 million Norwegian kroner. In the following, we retell the story, identifying and unfolding components of resilience capacity.

Cognitive resilience

The founder agreed to restart the firm on the premise that 'he could play ball with the best in production and the management team'; in other words, a restart depended on the former management team and employees joining the new firm. Starting with the same people increased the chance of success as their knowledge and expertise 'constitute the firm's foundation which is critical' (Founder).

The employees involved shared a strong belief that a restart would be successful, as the manager said, 'We have years of experience with this raw material and market, we know the mechanisms, and we know people. There is no reason that we should not make a good product in Alta'. This shared mindset, in addition to creative employees 'who understand fully what we do', is seen to be critical to '(knowledge) contributing to shorten the starting phase' (Marketing Manager).

Behavioural resilience

After the firm was re-established, it experienced restricted market access to the planned main market. This increased the pressure on the firm, but they were able to pursue an alternative strategy to 'come up with something new'. The founder recognized an opportunity in the fish farming industry and the management team, assisted by the production team, began to experiment to develop the idea into a full commercial product, the now patented HDPE fish-feeding pipe. A central element driving product development is the co-location of management and production. Co-location means daily meetings and easy flow of communication in the firm, which enables speedy all-round problem-solving and product testing and facilitates an 'environment where all employees dare to voice ideas and suggestions' (General Manager). These routines of collaboration make for 'practical real time problem-solving' (Technical manager). This further entails extensive dialogue with suppliers and customers, involving, in particular, the management team: 'We talk to the customers about the problems we can solve for them and we get ideas' (Founder). The production team also meets customers as many visits include a tour/inspection of the production hall where customers can talk directly to those planning and operating production: 'I talk to those who visit – I have a lot of plastic knowledge and knowledge about the process and the machinery' (Shift leader).

Contextual resilience

Once the dissolution of the original company in 2012 was a fact, the municipality invited the previous founder to investigate possibilities for a restart. Once the decision for a restart was taken, local entrepreneurs, local investors and a local public policy office became central to increase the pace of the restart phase. The history of the firm, its success and contributions to the local context and previous relations were important reasons for local engagement: 'When we came to the bank and to Innovation Norway with our idea, they said yes immediately, they knew our history' (Founder). The former mayor was quoted in the local newspaper as saying, 'The municipality of Alta will go the extra mile if that saves the firm' (Altaposten 7.9.2012). Arges also experienced support from local entrepreneurs when encountering a problem with the fish-feeding pipe during development: 'a team member with technical expertise just walked across the road to a mechanical firm and within 3 hours he had a solution to our problem' (Founder). Many of the local entrepreneurs are included in a local business network where the partners meet regularly to 'talk and learn about each other's problems and how they solve them' (General Manager). These networks are based on trust and although they are not viewed as contributing to direct problem-solving, they are important in maintaining a sense of community outside of the firm.

The analysis shows that the restart of the firm was supported through interaction with the local community. The feeling of community is strong, both inside and outside of the firm. This strengthens employees and manager's confidence and belief in future success.

Bjølvefossen

About the firm

Bjølvefossen was founded in 1905 in the industry village of Ålvik, located in the region of Kvam, 115 km east of Bergen, on the west coast of Norway. Since 1920, the firm has produced ferroalloys for the international iron and steel industry. The development of the small village has been largely affected by the industrial use of hydroelectric power resources and its national and international position as a producer of magnesium-ferrosilicon. The village emerged early as relatively modern and international with respect to living conditions and ways of life, compared to other villages and towns in Norway (Fossåskaret & Storås, 1999), but has remained highly dependent on the firm with respect to work opportunities. Historically, a large number of investors and entrepreneurs, both national and international, have contributed to develop the firm. The Elkem Company took over the firm in 2000. Today the firm is one of the world's largest producers of magnesium-ferrosilicon. The plant has around 160 employees, stable and mainly local staff, and a yearly turnover of 480 million Norwegian kroner. During its lifetime, the firm has experienced severe shocks and has been threatened with closure several times, but has proved able to adapt and prosper through change and crisis. The firm has continuously developed and applied new technology. During the 1990s, the firm implemented a team-based organization that has proved essential to sustaining its innovativeness.

The latest crisis struck in 2006, when the owner Elkem decided to move the production to Iceland. The main reason for this decision was the termination of the existent power regime ensuring low-priced energy to Norwegian industry.

In the analysis below, we concentrate on the subsequent period of crisis from 2006 to 2012. During this time, the firm functioned as a back-up plant, in case the planned transfer of production to Iceland failed. In addition, the owner Elkem initiated an innovative pilot project. This project in environmental recycling aimed to recover waste material from electrolysis cells in the aluminium industry. The project had an exploratory character, as a trial operation and demonstration plant, differing significantly from previous activity and practice.

Cognitive resilience

When confronted with the proposed move, the response of the workers at Bjølvefossen was characterized by uncertainty and scepticism. The trade union leader endeavoured to take a professional and positive role in relation to the shock, and tried to figure out 'how could we manage to turn this around, so that people saw an opportunity and were positive to it'.

Yet, he acknowledged it was a difficult task to sustain a positive spirit during the relatively long interval. For a short dramatic period of some months, all production at Bjølvefossen ceased:

> It was a very special situation. You have to remember that things have been rolling along here since 1927, around the clock. (HR manager)

The period clearly challenged the cognitive resilience of the firm.

The pilot project was challenging, as the workers had to find the motivation to build new knowledge which was necessary to introduce innovative production processes in the new operation. Because of the many crises and readjustments the firm had been through previously, it had developed a mindset and working culture that accepted change and sought improvement in order to overcome challenges, and a varied and solid organizational experience of working with new productions and processes.

> It is one of the things we are best at. To get things done. If we don't manage today, then we will at the very least manage it next time. (Quality manager)

> 'Bjølve has always been very open to testing new things, new technology, and we have been first out on many occasions … I think it has something to do with the fact that we have pretty much had our throats cut … and you have to do something' (Operator).

Behavioural resilience

The workers did not put much faith in the pilot project but sustained by habits and routines of collaboration engaged in new learning and upheld their loyalty, seeing this as the best prospect for maintaining their employment. The staff also displayed commitment to transferring knowledge to set up the production in Iceland, but this was coupled with some despair, as in reality they contributed to shut down their own plant.

The workers had embraced the team-based way of working implemented in the 1990s, and this strengthened the collective culture in the firm. Moreover, the staff had upgraded this team-based organization through the numerous challenges and crises the firm had been through. As well, the many crises through the years had enhanced the workers' willingness to overcome new challenges through engagement and learning. The following citation illustrates the firm's behavioural resilience capacity:

If there is an inquiry from a customer about something special, a problem or new quality demands, then the organization goes for it. The engineers tell us what is needed and there are no barriers to getting it done. We have understood what needs to be done, it is in our culture. (Production manager)

In 2012, Elkem decided to repatriate the production from Iceland to Bjølvefossen, as they had failed to establish the same quality and volume in the production in the new plant in Iceland. In addition, the change in the power regime did not affect the local firm negatively as anticipated.

Contextual resilience

The firm is strongly connected to the region. Throughout history, the firm has 'become' the place and the place has 'become' the firm. People working in the firm have few work opportunities nearby, a factor that strengthens their commitment and loyalty to the workplace.

… it's in the blood, we have had to be adaptable, – what else could we do – the whole place was under threat. (Trade union leader)

The workers are willing to engage in innovation and change, because they acknowledge the necessity of these activities – to keep their region alive.

The history of Bjølvefossen is very much about restructuring. Perhaps it is in the blood of the place, I have wondered about that. You observe that the world is changing, the market changes, and you have to do something, take hold of it. We have changed our product portfolio, many times, totally. (HR Manager)

Nøsted

About the firm

Nøsted is a family-owned company, established in 1939, with the fourth generation assuming the role of CEO of the firm in 2016. Today the firm is the only remaining chain producer in Norway. Nøsted owns ten factories in total, five in Norway and five abroad. The top management, the development department and the main production unit of chains are all located in the small town of Mandal, in the south of Norway.

Periods of growth and expansion have been followed by hard times and crises. After the Second World War, in the 1950s and 1960s the firm expanded its production. Since the 1970s, the firm has experienced several crises, but each time it has managed to face the new challenges, surviving and continuing its development. In the early 1970s, the leader and owner of the firm, the second generation of Nøsted, died unexpectedly. As the next generation was not yet old enough to lead the firm, an external manager was hired. Understanding the many informal rules that had developed between the owner/manager and the environment in the firm about how to do things was not an easy task for an outsider. For this and perhaps other reasons, growth stagnated until mid-1980s. At this time, the third generation took over the relay as the leader of the firm and a new growth path started.

Cognitive resilience

Through its sales organization in Canada, established in 1983, the firm realized that changes in the North American market subsequently reached Europe and Norway only later. By analysing trends in the North American market, the firm realized that the market for tyre chains, the most important product for the firm, was changing: Firstly, because of increased competition from producers in low-cost countries, and, secondly, because several 'green winters' in North America had resulted in a decreased demand for tyre chains. Cognitively this trend was easy to acknowledge, but given the firm's long tradition of producing tyre chains, constructing and implementing a new strategy, which entailed diversification into new products and markets, were demanding. By relying on their deep knowledge of chain production, the firm managed it. They branched into new markets with new types of chains, specifically the upcoming oil and gas industry in the North Sea and the fish farming industry. Both required high-quality anchoring chains. This type of creative response, where opportunity is seen in adversity, is typical of cognitive resilience that has been built up over time.

Behavioural resilience

A period of crisis in the 1990s forced the firm to develop new modes of behaviour. At the start of the period, the firm displayed few of the characteristics of behavioural resilience, as we will see in the narrative below, but through the crisis the firm was able to develop both new routines and flexibility and take counter-intuitive courses of action. The financial crisis in the beginning of the 1990 hit the firm hard because of leveraged investment in new technology, such as automatic welding machines.

Previous experience in the firm had shown that it was easy to implement change in the organization by investing in new machines. It was more difficult, but more affordable to work to change workers' attitudes to new methods, such as Lean manufacturing, that would increase production volume and decrease the waste in the production. However, the trade union and many workers were sceptical to new ideas about changes in the production process.

> There was a constant scepticism towards change. And I saw quite a lot of firms where things went much slower than here, so it was not just us. It was the times. (Factory Manager)

The scepticism reflected the context, the industrial culture in Mandal, developed over many years. In the 1970s, up to 15% of the workforce worked in industry. This group has been steadily reduced over the years by almost two-thirds. Also in Nøsted, many employees were dismissed. Only workers with expert knowledge about production were retained. The factory manager, at that time a newly educated engineer, described the situation not only as demanding and difficult, but also as an opportunity to find new solutions.

> But what was good was that you had to work at all levels in the firm. And so you were forced to get an overview of the whole firm. Instead of just getting stuck on a narrow engineering path. (Factory Manager)

Working on all levels in the factory gave a good insight into how production functioned in practice and into what needed to be changed in the organization. This knowledge was used to establish a revised division of labour within the firm. The most labour-intensive work was offshored to a new factory in Lithuania in 2003, while the most knowledge-intensive and automatic part of the production was retained in Mandal. In line with this knowledge development strategy, a development (R&D) department and a test laboratory were established in Mandal in 2014.

Contextual resilience

In a family firm as Nøsted, much of the interaction is informal, based on trust and influenced by the fact that the CEO is the owner of the firm. This makes communication and decisions easy as long as there is stability in the chain of persons who interact but are more sensitive to unexpected events with the involved actors. Social capital within the organization is both strong and vulnerable as it is reliant on the family ties.

The firm has sympathy and social capital in the local district. In the 1990s, the firm was threatened with bankruptcy, but the regional bank decided to show mercy due to the actions the firm had taken in order to survive and since it was a well-known firm in the region.

More recently, Nøsted has been involved in a number of projects in the region, such as the establishment and development of a Centre for Innovative Design and Production in 2014 and the establishment of a school for creative arts in Mandal in 2016. The aim of the cluster organization is to develop mutual R&D projects which individual firms are too small to handle alone.

Tranberg

About the firm

Tranberg AS is a small mechanical–electrical firm situated in the county of Rogaland, which today produces lighting, heating, enclosures and helideck products for three major industries: oil and gas, maritime and the helicopter industry. The firm was selected for this study as it epitomizes robustness and resilience. Throughout its over 100-year-long history, the firm has repeatedly demonstrated an ability to identify and enter into new markets, while at the same time maintaining a solid competitive production of old niche products. The firm has consciously maintained and strengthened its local affiliation. The production process, in its entity, from design, prototyping, testing and production, takes place in the regional locality. The firm has recently realized a long-term strategy and established a position in the Chinese market. Originally family owned, the firm joined the R. Stahl Technology Group in 2006.

Cognitive resilience

Respondents consistently refer to external shifts and shocks, whether these are the advent of new technology or changing and turbulent markets, as opportunities rather than as crises. 'Ok we think here is an opportunity for us. We find the solutions, present to the customers' (Head of marketing). The relatively small size of the company puts them at a higher risk of going under at such times, but they prefer to view their size as an advantage which gives them flexibility to change strategy quickly. 'We are small and flexible ... we make products that fit in and deliver when required' (Technical director).

> We have no control over the big things but we try to adapt to change (Head of marketing).

The market director describes how they entered into the helideck market from the oil industry. 'People needed to be transported, from land to offshore ... market for helicopter deck. ... We developed new lighting products ... and got a third place "niche" in the market. After a while this became a third of our turnover.' A more recent and developing business area is winterization, described as follows:

> A good example is the Goliath platform ... in the far north, winterization a whole new concept. Everything has to be ice free ... all supply boats too, at least four boats for each platform ... Ok we think, this is an opportunity, we find solutions, new area, new market, and we are there. (Head of marketing)

Similarly, they chose to view the more recent change in ownership as bringing new markets and access to testing facilities rather than as a loss of local identity. We interpret this conceptual orientation as typical of cognitive resilience.

Behavioural resilience

In each of the instances described above, the firm applied their core competence to develop new products for emerging markets, while at the same time maintaining production of original products.

Respondents maintain that this ability to act quickly and to develop new products is dependent on the organizational structure of the firm and on the competence of the staff. The organization is flat and team based. Internal transfer of knowledge is encouraged through regular meetings, which are open to discussion, suggestions and disputes. The technical, market and production departments meet weekly to plan together and work on projects. Project teams are constructed in line with the requirements of projects, thus ensuring ownership and varied workdays for workers. In this manner, employees gain self-confidence and are given opportunities for learning.

'Knowledge is in the people that work here. Besides technical skill, both the ability to fit into the culture of the firm and to learn fast are considered important when hiring new employees.' At the same time, the firm has worked systematically over many years to establish a database of technical specifications and drawings. 'We take good care of the golden egg' (Technical director).

Internally, the firm has made a dramatic shift from being a producer of single products to being a solution provider. Solutions are systems rather than single products. These solutions are incorporated in the design phase of larger projects such as shipbuilding, thus securing the market position. In addition, the firm is not competing with low-cost countries on producing series products.

> We follow the customer and adjust to them, rather than the opposite ... This is extremely important in order to survive. (Technical director)

Contextual resilience

Geographical location brought many opportunities for the firm in the 1970s, as establishing oil and service companies needed close contact. However, Tranberg has since expanded into new markets with new products and is no longer solely dependent on Norwegian customers or on the oil industry. It would seem that it is now more important for the company to be a member of an international global organization than to be a member of regional clusters or regional R&D collaborations. The owner group provides access to new markets, technology and testing facilities. The international nature of the shipping industry implies that it is not a disadvantage to be located in Stavanger. However, the company is still strongly tied to the local region of Jæren which is known for its entrepreneurial culture (Grove, 2016). Informants confirm that a problem-solving, creative orientation is deeply rooted in the local culture and the firm prefers to employ people from

Jæren. Once employed, workers tend to stay on and often recruit new employees from their family. Respondents suggest that 'real trade folk' are more capable than academics in developing new products.

Comparison of the case firms

The case analyses showed both commonalities and differences amongst the four firms. The three dimensions of resilience capacity were evident in all firms, but appeared as a complex and unique blend. Table 3 summarizes the case analyses.

A common feature amongst the firms was that cognitive resilience functioned to develop and sustain behavioural resilience. The firms interpreted and analysed externally induced shocks and shifts, and formulated responses, which resulted in appropriate adaptations in their behavioural repertoire.

A reliance on and respect for knowledge sharing resulted in nuanced and creative responses. Additionally, the analyses indicated that the firms had further developed cognitive resilience as a result of dealing with several shocks and shifts during their lifespan. In Bjølvefossen, Tranberg and Nøsted, this conceptual orientation has become deeply internalized in the firms over time. In Arges, we see an emerging cognitive resilience in an intentional response to a major threat, seeing opportunity rather than defeat. Behavioural resilience was commonly demonstrated in all firms in the internal team-based organization and in collaborative action. In Nøsted, the established industry culture challenged this way of working, but the firm was able to develop managing new production and surviving competitive threats.

The firms' long-term strategies in sustaining workforce competence have resulted in highly committed and innovative workforces, allowing them to move into international

Table 3. Summary of the case analysis.

Firm cases	Resilience capacity		
	Cognitive resilience	Behavioural resilience	Contextual resilience
Arges	High levels of reciprocity and commitment Shared values, purpose and strong feeling of community and trust	Small, dynamic teams increase flexibility and a hands-on approach Produce tailor-made solutions to new and existing markets High level of knowledge transfer within/between teams	Strong local support History strengthens local connection Collective project
Bjølvefossen	Positive mindsets and enduring attitude	Refined team-based organization High learning engagement and open for new technology	Strong and symbiotic-like relationship to the local place Resilience – inherent to the place
Nøsted	High adaptability developed through previous crisis	A flexible production aimed at serving customers' needs and external changes	Connected to the region through the long history Engage in activities with the aim of improving collaboration between local firms and knowledge organizations.
Tranberg	High level of ingenuity Opportunity seeking A strong sense of purpose, core values, a genius vision and deliberate use of language	Innovative, flexible – constant new markets and new products Shift from producing products to producing solutions Interesting and enjoyable tasks	Emphasis on the local regional culture and identity Doing-using-interaction mode ensures motivation, ownership and a stable staff

markets with competitive products. This modus operando may be regarded as business strategy, but the reported rational was based on strong relations to the region, 'the way we do things here', rather than economic theory.

The analyses of contextual resilience showed that each of the four firms had quite different relations to the region. However, these connections/relations emerged in the data as critical in sustaining resilience capacity for all firms and hence as a commonality amongst the firms. Bjølvefossen had developed a symbiotic-like relationship to its region through a shared history. The firm played a dominant role in shaping the region, with respect to living conditions and ways of life. The employees had few work opportunities outside of the firm, and the survival of the firm equalled the survival of the region. This insight sustained both cognitive and behavioural resilience. Arges used its social capital and local networks to re-establish the firm in the region. The firm also showed high commitment to this process, as it valued the local entrepreneurial milieu and local institutional actors such as investors and the public policy office. The dynamic interplay and interdependence between Arges and the surrounding regional actors sustained its resilience capacity. Tranberg showed a strong relation to the region, in physically maintaining their operations in the region, and in that the firm demonstrated a fervent, repeated and proud articulation of regional identity. The firm also emphasized the value of the locally recruited workforce with its associated competence and creativity, which, they contend, is deeply rooted in the region. This identity persists, clearly cultivated, in spite of the influences of both globalization and foreign acquisition, and functions as a driving force in sustaining resilience capacity. Nøsted has maintained strong relations to the region, as it has invested in local competence building and new machinery locally several times despite globalization and changing markets. The firm valued its locally recruited competence and continued to invest in relations with other regional firms to sustain its resilience capacity. Resilience is about handling such contextual factors in an enabling way in specific moments of change.

The research has revealed various ways in which resilient firms may relate to and interact with the region, thus specifically illuminating the contextual dimension of organizational resilience. In so doing, we add to the existing literature on organizational resilience. We have seen that the firm–region relation evolves such that the firm and its workforce are deeply connected to the region, economically and socioculturally. This strong interdependence contributes to sustain and build organizational resilience, perhaps because the workforce is cognizant of the negative consequences for themselves and for the firm of breaking the relationship. In general, in all cases the firm–region relation was displayed through a strong regional identity, where the locally recruited workforce and associated competence are highly valued and cultivated within the firm. Moreover, the firm–region relation may materialize through reciprocal commitment and support amongst a broad number of actors in the region and the firm.

Overall, our findings show that the region, in terms of pre-existing cultures and structures, has contributed positively to sustain resilience in the firms – an issue discussed in Boschma (2015). Yet, we argue that the firm-level perspective is essential in this matter. It is the firms' interpretation of the region as context and the consequent behavioural action that are of significance. Whereas other regional firms may see constraints in the region, these firms have focused on opportunities and inherent values in their region as a positive force sustaining organizational resilience. Hence, referring to Boschma

(2015), the key to understand how regions may develop new growth paths is to understand individual firms, and their responsiveness, as these agents interpret and deal differently with shifts and shocks.

Our research also supports the view of seeing resilience as an ongoing process, rather than as a recovery to a stable equilibrium state (Simmie & Martin, 2010, p. 31). Translated to the firm level, resilient firms adopt long-term strategies in order to be able to cope with new technologies, changes in markets and global competition. These strategies encompass an ongoing investment and cultivation of workforce competence and creativity, investments in the capacity to implement new technologies, productions and organizational innovations. Therefore, new growth paths are not detached from their past, but firms' path dependency in the form of the cultivated workforce culture and competence is possibly compatible with change, rejuvenated and redeployed in new combinations to cope with external shocks and shifts.

Conclusion

In this paper, we have endeavoured to develop a more comprehensive understanding of how firms develop and sustain resilience capacity over time. As stated earlier, understanding regional resilience implies an understanding of the resilience of individual firms (Swanstrom, 2008; based on Boschma, 2015). Regions are constructed through the activities of human action and interaction and, as a result, are in a constant process of transition. We found that firms' resilience capacity evolves in the interplay between the region and the firm over time. Culture and identity are established into the firm through the people, giving rise to shared values and enhanced commitment.

The four firms in this study contribute to regional resilience in various ways. Firstly, each promotes a culture of innovation and presents as an exemplary case. Such cases serve as inspiration and models in regional development. Individually, Tranberg, the only urban-based firm, contributes to industrial sector resilience. In addition, in all cases we found that the connection to a specific place with its associated culture matters (e.g. Massey, 1984).

To conclude, the history of the firms, as part of a global industry encompassing shocks and shifts, has deeply affected the firms and the region. Through the many shocks and shifts, the firms have developed a profound understanding of the need to adapt to the global market and to technological changes. The analysis shows that the firms have continuously developed and sustained resilience capacity over time and in interaction with the region. The relationship between the firms and the region is interdependent, creating a strong regional commitment to the firm and vice versa, which again sustains the firm's resilience capacity.

Limitations and directions for further research

The study is limited to a small number of firms. As such it has obvious limitations in regards to empirical generalization. (Flyvbjerg, 2006; Yin, 2013). However, the case study can contribute to theoretical generalization (Flyvbjerg, 2006; Yin, 2013), maturing both the theory of path development and the different resilience concepts explored in this research.

Further studies are needed to investigate the interplay between organizational resilience and regional resilience. In such studies, the number of firms studied in each region should be increased. Employing a mixture of qualitative and quantitative methods will allow for both empirical and theoretical generalization.

Acknowledgements

The authors would like to thank the two anonymous reviewers for their helpful comments on previous drafts of this paper.

Disclosure statement

No potential conflict of interest was reported by the authors.

Funding

The research was supported by The Research Council of Norway and the counties of Agder, Finnmark, Hordaland and Rogaland.

References

Akgün, A. E., & Keskin, H. (2014). Organisational resilience capacity and firm product innovativeness and performance. *International Journal of Production Research, 52*(23), 6918–6937. doi:10.1080/00207543.2014.910624

Annarelli, A., & Nonino, F. (2016). Strategic and operational management of organizational resilience: Current state of research and future directions. *Omega, 62*, 1–18. doi:10.1016/j.omega.2015.08.004

Balland, P.-A., Rigby, D., & Boschma, R. (2015). The technological resilience of US cities. *Cambridge Journal of Regions, Economy and Society, 8*(2), 167–184. doi:10.1093/cjres/rsv007

Boschma, R. (2015). Towards an evolutionary perspective on regional resilience. *Regional Studies, 49*(5), 733–751. doi:10.1080/00343404.2014.959481

Bristow, G., & Healy, A. (2014). Regional resilience: An agency perspective. *Regional Studies, 48*(5), 923–935. doi:10.1080/00343404.2013.854879

Christopherson, S., Michie, J., & Tyler, P. (2010). Regional resilience: Theoretical and empirical perspectives. *Cambridge Journal of Regions, Economy and Society, 3*(1), 3–10. doi:10.1093/cjres/rsq004

Coetzer, A., Redmond, J., & Sharafizad, J. (2012). Decision making regarding access to training and development in medium-sized enterprises: An exploratory study using the critical incident technique. *European Journal of Training and Development, 36*(4), 426–447. doi:10.1108/03090591211220348

Cooke, P. (1998). Introduction: Origins of the concept. In H.-J. Braczyk, P. Cooke, & M. Heidenreich (Eds.), *Regional innovation systems* (pp. 2–25). London: UCL Press.

Cope, J., & Watts, G. (2000). Learning by doing-an exploration of experience, critical incidents and reflection in entrepreneurial learning. *International Journal of Entrepreneurial Behavior & Research, 6*(3), 104–124. doi:10.1108/13552550010346208

Davoudi, S., & Porter, L. (2012). Resilience: A bridging concept or a dead end? *Planning Theory & Practice, 13*(2), 299–333. doi:10.1080/14649357.2012.677124

Dewald, J., & Bowen, F. (2010). Storm clouds and silver linings: Responding to disruptive innovations through cognitive resilience. *Entrepreneurship Theory and Practice, 34*(1), 197–218. doi:10.1111/j.1540-6520.2009.00312.x

Doran, J., & Fingleton, B. (2016). Employment resilience in Europe and the 2008 economic crisis: Insight from micro-level data. *Regional Studies, 50*(4), 644–656. doi:10.1080/00343404.2015.1088642

Flanagan, J. C. (1954). The critical incident technique. *Psychologial Bulletin, 51*(4), 327–358. doi:10.1037/h0061470

Flyvbjerg, B. (2006). Five misunderstandings about case-study research. *Qualitative Inquiry, 12*(2), 219–245. doi:10.1177/1077800405284363

Fossåskaret, E., & Storås, F. (1999). *Ferrofolket ved fjorden Globale tema i lokal soge – Bjølvefossen, Ålvik, Hardanger.* Bergen: John Grieg AS.

Grabher, G. (1993). The weakness of strong ties: The lock-in of regional development in the Ruhr area. In G. Grabher (Ed.), *The embedded firm: On the socioeconomics of industrial networks* (pp. 255–277). London: Routledge.

Grove, K. (2016). *På leit etter en vestnorsk arbeidarkultur Arbeiderhistorie 28.*

Hassink, R. (2010). Regional resilience: A promising concept to explain differences in regional economic adaptability? *Cambridge Journal of Regions, Economy and Society, 3*(1), 45–58. doi:10.1093/cjres/rsp033

Isaksen, A. (2005). *Den kreative klassen og regional næringsutvikling i Norge.*

Isaksen, A. (2015). Industrial development in thin regions: Trapped in path extension? *Journal of Economic Geography, 15*(3), 585–600. doi:10.1093/jeg/lbu026

Karlsen, J., & Larrea, M. (2016). Moving context from the background to the forefront of policy learning: Reflections on a case in Gipuzkoa, Basque country. *Environment and Planning C: Government and Policy.* doi:10.1177/0263774X16642442

Kraaijenbrink, J. (2012). Integrating knowledge and knowledge processes: A critical incident study of product development projects. *Journal of Product Innovation Management, 29*(6), 1082–1096. doi:10.1111/j.1540-5885.2012.00953.x

Lengnick-Hall, C. A., & Beck, T. E. (2005). Adaptive fit versus robust transformation: How organizations respond to environmental change. *Journal of Management, 31*(5), 738–757. doi:10.1177/0149206305279367

Lengnick-Hall, C. A., Beck, T. E., & Lengnick-Hall, M. L. (2011). Developing a capacity for organizational resilience through strategic human resource management. *Human Resource Management Review, 21*(3), 243–255. doi:10.1016/j.hrmr.2010.07.001

Martin, R., & Sunley, P. (2015). On the notion of regional economic resilience: Conceptualization and explanation. *Journal of Economic Geography, 15*, 1–42. doi:10.1093/jeg/lbu015

Massey, D. (1984). *Spatial divisions of labour. Social structures and the geography of production.* London: Macmillan.

Pal, R., Torstensson, H., & Mattila, H. (2014). Antecedents of organizational resilience in economic crises – an empirical study of Swedish textile and clothing SMEs. *International Journal of Production Economics, 147*, 410–428. doi:10.1016/j.ijpe.2013.02.031

Piekkari, R., Plakoyiannaki, E., & Welch, C. (2010). 'Good' case research in industrial marketing: Insights from research practice. *Industrial Marketing Management, 39*(1), 109–117. doi:10.1016/j.indmarman.2008.04.017

Selstad, T., & Onsager, K. (2004). *Regioner i utakt. Tapir akademisk forl.* Trondheim.

Shaw, K. (2012). Reframing' resilience: Challenges for planning theory and practice. *Planning Theory and Practice, 13*(2), 308–312. doi:10.1080/14649357.2012.677124

Sheffi, Y., & Rice Jr, J. B. (2005). A supply chain view of the resilient enterprise. *MIT Sloan Management Review, 47*(1), 41–48.

Simmie, J., & Martin, R. (2010). The economic resilience of regions: Towards an evolutionary approach. *Cambridge Journal of Regions, Economy and Society, 3*(1), 27–43. doi:10.1093/cjres/rsp029

Stake, R. E. (2013). *Multiple case study analysis.* New York, NY: Guilford Press.

Swanstrom, T. (2008). *Regional resilience: A critical examination of the ecological framework.* Berkeley, CA: University of California.

Teixeira, E. de O., & Werther, W. B. (2013). Resilience: Continuous renewal of competitive advantages. *Business Horizons, 56*(3), 333–342. doi:10.1016/j.bushor.2013.01.009

Yin, R. K. (2013). *Case study research: Design and methods.* Thousand Oaks: Sage.

Extra-regional linkages through MNCs in organizationally thick and specialized RISs: a source of new path development?

Heidi Wiig Aslesen, Katja Maria Hydle 🄳 and Kristin Wallevik

ABSTRACT

This paper explores how global innovation networks (GIN) within multinational companies (MNCs) act as extra-regional sources for path development in a regional innovation system (RIS) specializing in the oil and gas sector. We combine the literature on intra-firm knowledge dynamics in MNCs' GIN with the literature on RISs to better understand their interrelatedness and their dynamics. Based on interviews with 15 MNCs located in the south-west of Norway, we find that firms are highly dependent on competence throughout the MNCs' entire networks, as well as interaction with the overall RIS. The findings expose that MNCs' GINs can act as extra-regional sources for path 'extension' in thick and specialized RISs through intra-firm mobility, observation and sharing of routines and best practice, mainly resulting in incremental innovations. We find some signs of potential path 'renewal', including radical innovation ideas. However, there are hampering factors linked to strong internal competition for innovation projects, pressure for local profitability and ownership motivation. At the level of RISs, new initiatives going beyond existing cluster initiatives and specializations need support.

1. Introduction

Organizationally thick and specialized regional innovation systems (RISs) are seen as 'core centres of *continuity*' (Isaksen & Trippl, 2016). Furthermore, research suggests that extra-regional knowledge networks extend existing paths and create impulses to renew old paths (Bathelt, Malmberg, & Maskell, 2004; Binz, Truffer, & Coenen, 2014; Coenen, Benneworth, & Truffer, 2012). Multinational companies (MNCs) establish activity in regions with accumulated specific competences, innovation dynamics and well-functioning innovation systems (Cantwell & Piscitello, 2005; Crescenzi & Rodríguez-Pose, 2011). Furthermore, intra-firm networks of MNCs can be regarded as global innovation networks (GINs) (Liu & Liefner, 2016). In order to understand the dynamics and complementarities creating the potential for industrial development, firm-level accounts must be viewed within the wider regional environment which the firms are part of (Isaksen & Trippl, 2016). This paper explores learning and innovation through MNCs' GINs and the RISs they are embedded in. It is based on interviews with Norwegian firms that are part of MNCs located in the south-western part of Norway.

In the field of economic geography, uneven distribution of economic activity across space has been understood as an outcome of largely contingent, path-dependent, historical processes (Boschma & Frenken, 2011). The concept of path dependence has been used within several research fields in social science (Djelic & Quack, 2003; Garud & Karnoe, 2001; Sydow, Windeler, Müller-Seitz, & Lange, 2012), originating from the work of David (1985) and Arthur (1989) and defined as the historically contingent lock-in to one of a multiplicity of possible equilibrium states (David, 2005). The evolution from path dependence can, in periods of growth, follow the tracks of path 'extension', but continuing on the same path can lead to path 'exhaustion' and gradual decline (Hassink, 2010; Isaksen & Trippl, 2016). The theorizing around path dependence has been concerned with explaining the continuation and stability of existing pathways based on firm-specific intra-path incremental innovations. There has been less focus on renewal or new path creation that highlights elements in the wider regional environment influencing the innovation capability of regionally located firms, such as RISs (Isaksen & Trippl, 2016).

In order to better understand regional dynamics, scholars within economic geography and innovation systems agree that innovation research should explore multi-scalar processes in more detail, especially at the global scale (Binz et al., 2014; Bunnell & Coe, 2001; Carlsson, 2006). The previous neglect of multi-scalar interrelatedness has been criticized (Hassink, Klaerding, & Marques, 2014). This especially applies to the neglect of the embeddedness of firms in global production networks (GPN) (Mackinnon, 2012; Mackinnon, Cumbers, Pike, Birch, & Mcmaster, 2009, p. 139) as sources of development. There is a gap in the theorizing about the impact of GINs on industry formation (Coenen et al., 2012): GINs focus on the relevance of specific high-value-added activities (dispersed engineering, product development and R&D) across space, and the unit of analysis is the firm and the industry it is part of (Cooke, 2013; Parrilli, Nadvi, & Yeung, 2013). Hassink et al. (2014) also emphasize the need to go beyond firm-level approaches to understand economic development.

This paper addresses the above critique by looking at the interrelatedness between MNCs, GINs and RIS in analysing industrial development (Parrilli et al., 2013). Both firms and institutions operate on multiple scales, suggesting that the endogenous view of industrial development must be supplemented with extra-regional relations, since firms in a globalized world are part of global networks. The research questions are: How can MNCs' GINs act as extra-regional sources for path extension in organizationally thick and specialized RISs? How can path renewal be stimulated in a context with thick and specialized RISs with a number of MNCs?

The paper is organized as follows: Section 2 discusses the theory and Section 3 presents the methodology. The main empirical findings are presented in Section 4, followed by a discussion on the potentials for path extension and renewal in Section 5.

2. Regional path development, RISs and external knowledge flows through MNCs

Path dependence has been used as a concept for understanding social, cultural, institutional, organizational and political, as well as economic and technological, evolution

(Martin, 2010). The next section elaborates on the concept and links it to the discussion on regional path development and RISs. Research on extra-regional resources for path development, especially GINs and the role of MNCs in path development at the regional level, is also discussed.

2.1. Path dependence, de-locking and path development

The concept of path dependence has become important in understanding industrial development. It has been used to emphasize continuity rather than ongoing change, to understand why some development routes are intentionally chosen over others, and why change takes a particular direction (Grabher, 1993; Henning, Stam, & Wenting, 2013; Martin, 2010; Martin & Sunley, 2006). The concept has also been used to describe situations where actors are unable to move to a new state despite opportunities (Garud, Kumaraswamy, & Karnøe, 2010).

The concept of path dependence has been embraced by evolutionary economic geographers (Boschma & Frenken, 2006) where the construct of 'lock-in' is core. According to Martin (2010), the term lock-in has been used by numerous geographers to characterize the evolution of industrial districts, clusters and other localized forms of industrial specialization, referring to 'increasing returns'. Studies on the 'de-locking' of a stable state focus on change factors such as shocks or other triggering external events, assuming that local industries are not closed systems but subject to a variety of external forces that are not necessarily 'spasmodic events' (Martin, 2010). David (2001) assumed that only external shocks could move a technological path from lock-in and create a new path. Other scholars suggest a more gradual and transformative change (Djelic & Quack, 2003; Garud & Karnoe, 2001), where mechanisms for change also arise within systems. It is suggested that de-locking is linked to endogenous forces, such as agglomeration dis-economies, shifting into new paths, exhaustion of innovation by local firms (Martin, 2010), and learning and innovation in general. Learning processes require people to initiate and participate in the exchange and creation of knowledge (not as regions per se), and the regional level becomes important due to the social and institutional embeddedness of actors creating territorialized learning processes (Asheim, 2009).

Path dependence can have both positive and negative effects on regional economic performance. It can be positive when regional institutions and investments are adapted to enable the growth of a particular dominant industry, called 'path extension'; it can be negative when economies of specialization give rise to inertia even when new environmental conditions require adaptability, called 'path exhaustion' (Hassink, 2010; Henning et al., 2013). 'Path renewal' is defined as diversification of existing industries 'branching' into related ones, partly predetermining a region's structural diversification (Boschma, 2015; Boschma & Frenken, 2011; Isaksen & Trippl, 2016; Neffke, Henning, & Boschma, 2011). Industries will be created through endogenous spillover processes, where territorial embedded and recombined knowledge within clusters, or technological enclaves, are important (Frenken & Boschma, 2007). In the literature on 'path creation' (Garud & Karnoe, 2001), the primary explanation for technological development is the role of human agency and the way 'actors can and will mindfully deviate' from what appears to be the common expectation, in order to sample new experiences, explore new forms of practice and create new resources (Garud & Karnoe, 2001, p. 6). At the regional level, 'path creation' can be caused by inward investments and/or sectorial diversification and also be research driven (Henning et al., 2013; Isaksen & Trippl, 2016). The output of path creation can be new firms, spin-offs and/or industries that are new to the region, or result in firms having different variants of products, services, new techniques or new ways of organizing (Martin & Sunley, 2006; Tödtling & Trippl, 2013). Sydow et al. (2012) find that path extension mainly builds on consensus and follows a conservative mind-set, whereas path creation concerns the organization of conflict and entails a more disruptive way of thinking (p. 925). Path dependence and path creation involve context-sensitive actions (Meyer & Schubert, 2007); they are not contrasting as they are theoretically related and can be seen as two ends of a spectrum.

2.2. Types of RISs and path development

Well-functioning RISs can be characterized by the stimulation of collective learning by close inter-firm interactions, relevant knowledge and policy support infrastructure and the existence of formal and informal institutions that stimulate cooperation among different actors, reducing uncertainty in innovation processes (Asheim & Isaksen, 2002). Isaksen and Trippl (2016) differentiate between three types of RISs according to the number, size and types of firms and knowledge organizations, and the extent, breadth and reach of knowledge exchange. These are (1) organizationally thick and diversified RISs (advanced core regions), (2) organizationally thick and specialized RISs (old industrial areas/districts) and (3) organizationally thin RISs (peripheral areas). This paper analyses regions with organizationally thick and specialized RISs, characterized by a well-developed support structure strengthening prevailing pathways. These regions may have a lower capacity to attract related or unrelated knowledge due to lower anchoring capacity (Trippl, Grillitsch, & Isaksen, 2015), as the region is dominated by a few industries and their supporting infrastructure. The challenges of renewal capacity in thick specialized regions can be explained by local assets being strongly linked to their specialization and by low intra-regional related variety, which raise questions about the absorptive capacity of new knowledge as they are trapped in rigid specializations (Grabher, 1993). Regions also tend to diversify into related activities and shake off unrelated activities.

It has been suggested that promotion of extra-regional sources may induce changes in these 'core centres of continuity' (Trippl et al., 2015), which have the potential for path exhaustion due to a negative relation between specialization and renewal capacity (Boschma, 2015). External sources are suggested as a way to extend or combine existing knowledge (Boschma & Capone, 2014), where the combination of extra-regional connections and local ties may create innovativeness of actors, places and innovation systems (Bathelt et al., 2004). Path renewal is created within the firm and industry, and as the regional industry transforms and develops, the industrial structure will broaden into new or related areas (Boschma & Frenken, 2011). For this reason, it is important to address the multi-scalar interrelatedness and embeddedness of firms to understand path development (Hassink et al., 2014), since sources of change are often interdependent and potentially arise from causation between the various levels of analysis (Henning et al., 2013). The paper addresses this by looking at MNCs' GINs as external sources of path development and as such fills a gap in the literature on path development by including external sources and by looking at intra-firm relationships.

2.3. How MNCs' GINs can stimulate and hamper path extension and path renewal

Characteristics of the RIS and the existence of institutional support can attract organizations from outside the regions, such as MNCs. Innovative foreign investments through MNCs are based on regional assets and processes (Crescenzi, Pietrobelli, & Rabellotti, 2014), and MNCs establish activities in regions with accumulated specific competences (Cantwell & Piscitello, 2005; Narula & Zanfei, 2005), acting as extra-regional linkages inducing industrial development. For the MNCs, their presence in foreign locations and RISs broadens their search space and allows new opportunities and collaboration partners to be identified (Ebersberger & Herstad, 2012).

Neffke, Hartog, Boschma, and Henning (2014, p. 30) found that non-local agents induced significantly more structural changes to a region than agents from within the region, providing an important lesson for the relationship between extra-regional organizations and regional renewal. External firms may be critical to initiating a new technological or industrial path locally (Martin & Sunley, 2006). Regional features can, however, influence investments in functions associated with bringing new products or services to the market, suggesting that regional policy should focus on reinforcing general regional socio-economic conditions (Crescenzi et al., 2014).

Firms and institutions operate on multiple scales, that is, through connections, collaborations and location decisions and through their global production and innovation networks (Aslesen & Harirchi, 2015; Cooke, 2013; Liu, Chaminade, & Asheim, 2013). Multiscalar processes, especially at the global scale, need to be analysed in more detail (Binz et al., 2014; Carlsson, 2006) as such links are also associated with radical innovation (Coe, Dicken, & Hess, 2008; Laursen & Salter, 2006). The literature on GPN has gained academic recognition (Dicken, Kelly, Olds, & Yeung, 2001), but the relation to regional policy and development remains under-theorized and inadequately developed (Yeung & Coe, 2015). It is not only production but also innovation that happens in networks, where new industrial paths emerge from interaction in dispersed 'GINs' (Coe & Bunnell, 2003). GINs can be seen as a variant of 'global pipelines' (Bathelt et al., 2004), acting as a channel for communication and interaction between localized firms and external partners. The concepts of GPNs and GINs may interact, but GINs involve research and development, new knowledge or technologies for future value creation (Liu & Chaminade, 2015). However, little is known about the effects of such networks on industry formation (Coenen et al., 2012) and industrial development.

The literature on GINs tends to focus on inter-firm relationships and less on intra-firm relationships (Liu et al., 2013). Knowledge can be shared in many ways also within the boundaries of MNCs and knowledge exchange can be static or dynamic (Saxenian, 2007; Tödtling, Lehner, & Trippl, 2006), where static knowledge exchange refers to sharing of 'ready' pieces of information and knowledge from one unit to the other without further learning. Dynamic knowledge exchange relates to interactive learning and co-generation of knowledge among units and actors where new knowledge occurs through collaboration (Asheim & Gertler, 2005, p. 294). Linking this to knowledge flows between units in MNCs, static knowledge exchange will typically be mobility and exchange of individuals throughout the organization sharing experiences. Dynamic knowledge linkages within MNCs can be formalized collaborative linkages such as R&D projects and innovation projects in transnational teams. Through these knowledge linkages, the degree of interactive learning and potential innovation outcome will be higher than through the more static knowledge linkages.

Our understanding of innovation networks and GINs extends the definition of Herstad et al. as innovation collaboration to also include other forms of knowledge exchange, since MNCs' intra-firm networks are strengthened by common identity and language facilitating extensive and efficient knowledge sharing (Kogut & Zander, 1992). Hence, organizational proximity in the MNCs facilitates knowledge exchange and learning among individuals and units (Hydle, Kvålshaugen, & Breunig, 2014) and may substitute geographical proximity as an essential element for interactive learning (Aguiléra, Lethiais, & Rallet, 2012; Boschma, 2005). Boschma (2005, p. 65) refers to an intra-organizational relation of similarity and membership where strong ties stimulate the transfer of complex knowledge in product development projects.

This suggests that intra-organizational GINs might be an important external source for learning, innovation and path development. The effect, however, can be incremental innovation and thereof path extension (static knowledge exchange) versus more radical innovation and potential path renewal (higher probability with dynamic knowledge exchange). Outcomes are related to the allocation of necessary human resources and dedicated management attention (Ocasio, 1997) and can further be hampered by factors such as inflexibility in the organization, rivalry among subsidiaries competing for future investment, and mergers and acquisitions (Boschma, 2005; Dawley, 2011). Also, too strong ties within organizations can hamper novel insights and bureaucratic systems may inhibit new ideas (Boschma, 2005), leading to fewer initiatives for change (too much organizational proximity). Innovation requires flexible organizations and 'loose couplings', where decentralized autonomous units can explore new knowledge, and centralized coordination facilitates learning and sharing of experiences (Boschma, 2005, p. 65). Hence 'organizational distance' in the MNCs may be important to engage in new paths and exploration.

2.4. Combining the MNCs' GINs and RISs to better understand path development

From the theoretical contributions presented above, we find several gaps in the current literature that need to be addressed. It is necessary to go beyond firm-level approaches to understand economic development, included in the path dependency framework. We need to enhance the understanding of how change factors may lead to new paths, focusing on de-locking and on the elements that affect the innovation capability of regionally located firms in RISs. Multi-scalar processes need to be analysed in more depth, especially the relationship between firms in MNCs and their role in learning and innovation and their effect on industrial development. We propose an analytical framework combining the role of RISs and MNCs' GINs to understand not only firms' internal sources, but also the wider set of external sources and their interdependence and complementarity for path development. The table below summarizes the above discussion on what can stimulate and/or hamper path renewal and extension in thick and specialized RISs and in MNCs' GIN, respectively.

3. Case studies of MNCs

This paper explores whether GINs, through MNCs, can be a source of regional path extension or path renewal. We performed comparative case studies where a number of cases were chosen purposefully to investigate the topic under investigation (Stake, 1994). The selection criteria were that the firms are European and North American MNCs within the same industry and with headquarters in different continents. Furthermore, it was a desire to include companies representing different parts of the value chain, where engineering, production and services are the main activities. Fifteen MNCs from the Norwegian counties Rogaland and Agder were selected, two regions characterized by long industrial traditions, also in the oil and gas industry. Rogaland has approximately 460,000 inhabitants, whereas Agder (Aust- and Vest-Agder) has 290,000 inhabitants.

Looking at the 'industry structure', firms in these two regions support different parts of the value chain in the oil and gas sector. In 2015, the Agder region represented 37.6% of the total national revenue on the industry code for machinery and equipment (NACE 28*), 25% of the employees and 46.4% of the total national value creation on this code. A large portion of this value creation supports the oil and gas industry (own calculations based on information about firms from www.purehelp.no). In Rogaland the main emphasis is on services, exploration and recovery of oil and gas. Here, the industry code for drilling and other services to the oil and gas industry (NACE 09*) represents 67.6% of the national revenue, 67.3% of the employees and 61.2% of the total value creation on this code, giving an indication of the position this region has in this industry (www.purehelp.no). Most of our sample firms belong to one of these industry codes according to this regional division.

Looking at the 'RIS' in Agder and Rogaland, there are some similar characteristics. Both regions have a relatively young university in their close proximity. The University in Agder has an engineering specialization in mechatronics, underpinning the needs of the industry, including large research projects together with the industry. Also, the applied research institute Teknova recruits researchers to support its regional industry. In Rogaland, the University of Stavanger and the research institute International Research Institute of Stavanger (IRIS) have developed studies and research areas supporting the oil and gas industry over years. IRIS also offers advanced test facilities to ensure the industry's competitiveness. In addition to supporting the industry with research, both universities educate students in areas of relevance to its regional industry's requirements for future hire.

In 'our sample', we chose 10 MNCs within oil and gas service engineering in Rogaland, where 4 have headquarters in the US, 2 in Europe and 4 have their main headquarters in Norway. In Agder, we chose five MNCs within equipment for oil and gas, and of these five, three have headquarters in the US and two have European headquarters. The chosen firms operate within the field of engineering and equipment production and represent different parts of the value chain, and for this reason have different characteristics. Nevertheless, there were several similarities: being part of a larger MNC, affecting their global competitiveness and role in the region. Some of the sample firms are large integrated corporations with operations all over the globe. Others are smaller and more independent from the MNC, but representing value for the corporation. The sample represents not only a large number of employees and revenue, measured in billions of USD globally, but also a substantial part of the value creation in their respective regions. In order to preserve anonymity, we are not able to provide more details of the MNCs (see Table A1 in Appendix for more information).

In order to inquire about local and global innovation activities and regional embeddedness, we needed to talk to people who know about both local and global activities. From the initially identified 15 firms, we interviewed CEOs, board directors, chief executives, strategists and R&D directors. In total, we conducted 25 interviews with 35 people. The interviews lasted between 1.5 and 3 hours with one to four persons. All interviews were recorded and transcribed and further analysed in relation to the research questions. The interviews were semi-structured based on a predefined interview guide. The overall structure was designed to collect data relating to:

- Overall characteristics of the firm, including division of activities between locations;
- Importance of competence, knowledge sharing and knowledge infrastructure;
- Subsidiary-headquarters relations and intra-firm networks and
- Effect of partnerships and collaboration with industry, regional clusters and RISs.

Our sample firms represent an important part of the value creation in their respective regions, having an existing knowledge infrastructure supporting the firms, either the regional university or research institutes, in addition to a substantial amount of regional suppliers. In the next section, we discuss how the innovation activities are conducted in our sample firms and how being a part of an MNC affects these activities and practices.

4. Knowledge sharing from global and regional interactions

The firms operate in global markets with fierce competition, where both knowledge intensity and technology push require high levels of competence throughout the entire organization and in their relations with RISs. We first present knowledge flows in MNCs' GINs and then their relation to RISs.

4.1. MNCs' characteristics and their GINs

Through various global networks, both within and external to the MNC, the firms share knowledge, improving their competitiveness through competence, interdependence, access to resources and R&D networks.

4.1.1. Knowledge flows through mobility, experience sharing and implementation of routines in MNCs' GINs

The stimulating factor is competence in a variety of disciplines from the MNC, in addition to access to other production facilities, all representing a unique opportunity to remain competitive. One interviewee said:

> We have become a knowledge hub. When we do this in Brazil for instance, there are people from Brazil coming here to learn. And then we have of course a large professional group in our headquarters in the US, who also have learned a lot of that competence. So all of the learning does not happen here, but a lot of the locations choose to come here to learn ... (Firm D).

In general, mobility, observations and learning in other locations, access to resources, extended networks and markets are regarded as the biggest advantages of being part of an MNC.

Some of the companies that have been part of a merger or acquisition experience more focus on structure, routines and process documentation from their headquarters. Post-acquisition integration has improved their own systems and given them tools to better handle a variety of issues, from production planning to financial systems and as such given organizational and process innovations. Several of the subsidiaries experience pressure to increase efficiency and streamline operations including adapting the concept of Lean production, Six Sigma, improved routines on Health, Security and Environment, increased standardization of the product portfolio to reduce unit cost, as well as increased focus on effectiveness and resource efficiency. Several firms have implemented pro-fessional and structured innovation and product development processes globally. This has happened through a set of tools used by the MNC, with the Stage-gate model men-tioned by several of the informants. A majority of the firms argue that the increased emphasis on structure and procedures has a positive value. However, it was also seen as hampering as several of the firms mention increased bureaucracy and strong financial requirements for project approvals as hampering factors.

All the informants explain how employee-driven innovation is part of daily operations, since incremental innovation is based on customer demands and requirements. Some of these innovations, either services, products or processes, may qualify for patents or other protection instruments. Here the interviewed managers state that all legal processes regarding patents, trademarks and property rights are handled at the headquarters by specialized departments using internal lawyers for intellectual property rights. Some of the interviewed managers even state that the use of headquarters in these cases has increased their competitiveness.

4.1.2. Knowledge flows through innovation collaboration in MNCs' GINs

Some of the interviewed firms have R&D collaboration within the MNC with HQ super-vision involving different local experts in relation to their competence. Experts from Agder and Rogaland are either working in Norway or travelling to take part in the R&D activities and/or they take part in the process on distance depending on the innovation project and the time framing of the project. Other firms develop their own products or operation within the local entity and several have both R&D collaboration with other firms in the MNCs on large R&D projects and local innovation projects. Several state that they have substantial autonomy in executing process improvements, but less on product develop-ment. The autonomy depends on how integrated the local unit is in the value chain of the MNC. For the subsidiaries that are part of the value chain, the respondents argue that entering new fields is a difficult strategy. Many firms mentioned the importance of having ownership of products or processes in the local company to maintain access to cor-porate funds and develop regional competence. These funds are mainly financed through their own operations, but they still need approval from the corporate headquarters to pursue innovation and development. 'We will literally put together a business case for it. And it is like any other MNC; the size of the price justifies the priority and the resource needed for development' (Firm C).

There is a strong interdependence between the MNCs and the subsidiaries in Norway, with many examples of innovation from Norway being used across the MNC. Firm A explained: 'We have developed technology internally in the company that we have used first in Norway and then it has been distributed globally afterwards.' Although the MNC is dependent on the regional subsidiaries, they are well aware of their status. Firm B explained it like this:

> The challenge for the region is that we are competent to innovate, we have good competence to build up large things, and we are excellent in solving problems. But we are a branch region. We all work in international companies.

Some firms argue that they have their place in the value chain and that it may be difficult to orient themselves into new business areas, and hence possibly directly compete with other companies within the MNC. A few firms define their owners as more financial than long-term industrial owners, with local profitability as the main objective rather than division of labour within the corporation.

Some firms see that their competence can be used in different contexts or for new industries. A manager from firm A explained that their competence could be of use ' … on Mars. I got an invitation to actually talk in a conference together with a company that now will conduct operations on Mars. Part of the technology advances that are being made … are of course some of the same theme'. The manager further explained how part of the technology used in the industry has been further developed locally into the chemical and agriculture industry.

There are large variations in the sample concerning benefits from sharing experiences and learning from 'external' collaboration through other subsidiaries in the MNC. Most firms report a substantial amount of collaboration with customers, partners, suppliers and R&D institutions, and even competitors. The various forms of collaboration may include only the Norwegian part of the MNC or they may involve other entities in the corporation, with more widespread benefits.

The informants explained that the innovation competence in the regional subsidiaries can be used in other fields as well. Determining factors for such an extension could be the local firm's place in the global value chain, the general market development, the strategy of the MNC and the applicability of existing technology in new markets. The informants stated that profitability in the market place will determine the future development of the subsidiaries and the regions.

4.2. The MNCs' interaction with RIS

Regarding the RIS, the informants were asked how they perceived and related to the actors in this system for innovation purposes. Their responses were that a strong regional infrastructure for research, competence and collaboration in place increased the probability of creating regional path renewal, thereby contributing to the continued existence of the subsidiaries and, hence, attracting new firms to the region.

4.2.1. Educated workforce and local knowledge infrastructure
Most of the informants mentioned the importance of the regional knowledge infrastructure, including universities and research institutes, both for access to an educated

workforce and research collaboration. Several of the firms emphasized the necessity of having a solid and substantial local recruitment base, including both high general and specialized competence. One of the interviewed managers said that:

> On the flip side of the expensive work force, we have a highly educated work force. We also have a specifically educated work force, which can be bad for the area in the long run. But in the short-term or medium-term it's a good thing. Everybody here, not everybody, but a high percentage of the work force is specifically trained for the industry, in one way or another. (Firm C).

The interdependence between the MNC and the RIS is accentuated by close relations to research institutes and large regional customers. A top manager in firm D explained:

> This is because the MNC has 17 employees located next to the regional research institute, which is, according to the firm, a world leading actor in the industry. Another factor making the firm a strong provider of quality products is the fact that they build equipment according to the large regional customer's standard. The MNC is located in 115 countries, and at least 50 of these have an application of products that are made in Norway.

The interdependence between firms and RIS is clear. Firm B:

> It's good to know the history. It's a reason why we have made it so well here in this region .... and that is something. And it is clear it has built up much expertise, with facilities at the research institute and the research institute itself. That has helped tremendously ... the whole setting here is a combination of, if not global, then at least the regional setting where it's been built up expertise.

4.2.2. Other actors in RISs

Some equipment firms have all of their production in the region, some do engineering but produce elsewhere, while others combine the two. All the firms focus on competence, quality, reliability and proximity (time) as important factors when selecting suppliers. Many of the respondents argue that their local cluster increases their competiveness due to the exchange of ideas and competence and say that they want to develop the cluster further. Others are less active and argue that they have not reached the full potential of the cluster, while others even question the role of clusters. Several firms emphasize the importance of proximity to a mechanical industry and that this is crucial for the further development of their firm. One even stated that his MNC would be reluctant to establish themselves in a place without a strong local mechanical industry that can provide support to their development of equipment.

Other respondents focus on the need to cooperate with smaller niche companies that can bring new ideas into technology development, where both can gain from collaboration:

> On the small collaboration, it happens much more often. We have a collaboration right now going on with a small Norwegian innovator. We have agreed to work with them on a pilot project, to see if there is a benefit for both parties, technologically and contractually. (Firm K).

Overall, the relations between the MNCs and local and national authorities are considered to be close and constructive. The top manager of Firm J said: 'I do not see that there are any barriers that prevent us in any way to do things ourselves or to cooperate with authorities'. Some firms see that their competence 'could have been further extended' to other fields if there had been political backing or private investment. A manager in Firm D explained with a sigh: 'The expertise will deteriorate if it is not stimulated; we need intervention, also from a political point of view.'

5. MNCs' GINs and RISs combined

Our first research question was: How can MNCs' GINs act as extra-regional sources for path extension in organizationally thick and specialized RISs? At the time of the interviews, the subsidiaries were not characterized by lack of innovation, general decline, lack of renewal (Hassink, 2010) or other signs of path exhaustion. We find path extension (understood as incremental innovation) both as a result of MNCs' GINs and as a result of interaction with RISs. Regarding path renewal (understood as more radical innovations), we find that the preconditions are only partly in place.

Referring back to Table 1, we will discuss factors stimulating or hampering path extension and path renewal, respectively, with a special emphasis on the MNC and RIS interaction.

5.1. Path extension

5.1.1. Path extension as a result of MNCs' GINs

Can external linkages through MNCs' GINs induce further growth in an industry and a region, leading to path extensions? Looking at the 'stimulating' factors through MNCs' GIN linkages, the subsidiaries emphasize continuous learning by responding to a larger set of demanding customers (and strong regulations), through adapting to new internal managerial infrastructure, routines and processes (Keupp, Palmié, & Gassmann, 2011) which have offset organizational and process innovations, increasing efficiency in the subsidiaries. Subsidiaries report knowledge flow through observation, mobility and joint projects, suggesting that MNCs can be seen as a communication channel for knowledge.

> 'Hampering factors' mentioned are the growing bureaucracy, increasing the administrative workload and making the subsidiaries less flexible. Dynamic knowledge sharing through R&D and innovation collaboration has involved different actors in the MNC; however, the control and autonomy of such projects are dependent on how integrated the local unit is in the value chain. The regional subsidiaries are well aware of their status and role as branch region and emphasize rivalry for the approval of funding of innovation and development. Especially innovation projects that focus more on product innovations (as opposed to process innovations) are harder to get.

The organizational proximity within the MNCs' GINs creates strong ties, and firms report that knowledge flows both ways between the subsidiary and other units. The internal knowledge dynamics has worked as a push factor for continuous learning due to tough competition among the units. The MNCs' GINs have enabled knowledge sharing worldwide, through ownership and interdependence between the entities. The result of dynamic knowledge sharing within the MNCs' GINs can be incremental or more radical innovations, leading to learning and to knowledge exchange and innovation results and as such contribute to path extensions.

Table 1. Analytical framework.

	Path extension		Path renewal	
	Stimulated by	Hampered by	Stimulated by	Hampered by
Characteristics of path development in thick and specialized RISs	Strong economic specialization, intra-regional related variety is low with well-adapted organizational and institutional support both formally and informally. Consensus driven	Economies of specialization can give rise to inertia and exhaustion	Diversification and recombination of exogenous sources such as inward investment and MNCs to diversify knowledge and create innovation. More disruptive way of thinking	The need for disruptiveness can lead to conflicts. Lack of anchoring capacity in RISs for unrelated knowledge
Path development through MNCs' GIN	*Static knowledge exchange:* Accumulated specific assets and competence that are ready pieces of information and knowledge that can be transferred from one unit to the other in the MNC – Intra-organizational relations in MNCs can stimulate knowledge sharing through learning visits, mobility, informal contacts and common projects across locations and other more static forms of knowledge sharing, leading to incremental changes in the organization – Acquisitions of companies with related expertise	*Static knowledge exchange:* – Too strong ties, lack of transparency and inflexibility in organization, loss of future investments	*Dynamic knowledge exchange: stimulate:* – Interactive learning in innovation and development projects where there is interdependence between the actors/units and where new knowledge is evolving, and the facilitation of such – 'Loose couplings' between units combining knowledge	*Dynamic knowledge exchange: hamper:* – Intra-organizational structure that inhibits new ideas and organizational routines that lead to few initiatives for change. 'Organizational distance' – Lack of absorptive capacity and relevant human capacity and resources for innovative tasks – Lack of support from HQ to explore new ways to combine knowledge

5.1.2. Path extension as a result of interdependence between the MNCs and RIS

The specialized regional environment initially attracted the MNCs to the region, as emphasized in the interviews. The regional assets are regarded as positive and have influenced the innovation capability of the subsidiaries (Isaksen & Trippl, 2016). Through the specialized RIS, the MNCs have access to highly competent local resources (newly educated, specialized human capital and knowledge infrastructure) on which they are dependent to react quickly to the high innovation pressure and the demand for excellence through the MNC. Geographical proximity to actors in the value chain and to competitors was also perceived as important. The RIS has developed alongside the industry through the years, strengthening and extending prevailing pathways.

Based on the interviews, we argue that the ongoing knowledge flow and exchange, both static and dynamic, in MNCs' GINs and between the MNC and RIS contribute to learning and innovation at the subsidiary level that strengthen and extend its knowledge, leading to path extension in the region. Some of the respondents regard themselves as knowledge hubs and results are shared within the MNCs, and local innovation can be taken up by the MNCs' GINs and spread globally and vice versa. The reported positive dynamics between MNCs' GINs and the RIS indicate a virtuous circle, where learning and innovation happen as a result of 'organizational proximity' in MNCs' GINs and 'geographical proximity' to actors in the RIS. This complementary effect of global and local learning creates a dynamic path extension. Locally, the global competitive pressure and learning through MNCs' GINs create pressure on actors in the RIS, suggesting that the RIS also transforms over time.

5.2. Signs of path renewal?

The second research question was: How can path renewal be stimulated in a context with thick and specialized RIS with a number of MNCs? We question whether there are signs of path renewal such as diversification of existing industries through the MNCs' GINs and RIS interaction. Are there any signs that MNCs initiate new technological or industrial paths locally (Martin & Sunley, 2006) or is it up to the RIS to initiate such changes?

Formal innovation collaborations within the MNC were perceived as a competitive strength for the subsidiary as they were able to learn from other units and knowledge hubs within the enterprise. This has given increased competitiveness and as such enabled growth in current technological trajectories. Ownership of products or processes in the subsidiaries is regarded as important, giving bargaining power and access to resources within the MNC. Firms report that their technology and competence are in some ways generic, and could be used in other local industries; the potential following up such initiatives also seems to be dependent on types of ownership as not all owners are long-term industrial owners. However, there are few signs of 'branching' into related trajectories/industries or establishing new paths.

The hampering factor reported was that of being a branch plant with a specific place in the value chain, making it difficult to initiate or lead the development of 'new' business areas. Constantly competing with all other units in the MNC for approval and funding makes it harder to get funds for more radical and 'uncertain' innovation projects with uncertain outcome and market. Radical innovation and new technologies are long term and can be expensive and will challenge local profitability; these are considerations that the subsidiaries are faced against in the MNC. This is an important hampering factor for the potential for 'branching' or new paths spurred through the MNCs' GIN.

The MNCs have a centralized coordination system for innovation, enabling knowledge flows within MNCs' GINs. The downside of such systems is they can lead to less flexibility and openness to new ideas and knowledge. Further, our sample firms need to apply for funding for R&D projects, with high expectations of return on investments. Hence, MNCs need to regard both the subsidiary and the RIS they are part of as attractive sites for new technology development when making investment decisions.

One respondent challenged the existing regional knowledge infrastructure saying it needed be more globally connected, beyond MNCs' GINs, to be relevant in the future. This could be linked to the knowledge infrastructure's ability to both see and consider new paths and further the ability to anchor the related or unrelated external knowledge needed for path renewal in the region (Crevoisier & Jeannerat, 2009; Trippl et al., 2015). The strong organizational and institutional support to existing clusters could also be regarded as hampering new industrial development in the region. We found that smaller niche companies have brought new ideas and technologies into the specialized RIS. However, integration into existing initiatives could hamper their 'radical' innovation activity due to the development of more cognitive proximity with the already dominating regional firms and industries. Supplementary and new initiatives do, therefore, seem necessary in order to support niche firms.

The 'de-locking' of a stable state through branching or new technology development is demanding and incurs some level of disruptiveness at the levels of the MNC, the subsidiary and the RIS as it will demand that actors can and will mindfully deviate from what appears to be the common expectation (Garud & Karnoe, 2001, p. 6). The main learning is that the interdependence between the MNCs' GINs and RIS is tight and together form 'core centres of continuity' (Trippl et al., 2015). If new paths are to develop, either the MNCs need to give local autonomy and flexibility to develop in new directions through various means, and/or the RIS needs to develop new educational directions and new fields of research nurturing the development of new paths. Since our interviews, the 15 firms have experienced a major external shock with declining oil prices. MNCs are now making people redundant, stopping R&D projects and downsizing operations, but they are also seeking opportunities that could result in path renewal. From the RIS there is a push for potential path creation by looking at how engineering competence can be used for other purposes, such as welfare technologies, renewable energy, sea mining or other applications. How these initiatives will be grasped by the MNCs, and whether new initiatives from the MNCs will create new paths remain to be seen. To explore future path creation, we suggest that it is necessary to look at activities undertaken by the MNCs, the RIS and their mutual interaction.

5.3. Conclusion

We found clear signs of path extensions, with strong complementarities between MNCs' GINs and RISs, showing a dynamic interplay between the local and global forces. There are no clear signs of path renewal or path creation in the interdependence between MNCs' GINs and RISs. Path creation concerns the organization of conflict and entails a more disruptive way of thinking (Sydow et al., 2012, p. 925). Within the MNC, there might be 'tensions' between the internal processes (organizational proximity) and the geographical proximity experienced in its local environment to build the capacity necessary to harness technological or operational synergies across these two types of contexts (Herstad, Ebersberger, & Asheim, 2013).

We argue that the basis for path renewal may be in place due to the institutionalized cooperation and collaboration between the different actors in these regions. Internal dynamics in both MNCs' GINs and RISs have the potential to create new paths because resources and competences acquired and used in existing paths may be 'recombined' into new paths (Garud & Karnoe, 2001).

Disclosure statement

No potential conflict of interest was reported by the authors.

ORCID

Katja Maria Hydle ⓘ http://orcid.org/0000-0001-7112-0040

References

Aguiléra, A., Lethiais, V., & Rallet, A. (2012). Spatial and non-spatial proximities in inter-firm relations: An empirical analysis. *Industry and Innovation*, *19*, 187–202. doi:10.1080/13662716. 2012.669609

Arthur, W. (1989). Competing technologies, increasing returns, and lock-in by historical events. *The Economic Journal*, *99*(394), 116–131. doi:10.2307/2234208

Asheim, B. (2009). Guest editorial: Introduction to the creative class in European city regions. *Economic Geography*, *85*, 355–362. doi:10.1111/j.1944-8287.2009.01046.x

Asheim, B. T., & Gertler, M. (2005). The geography of innovation: Regional innovation systems. In J. Fagerberg, D. C. Mowery, & R. R. Nelson (Eds.), *The Oxford handbook of innovation* (pp. 291–317). Oxford: Oxford University Press.

Asheim, B. T., & Isaksen, A. (2002). Regional innovation systems: The integration of local 'sticky' and global 'ubiquitous' knowledge. *The Journal of Technology Transfer*, *27*, 77–86. doi:10. 1023/A:1013100704794

Aslesen, H. W., & Harirchi, G. (2015). The effect of local and global linkages on the innovativeness in ICT SMEs: Does location-specific context matter? *Entrepreneurship & Regional Development*, *27*, 644–669. doi:10.1080/08985626.2015.1059897

Bathelt, H., Malmberg, A., & Maskell, P. (2004). Clusters and knowledge: Local buzz, global pipelines and the process of knowledge creation. *Progress in Human Geography*, *28*, 31–56. doi:10. 1191/0309132504ph469oa

Binz, C., Truffer, B., & Coenen, L. (2014). Why space matters in technological innovation systems – Mapping global knowledge dynamics of membrane bioreactor technology. *Research Policy*, *43*, 138–155. doi:10.1016/j.respol.2013.07.002

Boschma, R. A. (2005). Proximity and innovation: A critical assessment. *Regional Studies*, *39*, 61–74. doi:10.1080/0034340052000320887

Boschma, R. A. (2015). Towards an evolutionary perspective on regional resilience. *Regional Studies*, *49*, 733–751. doi:10.1080/00343404.2014.959481

Boschma, R. A., & Capone, G. (2014). *Relatedness, diversification and institutions*. Working paper. Utrecht: Utrecht University.

Boschma, R. A., & Frenken, K. (2006). Why is economic geography not an evolutionary science? Towards an evolutionary economic geography. *Journal of Economic Geography*, *6*, 273–302. doi:10.1093/jeg/lbi022

Boschma, R. A., & Frenken, K. (2011). Technological relatedness and regional branching. In H. Bathelt, M. P. Feldman, & D. F. Kogler (Eds.), *Beyond territory. Dynamic geographies of knowledge creation, diffusion, and innovation* (pp. 64–81). London: Routledge.

Bunnell, T. G., & Coe, N. M. (2001). Spaces and scales of innovation. *Progress in Human Geography*, 25, 569–589. doi:10.1191/030913201682688940

Cantwell, J., & Piscitello, L. (2005). Recent location of foreign-owned research and development activities by large multinational corporations in the European regions: The role of spillovers and externalities. *Regional Studies*, 39, 1–16. doi:10.1080/0034340052000320824

Carlsson, B. (2006). Internationalization of innovation systems: A survey of the literature. *Research Policy*, 35, 56–67. doi:10.1016/j.respol.2005.08.003

Coe, N. M., & Bunnell, T. G. (2003). 'Spatializing' knowledge communities: Towards a conceptualization of transnational innovation networks. *Global Networks*, 3, 437–456. doi:10.1111/1471-0374.00071

Coe, N. M., Dicken, P., & Hess, M. (2008). Global production networks: Realizing the potential. *Journal of Economic Geography*, 8, 271–295. doi:10.1093/jeg/lbn002

Coenen, L., Benneworth, P., & Truffer, B. (2012). Toward a spatial perspective on sustainability transitions. *Research Policy*, 41, 968–979. doi:10.1016/j.respol.2012.02.014

Cooke, P. (2013). Global production networks and global innovation networks: Stability versus growth. *European Planning Studies*, 21, 1081–1094. doi:10.1080/09654313.2013.733854

Crescenzi, R., Pietrobelli, C., & Rabellotti, R. (2014). Innovation drivers, value chains and the geography of multinational corporations in Europe. *Journal of Economic Geography*, 14, 1053–1086. doi:10.1093/jeg/lbt018

Crescenzi, R., & Rodríguez-Pose, A. (2011). *Innovation and regional growth in the European Union*. Berlin: Springer Science & Business Media.

Crevoisier, O., & Jeannerat, H. (2009). Territorial knowledge dynamics: From the proximity paradigm to multi-location milieus. *European Planning Studies*, 17, 1223–1241. doi:10.1080/09654310902978231

David, P. A. (1985). Clio and the economics of qwerty. *American Economic Review*, 75, 332–337.

David, P. A. (2001). Path dependence, its critics and the quest for 'historical economics'. In P. Garrouste & S. Ioannides (Eds.), *Evolution and path dependence in economic ideas: Past and present*. Cheltenham: Edward Elgar Publishing.

David, P. A. (2005). Path dependence in economic processes: Implications for policy analysis in dynamical systems contexts. *The Evolutionary Foundations of Economics*, 151–194.

Dawley, S. (2011). Transnational corporations and local and regional development. In A. Pike, A. Rodriguez-Pose, & J. J. Tomaney (Eds.), *Handbook of local and regional development* (pp. 394–412). London: Routledge.

Dicken, P., Kelly, P. F., Olds, K., & Yeung, H. W.-C. (2001). Chains and networks, territories and scales: Towards a relational framework for analysing the global economy. *Global Networks*, 1, 89–112. doi:10.1111/1471-0374.00007

Djelic, M.-L., & Quack, S. (2003). *Globalization and institutions. Redefining the rules of the economic game*. Cheltenham: Edward Elgar.

Ebersberger, B., & Herstad, S. J. (2012). Go abroad or have strangers visit? On organizational search spaces and local linkages. *Journal of Economic Geography*, 12(1), 273–295. doi:10.1093/jeg/lbq057

Frenken, K., & Boschma, R. A. (2007). A theoretical framework for evolutionary economic geography: Industrial dynamics and urban growth as a branching process. *Journal of Economic Geography*, 7, 635–649. doi:10.1093/jeg/lbm018

Garud, R., & Karnoe, P. (2001). Path creation as a process of mindful deviation. In R. Garud, & P. Karnoe (Eds.), *Path dependence and creation* (pp. 1–38). New York, NY: Lawrence Earlbaum Associates.

Garud, R., Kumaraswamy, A., & Karnøe, P. (2010). Path dependence or path creation? *Journal of Management Studies*, 47, 760–774. doi: 10.1111/j.1467-6486.2009.00914.x

Grabher, G. (1993). *The embedded firm*. London: Routledge.

Hassink, R. (2010). Locked in decline? On the role of regional lock-ins in old industrial areas. In R. Boschma & R. Martin (Eds.), *Handbook of evolutionary economic geography* (pp. 450–468). Cheltenham: Edward Elgar.

Hassink, R., Klaerding, C., & Marques, P. (2014). Advancing evolutionary economic geography by engaged pluralism. *Regional Studies, 48*, 1295–1307. doi:10.1080/00343404.2014.889815

Henning, M., Stam, E., & Wenting, R. (2013). Path dependence research in regional economic development: Cacophony or knowledge accumulation? *Regional Studies, 47*, 1348–1362. doi:10.1080/00343404.2012.750422

Herstad, S. J., Ebersberger, B., & Asheim, B. (2013). *MNC affiliation, knowledge bases and involvement in global innovation networks (No. 2013/12)*. Lund: CIRCLE-Center for Innovation, Research and Competences in the Learning Economy, Lund University.

Hydle, K. M., Kvålshaugen, R., & Breunig, K. J. (2014). Transnational practices in communities of task and communities of learning. *Management Learning, 45*, 609–629. doi:10.1177/1350507613500881

Isaksen, A., & Trippl, M. (2016). Path development in different regional innovation systems: A conceptual view. In M. D. Parrilli, R. D. Fitjar, & A. Rodriguez-Pose (Eds.), *Innovation drivers and regional innovation strategies* (pp. 66–84). New York, NY: Routledge.

Keupp, A. P. M. M., Palmié, P. C. M., & Gassmann, O. (2011). Achieving subsidiary integration in international innovation by managerial 'tools'. *Management International Review, 51*, 213–239. doi:10.1007/s11575-011-0072-5

Kogut, B., & Zander, U. (1992). Knowledge of the firm, combinative capabilities, and the replication of technology. *Organization Science, 3*, 383–397. doi:10.1287/orsc.3.3.383

Laursen, K., & Salter, A. (2006). Open for innovation: The role of openness in explaining innovation performance among UK manufacturing firms. *Strategic Management Journal, 27*, 131–150. doi:10.1002/smj.507

Liu, J., & Chaminade, C. (2015). *A case study on multinational companies' global innovation networks and global production networks: Toward a theoretical conceptualisation (No. 2015/45)*. Lund: CIRCLE-Center for Innovation, Research and Competences in the Learning Economy, Lund University.

Liu, J., Chaminade, C., & Asheim, B. (2013). The geography and structure of global innovation networks: A knowledge base perspective. *European Planning Studies, 21*, 1456–1473. doi:10.1080/09654313.2012.755842

Liu, J., & Liefner, I. (2016). *The joint influencing mechanism of proximities and knowledge base on multinational companies' global innovation networks (No. 2016/4)*. Lund: CIRCLE-Center for Innovation, Research and Competences in the Learning Economy, Lund University.

Mackinnon, D. (2012). Beyond strategic coupling: Reassessing the firm–region nexus in global production networks. *Journal of Economic Geography, 12*, 227–245. doi:10.1093/jeg/lbr009

Mackinnon, D., Cumbers, A., Pike, A., Birch, K., & Mcmaster, R. (2009). Evolution in economic geography: Institutions, political economy, and adaptation. *Economic Geography, 85*, 129–150. doi:10.1111/j.1944-8287.2009.01017.x

Martin, R. (2010). Roepke lecture in economic geography: Rethinking regional path dependence: Beyond lock-in to evolution. *Economic Geography, 86*, 1–27. doi:10.1111/j.1944-8287.2009.01056.x

Martin, R., & Sunley, P. (2006). Path dependence and regional economic evolution. *Journal of Economic Geography, 6*, 395–437. doi:10.1093/jeg/lbl012

Meyer, U., & Schubert, C. (2007). Integrating path dependency and path creation in a general understanding of path constitution: The role of agency and institutions in the stabilisation of technological innovations. *Science, Technology & Innovation Studies, 3*, 23–44.

Narula, R., & Zanfei, A. (2005). *Globalisation of innovation*. Oxford: Oxford University Press.

Neffke, F., Hartog, M., Boschma, R., & Henning, M. (2014). *Agents of structural change. The role of firms and entrepreneurs in regional diversification*. Papers in evolutionary economic geography, Utrecht University, Utrecht.

Neffke, F., Henning, M., & Boschma, R. (2011). How do regions diversify over time? Industry relatedness and the development of new growth paths in regions. *Economic Geography, 87*, 237–265. doi:10.1111/j.1944-8287.2011.01121.x

Ocasio, W. (1997). Towards an attention-based view of the firm. *Strategic Management Journal, 18*, 187–206. doi:10.1002/(SICI)1097-0266(199707)18:1+<187::AID-SMJ936>3.3.CO;2-B

Parrilli, M. D., Nadvi, K., & Yeung, H. W. C. (2013). Local and regional development in global value chains, production networks and innovation networks: A comparative review and the challenges for future research. *European Planning Studies, 21*, 967–988. doi:10.1080/09654313.2013.733849

Saxenian, A. (2007). *The new argonauts: Regional advantage in a global economy.* Cambridge, MA: Harvard University Press.

Stake, R. E. (1994). Case studies. In N. K. Denzin & Y. S. Lincoln (Eds.), *Handbook of qualitative research* (pp. 236–247). Thousand Oaks, CA: Sage.

Sydow, J., Windeler, A., Müller-Seitz, G., & Lange, K. (2012). Path constitution analysis: A methodology for understanding path dependence and path creation. *BuR Business Research, 5*, 155–176. doi:10.1007/BF03342736

Tödtling, F., Lehner, P., & Trippl, M. (2006). Innovation in knowledge intensive industries: The nature and geography of knowledge links. *European Planning Studies, 14*, 1035–1058. doi:10.1080/09654310600852365

Tödtling, F., & Trippl, M. (2013). Transformation of regional innovation systems: From old legacies to new development paths. In P. Cooke (Eds.), *Reframing regional development* (pp. 297–317). London: Routledge.

Trippl, M., Grillitsch, M., & Isaksen, A. (2015). External 'energy' for regional industrial change: Attraction and absorption of non-local knowledge for new path development (Papers in Innovation Studies No. 2015/47). Lund: Lund University, Centre for Innovation, Research and Competence in the Learning Economy (CIRCLE).

Yeung, H. W. C., & Coe, N. (2015). Toward a dynamic theory of global production networks. *Economic Geography, 91*, 29–58.

Appendix

Table A1. Interviewed firms.

Firms anonymized	HQ corporate – and HQ functions in other regions	Number of employees globally
Alpha	Corporate HQ: USA	80,000
	Operational HQ: USA/Middle East	
Beta	Corporate HQ: USA	70,000
Gamma	Corporate HQ: USA	65,000
Delta	Corporate HQ: Europe	60,000
	Operational HQ: USA	
Epsilon	Corporate HQ: USA	125,000
Zeta	Corporate HQ: Europe	15,000
	Operational HQ: Great Britain	
Eta	Corporate HQ: Europe	2000
Theta	Corporate HQ: Europe	1000
Iota	Corporate HQ: Europe	30,000
Kappa	Corporate HQ: Europe	1000
Lambda	Corporate HQ: USA	65,000
My	Corporate HQ: USA	25,000
Ny	Corporate HQ: Europe	10,000
Ksi	Corporate HQ: USA	10,000
Omikron	Corporate HQ: Europe	100,000

Foreign direct investment and renewal of industries: framing the reciprocity between materiality and discourse

Arnt Fløysand, Rune Njøs, Trond Nilsen and Vigdis Nygaard

ABSTRACT
Informed by the evolutionary literature on economic geography, this paper develops a conceptual framework for analysing the complexity between foreign direct investment (FDI) and renewal of industries. Present contributions tend to explain the impact of FDI on regional industry evolution as a static, output-oriented phenomenon, that is, informed by an instrumental rationale in which the dynamism of FDI and regional industry development is linked to polarization of stagnation/decline vs. growth/development. Opposing this, we argue for an epistemological shift in approach to the reciprocity between FDI and renewal of industries as dynamism between material outcomes and discursive processes. To accomplish this, we build on key concepts and understandings from evolutionary economic geography; review the regional effects of FDI literature and build a framework sensitive to contextual dimensions of FDI. We focus on multinational companies' practices and material outcomes in terms of regional spillovers and the discursive processes in terms of FDI narratives. This framework is exemplified by data from the salmon farming industry and the subsea industry in Hordaland and the oil and gas industry and the mining industry in Finnmark.

1. Introduction

For decades, economic geography researchers have attempted to understand and explain economic internationalization processes. One prominent feature is that today's regional economies are more and more influenced by capital flows from foreign direct investment (FDI) between geographical settings and nations, and by the related practices of multinational companies (MNCs) (Dicken, 2007). Global FDI stock rose by 9% from 2012 to 2013, to an incredible USD 25.5 trillion (UNCTAD, 2014). FDI growth has led to both optimism about potentials for rejuvenating and developing subnational regional economies and their industries through attracting inward FDI, and scepticism over counterproductive abilities of FDI for renewal of industries and wider processes of regional development. Moreover, the continuous growth of FDI importance has also led to an extensive discussion about its effects on broader development issues (Blomström & Kokko, 1998; Enright, 2000). Topics of real interest here include how the theory-based literature and empirical accounts narrate the interplay between regional development, FDI and MNC practice. The literature tends to highlight FDI as a material phenomenon causing an unsolved discourse on its regional effects. We believe this could be adjusted by looking at FDI as a relational phenomenon that is mutually constituted by material and discursive conditions.

From the evolutionary approach, industry renewal is understood as a continuum between continuation (low ability to adapt to changing circumstances) and substantial change (high ability to adapt to changing circumstances) (Boschma & Martin, 2010; Martin & Sunley, 2006; Sydow, Schreyögg, & Koch, 2009). Other key issues have been how ' ... the emergence of self-reinforcing effects steer a technology, industry or a regional economy along one path rather than another' (Martin, 2009, p. 3) and whether it is possible to observe different development paths within a system (Martin & Sunley, 2010). While the literature stream on evolutionary economic geography has been particularly concerned with attempts to conceptualize how industries develop along different paths, it has been less successful in conceptualizing how paths relate to discursive processes (Fløysand, Jakobsen, & Bjarnar, 2012; Iammarino & McCann, 2013). Moreover, in the spectacle of regional development, while industries evolve within regions, at the same time different sublevels (for instance, industries or firms) also follow particular paths. These considerations are particularly evident in the empirical portion of this paper, as we compare FDI and related MNC practices in two regions of Norway. The regions we study are based heavily on natural resource management; yet they used to exemplify different forms of 'local' capitalism in the past represented by 'private enterprise' in Hordaland and a 'governmental enterprise' in Finnmark. The industries we study are salmon farming and subsea operations in Hordaland, while oil & gas and mining are under scrutiny in Finnmark. In short, we ask:

- How do narratives of FDI and material outcomes of MNC practice communicate in processes of industry renewal?
- What are the theoretical implications of treating FDI and MNC practice as an interplay between materiality and discourse?

The study shows co-evolution between materiality and discourse with different effects upon the industries' path development. 'Path exhaustion' or 'path extension' is observed when FDIs are capital dominated and contain limited spillover effects and contra-FDI narratives, while 'path renewal' or 'path creation' occurs when FDIs arrive as a capital–network–knowledge package and there are substantial regional spillovers and pro-FDI narratives. Moreover, industry distinctive and MNCs' strategies seem to be more important for FDI-related path development than regional particularities in the four cases studied. Finally, we return to the concept of 'continuum' in integrating our findings in a model indicating how narratives of FDI and material outcomes of MNC practice relate to industry renewal. These dimensions are normally treated separately, and by considering their reciprocity we also highlight the evolutionary dynamism of such processes. Doing so, we contribute to the literature through emphasizing the duality of materiality and discourse in processes of renewal of industries.

2. FDI and the co-evolution of material and discursive processes

2.1. Evolutionary geography and the dynamism of industry renewal

Paradigmatic theories on regional development and innovation highlight the importance of balancing regional endogenous growth (Tödtling & Trippl, 2005) with processes of internationalization (Bathelt, Malmberg, & Maskell, 2004). Furthermore, global–local interaction is a key determinant in the innovation literature. The contributions of regional development and systems of innovation – and their interplay – often take as a starting point that (regional) economic development is influenced and guided by former contingencies and choices taken in regional configurations (i.e. systems). Such evolutionary perspectives do not, however, see development as historically determined, but rather as a process of decreasing contingencies and choices where aligned events foster the course of a path in an overall direction. This process is driven by positive feedback, adaptations and learning effects (Sydow, Windeler, Müller-Seitz, & Lange, 2012) in which self-reinforcing processes imply institutionalization. Thus, the development of more standardized interaction patterns (i.e. practice), and formal regional institutions and policies influence how an industry evolves (Jakobsen et al., 2012). Generally, an industry is characterized by specific technology solutions, taken-for-granted practice and institutionalized rules. This may, however, lead an industry into a state of lock-in, that is, a situation characterized by rigidity and erosion of adaptability (Hassink, 2005). Hence, a path may become '[…] confined to a single solution that does not need to be efficient' (Sydow et al., 2012, p. 159). Theories of path dependence are also central when facilitation of linkages between differentiated actors is considered crucial to cobble together innovation systems and to spur regional economic growth (Fagerberg, 2005). Accordingly, evolutionary concepts of path evolution and path dependence have become influential, both in the academic literature and in policy-making.

A central topic in this field is linked to explaining how industries and regions become locked in and how these developments can be avoided initially (Kogler, 2015; Njøs & Jakobsen, 2016). The underlying rationale is that renewal (Boschma & Martin, 2010; Pike, Dawley, & Tomaney, 2010) is key to avoiding path exhaustion and/or negative lock-in (e.g. detrimental regional industry development and lack of innovation ability) and to upholding or increase economic growth, employment, social welfare, etc. This should be classified as a continuum, between polarizations of continuity and change. Thus, the evolutionary approach places emphasis on 'degrees of renewal' within different systems. Such degrees of renewal are linked to firms', industries' and regions' individual development paths. From the literature on economic geography and innovation, we know that industry renewal is considered interwoven at different spatial scales, but that regional contexts are especially important (Cooke, Gomez Uranga, & Etxebarria, 1997; Henderson, Dicken, Hess, Coe, & Yeung, 2002; Porter, 1990). In this complex arena, industry actors (including local firms and MNCs), regional policy actors, industry/cluster facilitators, national policy institutions, customers and non-governmental institutions are all important (Fløysand & Jakobsen, 2011). Influential concepts and theories include industry clusters (Porter, 1990), regional innovation systems (Cooke et al., 1997), triple helix (Etzkowitz & Leydesdorff, 2000) and smart specialization (European Commission, 2012). One central concept that has received increased attention in recent years is the concept of related variety (Boschma, 2005; Boschma & Frenken, 2011;

Nooteboom, 2000), which represents, among other issues, an attempt to conceptualize – and operationalize – key dimensions of regional renewal (Bathelt et al., 2004; Hassink, 2005; Pike et al., 2010). Conditions for renewal are linked to a certain materiality:

> The higher the number of technologically related sectors in a region, the more variety in related sectors, the more learning opportunities there are for sectors in that region, and the more intersected knowledge spillovers are likely to take place, resulting in higher regional growth. (Boschma and Frenken, 2011, p. 188)

There are fewer studies regarding discursive processes. Regional industry development is conceptualized as guided by interrelated events '[…] in which one of the available techno-logical, institutional or organizational options gains momentum in time-space' (Sydow et al., 2012, p. 159). Thus, as logically deduced from such conceptualizations, evolution may lead to decreasing numbers of contingencies, whereas positive feedback, adaptations and learning effects (Sydow et al., 2012) may lead to self-reinforcing processes that imply institutionalization such as more standardized practices, formal institutions and policies, which eventually end up as negative path dependency and lock-in. Nevertheless, before returning to the discursive dynamics of FDI and how it relates to path development and renewal of industries, we need to take a closer look at how the literature considers FDI in explaining regional development.

2.2. FDI as material outcome

Apart from FDI as a source of economic capital and employment, an important way in which the economy of a region may benefit from FDI is through regional spillover effects. This refers to the effect of FDI on raising productivity in regional firms, increasing flows of knowledge in regional networks and strengthening the innovation capabilities of regions and their institutions. Such spillover effects have been widely studied. However, the results are anything but clear (Smeets, 2008). Regional spillover effects of FDI have traditionally been measured as job creation and regional purchases of goods and services (Dunning, 1993). However, Andersson and Forsgren (1996) argue for a shift in the under-standing of FDI in relation to MNCs. FDI should be understood as not only the source of a branch plant economy with primarily backward supply linkages to the regional economy (Phelps, 1992; Watts, 1981). It is also necessary to emphasize the flow of knowledge and competence caused by FDI in a region (Ivarsson, 1999). Very often, FDI provides MNCs with regional linkages to the competence and technology of regional firms (Dunning, 1993). It is claimed that FDI benefits the regional economy since MNCs can fully exploit economies of scale and scope. This means that a region with FDI can adjust more quickly to changes in technology and demand (Dunning, 1993).

Other contributions discredit a presupposed direct link between FDI and regional benefit and assume that, due to relational circumstances, there can be both positive and negative regional outcomes from FDI. Bellandi (2001) argues that close ties between the subsidiaries of MNCs and regional firms are most likely to develop when the regional pro-duction culture (referring to regional codified standards and knowledge in clustering industries) is neither 'too weak', nor 'too strong'. A 'too strong' culture can block network sharing and the exchange of technology and ideas. Borensztein, De Gregorio, and Lee (1998) argue that FDI contributes to economic growth only when the regional economy is sufficiently able to absorb the advanced technologies. These authors' main conclusion is that a region is more likely to benefit from FDIs if they are integrated into the region's development and technological plans (Milberg, 1999). However, while there are examples of regions in countries such as China and Malaysia that have been successful in regulating FDI, others show spillover effects that defy regulatory attempts. Agostin and Mayer (2000) investigated an important aspect of spillover effects by asking whether FDI in host countries 'crowds in' further investment by regional firms, or 'crowds out' existing investments of these firms as a consequence of increased competition and hence lower profits. Their results suggest that between 1970 and 1996, there was strong 'crowding in' in Asia, 'crowding out' in Latin America and more or less neutral effects in Africa and conclude that, on a national level, 'the positive impacts of FDI on domestic investment are not assured' (2000, p. 14). Te Velde (2003, p. 4) asserts that:

> While FDI may have been good for development (e.g. we find positive correlations between FDI and GDP, or productivity, or wages) this masks the fact that different countries with different policies and economic factors tend to derive different benefits and costs of FDI.

Machinea and Vera (2006, p. 38) also note that the effects of FDI on GDP growth are highly variable, with negative impacts in the primary sector, positive impacts in manufacturing and ambiguous impacts in services, 'In certain enclave-based primary activities, no such effects [positive effects on GDP] are generated and, in some cases, the only impact is the depletion of natural resources and massive capital outflows in the form of royalties and dividends.' They argue for a more selective 'use' of FDI by national governments in order to maximize the potentially positive domestic impacts (Machinea & Vera, 2006, p. 43):

> In any event it seems clear that – as in the case of trade liberalization – the benefits of FDI have been exaggerated ... As part of their creation of an FDI-friendly environment, the countries of the region should make an effort to attract the kinds of FDI that will have a greater impact on terms of linkages and R&D resources.

In a review on the relationship between FDI and regional development, Jakobsen, Rusten, and Fløysand (2005) summarize two main positions: 'FDI as progress' and 'FDI as dependency'. 'FDI as progress' is characterized by extensive regional spillover effects of FDI, such as technology transfer, spin-offs, innovation networks and transfer of knowledge. 'FDI as dependency' is characterized by situations in which the regional economy is dominated by the FDI, but involves negative effects such as social and employment dislocation, environmental disruption, corruption and 'outcrowding'. Generally, investments are returned to the investing region. They further stress that the entrepreneurial culture in the receiving region of FDI is decisive for whether the outcome of FDI will be dependency or progress (Jakobsen et al., 2005). However, such contributions tend to highlight the importance of time in explaining the regional impact of FDI, while at the same time treating FDI as a static outcome. If we look towards evolutionary literature, the axiomatic understanding within evolutionary geography is that regions differ according to culture and history, among others. This is of course a reasonable assumption. Nevertheless, the dynamism of industry renewal is under-communicated in these approaches. Through reflecting on 'degrees of renewal' through the continuum of continuation and change, we argue for understandings of the 'dynamic' interplay between narratives of FDI and material outcomes of MNC practice on an industry level. This requires bringing discourse more into play, indicating that we need to reconsider notions of FDI.

2.3. FDI as discursive process

In financial analysis, FDI is defined as a cross-border investment in which an investor intends to establish lasting financial interest and exert an effective influence on the activities of the investment object. In our view, this understanding, operationalized through highly technical measures, needs to be altered through an 'epistemological shift' to capture how FDI and related MNC practices engage with path development and regional renewal. As a start, we define an FDI as complex involving what we label the 'time–spatial characteristics of FDI', or the degree to which an FDI and its related MNC practices involve shared capital interests, networking and transfer of knowledge on a firm level. Reviewing the dichotomy between FDI as progress and dependency, we believe that such an analytical approach should start by emphasizing the encounter between MNCs and regional industry contexts (see also Fløysand & Jakobsen, 2011). Such encounters can encourage networking between FDI and regional firms, transfer of skills and knowledge, or shared interest through the transfer of capital (as illustrated by the grey ellipse in Figure 1). We believe that the outcome of such encounters is conditioned by the interplay between regional entrepreneurial culture and characteristics of the FDI. In cases where there is a 'positive' outcome, the characteristics of FDI and regional conditions communicate, whereas negative outcomes are the result of a mismatch between FDI characteristics and receiving context.

Linking FDI to MNC practice in this way makes the phenomenon much more complex than a simple economic transaction. It becomes an encounter between MNCs and local conditions in which the material as well as discursive outcomes partly depends on the particular business practices it generates in the region. Depending on the contextual condition, an FDI can promote and obstruct path development of regional industries.

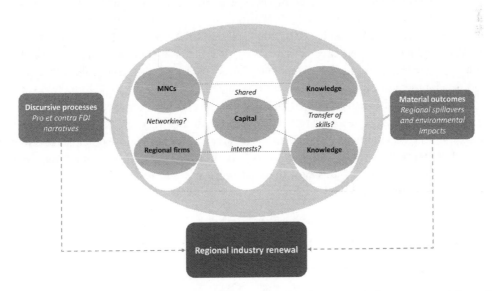

Figure 1. The encounter between FDI and regional conditions, the reciprocity between materiality and discourse, and regional industry renewal.

To uncover this, it is important to shed light on the material outcomes of FDI/MNC practices in terms of regional spillover effects (Figure 1), but an 'epistemological shift' also requires investigating the discursive processes of an FDI and related MNC practices.

Two main bodies of discourse theories can be observed within social sciences: traditional discourse theory and critical discourse analysis based in the more post-structural epistemologies. Traditional discourse theory views the social world as a discursive construction and was developed by Foucault (1991), while critical discourse analysis has been credited to the work of Fairclough (1995) and Lauclau and Mouffe (2001). In the theory of Foucault, discourses are seen as the fundamental structure in the world and constitute the basis for all social practice, whereas the critical discourse analysis position emphasizes changing paradigms of meaning and knowledge and political claim-making. Discourses are equally constitutive and constituted by social practice, but they are rooted in ideology. For example, Lauclau and Mouffe (2001) stress the practices of 'articulation' of claims and see them as attempts to fix meaning in political struggles. The methodologies of post-structural epistemologies are fuzzier. The linguistic approach of Fairclough (1995) concentrates on text analysis and distinguishes between the stages of description, interpretation and division. Our discourse approach draws less on Foucault and more on both Laclau and Mouffe, and Fairclough. Yet, to capture the voices of regional industrial politics, we find it useful to supplement their concept of articulation with the concept of narratives.

We define discourse as the process used to produce the meaning of a topic that inherently structures the perceptions and practices of the participants, although without their necessarily being conscious of being controlled (Rose, 2001, p. 138). Thus, narratives become the specific perceptions or modes of explanations promoted by an actor or group of actors located within a certain topic (Roe, 1991; Swift, 1996). The concept of narratives reduces the importance of unconscious knowledge in discursive practice in exchange for reflexive actors' interests. In our framework, narratives involve specific perceptions or modes of explanations promoted by stakeholders on how MNC practices relate to regional development in terms of 'pro et contra' FDI narratives (Figure 1). Our analysis of FDI and related narratives on how FDI affects processes of industry renewal focuses on questions such as: to what degree is it articulated that MNCs are sustaining regional development; and to what degree is it articulated that material outcomes of FDI stimulate industry renewal? As argued by Henderson et al. (2002, p. 446), implications for firms and development at each spatial level cannot be 'read off' from the logic of the network's organization and the distribution of power within it. Firms, other stakeholders and governmental bodies have different rationalities and priorities vis-à-vis profitability, growth and economic development (e.g. FDI narratives may differ between regional stakeholders and MNC representatives). In the following, we illustrate this through four examples of how reciprocity between industries' material outcomes and discursive processes relates to path evolution and renewal.

3. FDI and renewal of industries in two Norwegian regions

3.1. The stock of FDI in Norway

Statistics Norway does not make available numbers on inward and outward FDI at the regional level, but the Norwegian economy was among the top 20 economies for FDI

Table 1. Stock of inward and outward FDI, Norway, for selected years.

	1990	2000	2013
Stock of inward FDI	12	30	192
Stock of outward FDI	11	34	231

Note: Numbers in trillion USD (UNCTAD, 2014, p. 209).

outflows during 2012–2013, with an outflow of FDI of USD 18 billion (ranking 18th) (UNCTAD, 2014, p. xv). In 2013, the stock of FDI into/out of Norway aggregates to a level 18 times that of 1990 (Table 1). The importance of FDI is also underlined when looking at MNCs. Data from 2009 show that there were 82,000 MNCs globally, comprising 810,000 foreign affiliates (UNCTAD, 2009). In 2012, 6251 foreign enterprises had activities in Norway (employing 306,000 people), while 4200 Norwegian enterprises had transnational activities (employing 280,000 people) (http://ssb.no/utfono/).

3.2. Selection of regions and industries

With these indices in mind, the following discussion takes a closer look at FDI and related MNC practices in two Norwegian regions. The rationality behind our selection of regions was twofold as we looked for regions characterized by corresponding industrial structure, but regional economic particularity. Following up this, two industries were selected in each region: the salmon farming industry and the subsea industry in Hordaland, and the oil and gas industry and the mining industry in Finnmark, representing regional embedded industries based on natural resources with a relatively high standing in their respective regional economies. In each case, we scale the discussion by focusing on the practice of MNCs at the firm level and how material outcomes and FDI narratives relate to path evolution and processes of renewal at the industry level. To accomplish this, we have conducted 38 interviews with industry representatives (MNCs), industry facilitators (e.g. interest organizations) and regional government representatives (e.g. politicians), using a semi-structured interview guide developed for this study. Second, we have surveyed the coverage of FDI and MNC practices in the regional media during the period 2010–2015.

3.3. Hordaland region

3.3.1. The salmon farming industry: contra-FDI narrative and path extension

The salmon farming industry in Hordaland is part of a production system that turned Norway into the world's largest producer of Atlantic salmon (accounting for 65% of global production in 2010). Nationally, the salmon industry produces 1.25 million tons annually and production takes place at approximately 1000 locations. As the second fastest growing industry in Norway, it has become the third largest export industry in the country with a value of EUR 4.7 billion and provides approximately 25,000 jobs. Hordaland has a prominent position in this industry and the material outcomes are substantial. The region accounts for the highest number of licences (221) in Norway, one-third of the total turnover and one-fourth of total employment. Hordaland also hosts the headquarters of the leading firms, and thus includes significant research and development activities. Nevertheless, outward FDI characterizes the MNC practice. In the few cases of inward FDI, there is no evidence of regional spillover effects. In fact, the regional firms have been rather negative to 'intruders'. This became highly evident in an inward FDI of a Norwegian state-controlled firm in 2014:

> I see nothing positive in selling the salmon farming industry out of the country ... the industry is built up in Norway from nothing to become a huge success. It is here that the experts are located and research takes place. And then pundits in Oslo (the capital of Norway) argue, with support from (pundits at) NHH [the main business college], that such acquisitions that Mitsubishi will make are interesting and positive ... Apparently, it is trendy to see it as positive that foreigners buy Norwegian companies. I can't understand what's so positive about the farming industry along the Norwegian coast being owned by foreigners. [Industry representative] (Bergens Tidende, 23 September 2014)

The core claim of this contra-FDI narrative, that the region should avoid inward FDI/acquisitions from abroad, is a striking position considering that this industry has globalized over the past 40–45 years (Barton & Fløysand, 2010). Whether this explains why the industry has been accused of an unsustainable technological platform is hard to determine. However, the industry has relied on open net-pen technology that has several negative impacts on the fjords in which it is housed, in spite of its productivity. Based on reported emissions of organics and nutrients from the farms, production is equivalent to untreated sewage from 10 to 20 million people (Bergheim & Braaten, 2007). In addition, salmon farming in open net pens has been identified as a risk to the fjord environment as it causes increased load of salmon lice on wild fish, as well as the risk of genetic pollution of wild salmon stock through escapes (Taranger, Svåsand, Madhun, & Boxaspen, 2011; White Paper, 2014–2015). The Norwegian Seafood Federation (FHL) is contesting these matters:

> The Norwegian Seafood Federation (FHL) supports the proposition (White Paper 16 2014–2015/ Meld. St. 16 2014–2015) that only the lice load is suitable as an environmental indicator for a fiscal rule, but believes it is wrong that this shall be assessed from lice levels based on wild salmon stocks. Given the fact that there are great variations in lice abundance on wild fish in areas without aquaculture activities, it is unreasonable that natural fluctuations in sea lice populations are to regulate the growth of the aquaculture industry. [Industry facilitator] (The Norwegian Seafood Federation, 2015)

However, the world-leading and region-controlling MNC disagreed with this, which surprised the rest of the industry in the region and nation. The argument for abandoning the federation was related to environmental issues:

> Our position is that the industry should deal with lice before the industry can expand. Therefore, we have consistently opposed the wishes of the industry to increase production temporarily or permanently without relating to criteria for sustainable growth. We are sustaining food production in an eternal perspective, and then you have to adhere to the limits of nature. [Industry representative] (Dagens Næringsliv, 20 March 2015)

Summing up, the co-evolution of materiality and narratives is paradoxical. Hordaland region is a nucleus in a booming global production system of farmed Atlantic salmon that is experiencing positive regional spillover effects from the MNC-controlled regional capital. Yet this is characterized by a technological lock-in maintained by steadily increased productivity and high profits, as well as by scepticism towards inward FDI and a narrative within the environmental discourse challenging the industry. In sum, this seems to stimulate 'path extension' on an industry level.

3.3.2. The subsea industry: pro-FDI narrative and path renewal

In the 1960s and 1970s, it became evident that Norway possessed commercially recoverable oil and gas resources. The competence and resources needed to exploit this natural resource were not found in Norway. Consequently, foreign firms and their expertise fuelled the petroleum activity. However, regulations ensuring that firms be located in Norway, with state ownership of oil and gas resources, were implemented to stimulate industrial path creation on a national level. An informant reflected upon this:

> They [the foreign MNCs] brought with them some products from an international, global setting. Then you have mixed those products with Norwegian knowledge, and Norwegians have continued to develop these products. So, what is at the core here – if we think in terms of development – is that we have taken single elements from a global setting, and then we have further developed these with our engineering knowledge, resulting in a set of products which, at the time, was a global set of hardware products within the subsea industry. [Industry representative]

In 2014, 250,000 individuals were employed in this sector, which supplies services and products. This represents 10% of the total employment in Norway. The industry is concentrated in south-western Norway, demonstrating that Hordaland is an influential oil and gas region. This region has the highest absolute subsea employment and approximately 11% of the workforce in the region is employed in petroleum-related jobs (Blomgren et al., 2013). In contrast, northern Norway – where the Finnmark region is located – accounts for 4% of the Norwegian employment in this sector (see Section 3.4).

The subsea industry in the Hordaland region is relatively new, but since 1980 it has experienced rapid growth and has been proclaimed to be among the most innovative in the world (Sasson & Blomgren, 2011). It has always involved a high degree of FDI, both inwards and outwards. For instance, in 2014, 18% of the subsea firms in Hordaland were owned (shareholder majority) by foreign actors, 29% of the owners were located elsewhere in Norway and 53% were owned regionally ($N = 62$) (Jakobsen & Fløysand, 2011). Our informants point out that foreign actors were crucial in the early stages of subsea industry development in the region, and even though national companies are world-leading in subsea production of oil and gas, the importance of capital and market access, research and development, knowledge and other aspects of globalized business is considered crucial for further growth of the industry. Several influential MNCs perform a wide-ranging set of activities in the region, providing a global hub of expertise for subsea processing solutions, a Centre of Excellence within multiphase metering and FMC Technologies' regional headquarters for Customer Support. In general, influential MNCs of both national and foreign ownership have a solid presence in the Hordaland region. A cluster initiative, GCE Subsea, has been established, comprising 130 members, totalling 22,000 employees and NOK 51 billion in turnover in 2013.

Stakeholders voice a nearly unanimous positive attitude towards the MNC activity, highlighting that it constitutes an important dimension for the industrial development of the region. They emphasize that the MNC activity contributes to increased industry competitiveness and innovation:

> There are no local markets in this industry, only global markets. [Industry facilitator]

As far as I know, there have not been any closures [of acquisitioned regional firms]. We have one example of an acquisition leading to some movement of activity, but that's it. [Industry facilitator]

What they [foreign MNCs] bring in, and contribute with, is that they offer people an environment – and a network – which you do not have if you are a local firm. And that is attractive. [...] That, in turn, helps you internationalize, it helps you culturally, you achieve sharing of experience; that is, you get diversity – you get development. [Industry representative]

In sum, the subsea industry in Hordaland is a well-functioning, dynamic and innovative industry where FDI and related MNC practices have had substantial regional spillover effects including a cluster initiative. Not surprisingly, this is sustained by a pro-FDI narrative among the hegemonic stakeholders. At the industry level, this seems to stimulate 'path renewal'.

3.4. Finnmark region

3.4.1. The oil and gas industry: pro-FDI narrative and path creation

In contrast to Hordaland, fisheries and local municipalities in Finnmark used to be sceptical about petroleum activities in the region; they saw them as threatening to their fishery-dependent economy. Nevertheless, the petroleum activity in Norway spread northwards with a substantial impact on development in Finnmark. Until 2000, the region experienced a decline in population partly as an effect of declining demand for labour in the fishery sector. In particular, young people left the area in search of better education and job opportunities. The emergence of petroleum activities in the region changed this. The region's proportion of employment in the oil and gas industry increased from 30 employees in 2000 to 1430 in 2013. In some municipalities, the oil and gas industry reversed the trends in parts of the local economies: there was a shift from jobs decline to growth; young people moved back and settled; the labour market became more integrated; etc. Parallel to such prospering, articulation of the impacts of the oil and gas industry as being purely negative vanished.

Yet, the region is sparsely populated and had few local firms within the industry. Accordingly, the national government in cooperation with industry representatives (MNCs) put forward a 'local content' policy in order to qualify regional firms, establish a regional businesses environment, encourage research and development activities and locate MNC offices in the region. The 'local content' policy encouraged MNCs to participate and engage in projects resulting in regional spillovers. Located 2000 kilometres north of the nearest relevant oil and gas innovation hub, transportation costs, costs associated with expatriate staffing, etc., made it reasonable for MNCs to facilitate networking and share knowledge with regional firms. Thus, MNC practices were from the very beginning characterized by shared interests, networking and knowledge spillover. Parallel to this, a pro-FDI narrative portraying the new oil and gas industry as a window of opportunities for the region emerged:

The entry of international oil companies has introduced a totally new market for firms in the region, not only with regard to specialized oil and gas supplies but also for regional firms in construction, transportation, catering and general service industries. [Regional government representatives]

> From a regional perspective the growth of petroleum-related services gives the region new possibilities in terms of business growth, employment and also local and regional firms upgrade their knowledge and competencies – skills that can be applied in other sectors parallel to oil and gas industries. [Industry facilitators]

Industry facilitators also pointed to how the local industry and communities can take advantage of being close to coastal oil and gas resources to attract FDI, and that this benefits the region:

> Building up a critical mass of infrastructure and service functions in the [municipality] will be a strategic effort in order to handle operations in the Barents Sea in the future. The build-up of a supply base, heliport, oil spill contingency base, and establishment of operational offices in [municipality] for multinational oil companies, underlines this. [Industry facilitators]

> The Barents Sea may hold huge undiscovered petroleum resources. While over 1000 wells have been drilled in the North Sea, only 105 have been drilled in the Barents Sea. In the years to come, drilling activity into these areas will increase and we may also observe a shift where the Barents Sea will be the next large reserve resource magnitude on the Norwegian Continental Shelf. These operations will be served from [municipality]. [Industry representatives]

In summary, the informants in the oil and gas industry in the Finnmark region articulate a pro-FDI narrative. The basis for this is that MNC dynamics have had an impact after the oil and gas firms began settling in the region. The 'local content', and the efforts of the MNC in taking on a broader social role and responsibility, has created arenas of learning for local firms. This has co-evolved into a new industry (Nilsen, Karlstad, & Nilssen, 2013). As such, the co-evolution of narratives and material outcomes within the oil and gas industry in the Finnmark region can be considered as regional 'path creation'.

3.4.2. The mining industry: contra-FDI narrative and path exhaustion

Finnmark is also an important mining region in Norway, so that the Norwegian Government has prioritized it as a key component for regional industrial development in its 2006 'High North policy'. Moreover, the introduction of a new Mining Act by the Norwegian Government in 2009 encouraged more FDI into the industry. Before bankruptcy in late 2015, an iron mine was the most significant of the three remaining operating mines in the region. Up until its closure in 1996 (after 90 years of iron ore production), it was state owned. In 2009, inward FDI led to its reopening. Before bankruptcy, it employed 400 people and engaged a considerable number of local sub-suppliers. Two smaller mines have also been through a process of internationalization. As in the case of the iron mine, they recently experienced a shift from Norwegian to foreign ownership, with a subsequent inflow of FDI.

In short, FDI in the mining industry has been capital dominated. Contrary to the oil and gas industry in Finnmark, it is not regulated by a 'local content' policy. Whether or not this explains the MNC practice in the industry is unclear, but the entry of FDI has not contributed towards much innovation or regional development. For example, the iron mine enterprise originally included pellet processing. This was not sustained by the inward FDI. Rather, the mine went back to low-cost product production after the takeover. The FDI also caused a shift in technology when the MNC brought in 'new' production technology from abroad. Ironically, this technology failed to work well in the arctic climate, causing production to halt. This led some regional stakeholders to claim that regional knowledge on how to run the mine was neglected. Whatever the reason, the company was unable to meet production targets, causing financial deficits for the firm. This again negatively affected regional financial institutions. Subcontractors also struggled to receive payments. Therefore, although the reopening of the mine certainly gave local service and manufacturing firms new opportunities, long-term survival of the MNC failed. The FDI narrative related to the mining sector has been relatively outspoken and negative:

> The new owners underestimated the need for FDI in the start-up phase. They thought it would be easy and cheap, and failed to use the best available technology. The local community and the environment will have to pay the price. [Industry facilitator]

Environmental issues also affect the articulations of statements. Norway is one of few countries in the world permitting sea deposits of mining waste. The iron mine involved a sea deposit requiring a considerable amount of flocculence and floating chemicals, practically killing most of the life in the deposit fjord. Not surprisingly, this has caused negative claims:

> Our fjords are not for dumping of waste! Food producers, locals, environmentalists, reindeer herders and the tourist industry unite in this protest. [Industry facilitator]

Similar claims have been raised in relation to FDI plans, including those for new copper and gold mines. Most disputed is the copper mine as it involves a sea deposit claimed to violate the EU water directive and the rights of the indigenous population, and to undermine protected natural reservations:

> Twelve environmental and fishery organizations have now sent an appeal to European Space Agency to stop the plans to use the fjords as dumping sites for mining waste. [Complaint, Naturvernforbundet dated 19.05.2015]

In addition, plans for new mines in Finnmark face a new legal framework protecting the rights of the indigenous population and providing a greater say of the local government:

> The company violates human rights if it rejects the demands of the reindeer herders who are affected. [Industry facilitator]

The negative experience with loss of control over the mineral resources to an MNC has led to an apparently hostile attitude towards parts of the mining industry in this region. The contra-FDI narrative produced is that of the MNC exploiting the regional resources without leaving much ripple effect in the region:

> The mineral industry is out of our control … We have no possibility to secure the values locally. [Regional government representative]

In sum, even though FDI can be assumed to have had some spillover effects in the communities where mining has taken place, the FDI narrative in the region is mainly negative. Along with this, the sector struggles with negative economic returns and environmental challenges. In short, repercussions of the present co-evolving material and discursive processes in the mining industry in the Finnmark region seem to be characterized by 'path exhaustion'.

4. Towards a model

Section 3 has illustrated the analytical framework (see Figure 1) developed in Section 2. Our examples illustrate how the heterogeneity of encounters between MNCs and regional industry contexts contributes to a nuanced understanding of the reciprocity between materiality, discourse and renewal of industries. The reciprocity between materiality and discourse can be observed as dialectic dynamism between material 'outcomes', in terms of regional spillover and effects/environmental impacts, and discursive 'processes', in terms of narratives encouraging/countering FDI. Returning to the questions raised in the Introduction, the examples discussed here certainly demonstrate that FDI and related MNC practices spark different material outcomes and FDI narratives on an industry level. In the fish farming (path extension) and mining (path exhaustion) examples, we observe a contra-FDI narrative coupled with minor regional spillovers. On the other hand, we exemplify how the subsea (path renewal) and petroleum (path creation) examples represent pro-narratives to FDI, and also how this is coupled with substantial regional spillovers. Thus, communication between narratives of FDI and material outcomes of MNC practice appears to influence processes of industry renewal. The evolutionary argument of a 'regional particularity' is harder to spot as neither the 'private enterprise' culture in Hordaland, nor the 'governmental enterprise' in Finnmark emerges across the industry cases. On the contrary, the material outcomes and discourses are considerably different at the industry level in both regions.

So, what are the theoretical implications of treating, through a regional development perspective, FDI and MNC practice as an interplay between materiality and discourse for our understanding of regional renewal? We argue that substantial change is taking place in industries relying on a discursive environment of pro-FDI narratives and substantial regional spillovers, while continuation occurs when an FDI is surrounded by contra-FDI narratives and minor regional spillovers. We also argue that FDI-related MNC practice characterized by a lack of shared capital interests, networking and transfer of knowledge creates processes of continuation, whereas high degrees of shared capital interests, networking and transfer of knowledge generate processes of change. This is illustrated in the model in Figure 2.

It follows from the model that outcomes of FDI on processes of industry renewal cannot be 'read off' from analyses isolating material or discursive characteristics of FDI and MNC practice alone. For example, if we were to investigate the marine industry in Hordaland through only considering its materiality, we would most likely end up in a description emphasizing the (financial) success of the industry, its innovative capability and its beneficial conditions for regional growth. However, through including narratives in our analytical framework, we also illustrate how hostility towards foreign capital may hamper innovation and sustainability, influencing degrees of renewal within the industry. On the contrary, if we were to investigate interplays between FDI and industry renewal through only looking at discourses in the petroleum industry in Finnmark, we would most likely end up with accounts glorifying its conditions for future economic growth in the region.

The model also indicates how, through directed policy action, one can influence the reciprocity between discourse and materiality. The dynamics of the model surface when change in FDI-related MNC practice moves industries between positions in the model.

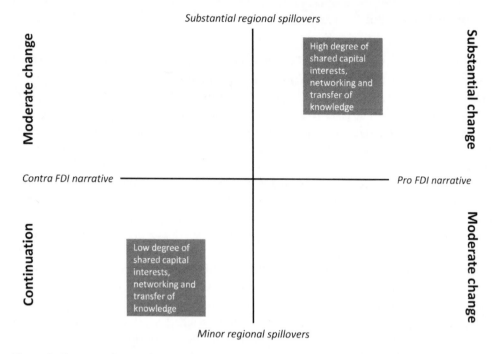

Figure 2. The co-evolution of material outcomes and FDI narratives and degrees of regional industry renewal.

In an evolutionary perspective, such moves have most prominently been linked to notions of 'external shocks' (Arthur, 1989; David, 1985). However, more recently it has been argued that deliberate action can contribute to altering industry development paths (Garud, Kumaraswamy, & Karnøe, 2010; Njøs, Jakobsen, & Rosnes, 2016; Sydow et al., 2009; Vergne & Durand, 2010). As such, policy should be considered crucial in guiding the interplay between FDI, path development and renewal of industries. Following our model, the aim should be to monitor the degree to which an FDI-related MNC practice involves shared capital interests, networking and transfer of knowledge.

But our approach does not come without limitations. As exemplified in the model, snapshots of renewal of industries can inform us on whether an industry is developing along beneficial or less beneficial paths, but it cannot inform our understanding of longer term processes of industry renewal and regional development more broadly. Thus, to provide greater nuance on the reciprocity between discourses and materiality, there is a need to investigate, over time, the evolving dynamics of individual industries as well as how multiple industry paths relate to wider processes of 'regional' renewal. What we can assume is that a region characterized by a high degree of continuation in important industries is less prone to renewal than a region characterized by high abilities to change.

5. Conclusions

We have highlighted the relations between FDI, related MNC practices and renewal of industries by engaging in theoretical, methodological and empirical discussions. Informed by discussions within the evolutionary literature, we have argued for an understanding of industry renewal that emphasizes 'degree of renewal', defining industry renewal as a continuum between continuation (low abilities to adapt to changing circumstances) and substantial change (high abilities to adapt to changing circumstances). Second, we have declared that an 'epistemological shift' stressing the co-evolution of discursive and material processes of FDI is needed when studying how FDI relates to regional renewal. In short, the framework stresses the degree to which an FDI and its related MNC practices involve shared capital interests, networking and transfer of knowledge at the firm level; material outcomes of FDI/MNC practices in terms of spillover effects on an industry level; and how this is linked to 'pro et contra' FDI narratives. Finally, we have put the framework into practice through an empirical discussion of four industries in two regions of Norway. This indicates that the impact of FDI and MNCs on industry renewal depends on the degree of coherence between observable material outcomes and FDI narratives, but that case particularity – rather than regional distinctive conditions – explains the FDI-related path development in the four industries. Regarding the question on how narratives of FDI and material outcomes of MNC practice 'communicate', the discussed industries display 'path exhaustion' or 'path extension' in cases of minor spillover effects in co-evolution with contra-FDI narratives, while 'path renewal' or 'path creation' occurs in the cases of severe regional spillovers and pro-FDI narratives. The way this links to industry renewal seems to be that a high degree of 'positive' coherence encourages change, whereas a high degree of 'negative' coherence leads to continuation. Although more (thoroughgoing) studies are needed to confirm the representativeness of these findings, the observed co-evolution of material outcomes and narratives is comprehensive on an industry level and should not be overlooked in studies of FDI and regional development. In order to avoid static understandings of FDI and renewal of industries, our analytical frameworks need to consider the reciprocity of (changing) interplays between discursive processes and material outcomes. However, if such studies are going to inform regional policies, there is a need to further develop our theoretical framework through also incorporating wider regional industry structures.

Acknowledgements

The authors would like to thank Arne Isaksen and the two anonymous reviewers for their helpful comments on previous drafts of this paper.

Disclosure statement

No potential conflict of interest was reported by the authors.

Funding

This research was made possible by funding from the Research Council of Norway, Hordaland county municipality and Finnmark county municipality.

References

Agostin, M., & Mayer, R. (2000). *Foreign direct investment in developing countries: Does it crowd in domestic investment?* UNCTAD Discussion Paper 146.

Andersson, U., & Forsgren, M. (1996). Subsidiary embeddedness and control in the multinational corporation. *International Business Review, 5*, 487–508. doi:10.1016/0969-5931(96)00023-6

Arthur, W. B. (1989). Competing technologies, increasing returns, and lock-in by historical events. *The Economic Journal, 99*, 116–131. doi:10.2307/2234208

Barton, J. R., & Fløysand, A. (2010). The political ecology of Chilean salmon aquaculture, 1982–2010: A trajectory from economic development to global sustainability. *Global Environmental Change, 20*, 739–752. doi:10.1016/j.gloenvcha.2010.04.001

Bathelt, H., Malmberg, A., & Maskell, P. (2004). Clusters and knowledge: Local buzz, global pipelines and the process of knowledge creation. *Progress in Human Geography, 28*, 31–56. doi:10.1191/0309132504ph469oa

Bellandi, M. (2001). Local development and embedded large firms. *Entrepreneurship & Regional Development, 13*, 189–210. doi:10.1080/08985620110051103

Bergheim, A., & Braaten, B. (2007). Modell for utslipp fra norske matfiskanlegg til sjø. Rapport fra IRIS, 2007/180. 35 s.

Blomgren, A., Quale, C., Brosvik Bayer, S., Nyvold, C. E., Steffensen, T., Tovmo, P., … Hagen, S. E. (2013). *Industribyggerne: Norsk olje-og gassnæring ut med havet og mellom bakkar og berg* [Industry entrepreneurs: Norwegian oil and gas industry by the ocean and between mountains]. Stavanger: Rapport IRIS - 2013/031, International Research Institute of Stavanger.

Blomström, M., & Kokko, A. (1998). Multinational corporations and spillovers. *Journal of Economic Surveys, 12*, 247–277. doi:10.1111/1467-6419.00056

Borensztein, E., De Gregorio, J., & Lee, J.-W. (1998). How does foreign direct investment affect economic growth? *Journal of International Economics, 45*, 115–135. doi:10.1016/S0022-1996(97)00033-0

Boschma, R., & Frenken, K. (2011). Technological relatedness, related variety and economic geography. In P. Cooke, B. Asheim, R. Boschma, R. Martin, D. Schwartz, & F. Tödtling (Eds.), *Handbook of regional innovation and growth* (pp. 187–197). Cheltenham: Edward Elgar.

Boschma, R. A. (2005). Proximity and innovation: A critical assessment. *Regional Studies, 39*, 61–74. doi:10.1080/0034340052000320887

Boschma, R. A., & Martin, R. R. L. (2010). *The handbook of evolutionary economic geography.* Cheltenham: Edward Elgar.

Cooke, P., Gomez Uranga, M., & Etxebarria, G. (1997). Regional innovation systems: Institutional and organisational dimensions. *Research Policy, 26*, 475–491. doi:10.1016/S0048-7333(97)00025-5

David, P. A. (1985). Clio and the economics of QWERTY. *The American Economic Review, 75*, 332–337. Retrieved from http://www.jstor.org/stable/1805621

Dicken, P. (2007). *Global shift: Mapping the changing contours of the world economy.* London: Sage.

Dunning, J. H. (1993). *Multinational enterprises and the global economy.* Wokingham: Addison-Wesley.

Enright, M. J. (2000). Regional clusters and multinational enterprises: Independence, dependence, or interdependence? *International Studies of Management & Organization, 30*(2), 114–138. doi:10.1080/00208825.2000.11656790

Etzkowitz, H., & Leydesdorff, L. (2000). The dynamics of innovation: From National Systems and 'Mode 2' to a Triple Helix of university–industry–government relations. *Research Policy, 29*, 109–123. doi:10.1016/S0048-7333(99)00055-4

European Commission. (2012). *Guide to research and innovation strategies for smart specialisations.* Luxembourg: Regional Policy.

Fagerberg, J. (2005). Innovation. A guide to the literature. In J. Fagerberg, D.C. Mowery, & R.R. Nelson (Eds.), *The Oxford handbook of innovation* (pp. 1–28). Oxford: Oxford University Press.

Fairclough, N. (1995). *Critical discourse analysis. The critical study of language.* London: Longman.

Fløysand, A., & Jakobsen, S.-E. (2011). The complexity of innovation: A relational turn. *Progress in Human Geography, 35*, 328–344. doi:10.1177/0309132510376257

Fløysand, A., Jakobsen, S. E., & Bjarnar, O. (2012). The dynamism of clustering: Interweaving material and discursive processes. *Geoforum, 43*, 948–958. doi:10.1016/j.geoforum.2012.05.002

Foucault, M. (1991). *Discipline and punish: The birth of prison.* Hammondsworth: Penguin Books.

Garud, R., Kumaraswamy, A., & Karnøe, P. (2010). Path dependence or path creation? *Journal of Management Studies, 47*, 760–774. doi:10.1111/j.1467-6486.2009.00914.x

Hassink, R. (2005). How to unlock regional economies from path dependency? From learning region to learning cluster. *European Planning Studies, 13*, 521–535. doi:10.1080/09654310500107134

Henderson, J., Dicken, P., Hess, M., Coe, N. M., & Yeung, H. W.-C. (2002). Global production networks and the analysis of economic development. *Review of International Political Economy, 9*, 436–464. doi:10.1080/09692290210150842

Iammarino, S., & McCann, P. (2013). *Multinationals and economic geography. Location, technology and innovation.* Cheltenham: Edward Elgar.

Ivarsson, I. (1999). Competitive industry clusters and inward TNC investment: The case of Sweden. *Regional Studies, 33*, 37–49. doi:10.1080/00343409950118904

Jakobsen, S. E., Byrkjeland, M., Båtevik, F. O., Pettersen, I. B., Skogseid, I., & Yttredal, E. R. (2012). Continuity and change in path-dependent regional policy development: The regional implementation of the Norwegian VRI programme. *Norsk Geografisk Tidsskrift – Norwegian Journal of Geography, 66*, 133–143. doi:10.1080/00291951.2012.681686

Jakobsen, S. E., & Fløysand, A. (2011). *Subseabedriftenes regionale forankring. Funn fra en spørreundersøkelse gjennomført blant subseabedrifter i Hordaland.* SNF-arbeidsnotat 48/10. Bergen: Samfunns- og næringslivsforskning.

Jakobsen, S. E., Rusten, G., & Fløysand, A. (2005). How green is the valley? Foreign direct investment in two Norwegian towns. *Canadian Geographer / Le Géographe canadien, 49*, 244–259. doi:10.1111/j.0008-3658.2005.00093.x

Kogler, D. F. (2015). Editorial: Evolutionary economic geography – theoretical and empirical progress. *Regional Studies, 49*, 705–711. doi:10.1080/00343404.2015.1033178

Lauclau, E., & Mouffe, C. (2001). *Hegemony and socialist strategy: Towards a radical democratic politics.* London: Verso.

Machinea, J. L., & Vera, C. (2006). *Trade, direct investment and production policies.* Santiago: CEPAL.

Martin, R. (2009). *Rethinking regional path dependence: Beyond lock-in to evolution.* Papers in Evolutionary Economic Geography, 09.10. Utrecht: Utrecht University.

Martin, R., & Sunley, P. (2006). Path dependence and regional economic evolution. *Journal of Economic Geography, 6*, 395–437. doi:10.1093/jeg/lbl012

Martin, R., & Sunley, P. (2010). The place of path dependence in an evolutionary perspective on the economic landscape. In R. A. Boschma & R. R. L. Martin (Eds.), *The handbook of evolutionary economic geography* (pp. 62–92). Cheltenham: Edward Elgar.

Milberg, W. (1999). *Foreign direct investment and development: Balancing costs and benefits. International monetary and financial issues for the 1990s.* United Nations Conference on Trade and Development, XI, 99–115.

Nilsen, T., Karlstad, S., & Nilssen, I. (2013). Norsk leverandørindustri sin konkurranseevne i en global offshorenæring. Leveranser til Goliatprosjektet i Barentshavet. Norut Alta-rapport 2013:11.

Njøs, R., & Jakobsen, S.-E. (2016). Cluster policy and regional development: Scale, scope and renewal. *Regional Studies, Regional Science, 3*, 146–169. doi:10.1080/21681376.2015.1138094

Njøs, R., Jakobsen, S.-E., & Rosnes, V. (2016). Market-driven organizational lock-in: A case study of a former first mover. *Norsk Geografisk Tidsskrift – Norwegian Journal of Geography, 70*(3), 140–151. doi:10.1080/00291951.2015.1116601

Nooteboom, B. (2000). *Learning and innovation in organizations and economies.* Oxford: Oxford University Press.

Phelps, N. A. (1992). Branch plants and the evolving spatial division of labour: A study of material linkages change in the northern region of England. *Regional Studies, 27*, 87–101. doi:10.1080/00343409312331347405

Pike, A., Dawley, S., & Tomaney, J. (2010). Resilience, adaptation and adaptability. *Cambridge Journal of Regions, Economy and Society, 3*(1), 59–70. doi:10.1093/cjres/rsq001

Porter, M. E. (1990). *The competitive advantage of nations.* London: Macmillan.

Roe, E. M. (1991). Development narratives, or making the best of blueprint development. *World Development*, *19*, 287–300. doi:10.1016/0305-750X(91)90177-J

Rose, G. (2001). *Visual methodologies: An introduction to the interpretation of visual material*. London: Sage.

Sasson, A., & Blomgren, A. (2011). *Knowledge based oil and gas industry*. Report no. 4. Et kunnskapsbasert Norge. BI & IRIS – International Research Institute of Stavanger.

Smeets, R. (2008). Collecting the pieces of the FDI knowledge spillovers puzzle. *The World Bank Research Observer*, *23*, 107–138. doi:10.1093/wbro/lkn003

Swift, J. (1996). Desertification: Narratives, winners & losers. In M. Leach & R. Mearns (Eds.), *The lie of the land: Challenging received wisdom on the African environment* (pp. 73–90). Oxford: Heinemann.

Sydow, J., Schreyögg, G., & Koch, J. (2009). Organizational path dependence: Opening the black box. *Academy of Management Review*, *34*, 689–709. doi:10.5465/AMR.2009.44885978

Sydow, J., Windeler, A., Müller-Seitz, G., & Lange, K. (2012). Path constitution analysis: A methodology for understanding path dependence and path creation. *Business Research*, *5*, 155–176. doi:10.1007/BF03342736

Taranger, G. L., Svåsand, T., Madhun, A. S., & Boxaspen, K. K. (2011). *Risikovurdering – miljøvirkninger av norsk fiskeoppdrett*. Bergen: Havforskningsinstituttet.

Te Velde, D. W. (2003). *Foreign direct investment and income inequality in Latin America: Experiences and policy implications*. London: Overseas Development Institute.

The Norwegian Seafood Federation. (2015). Resolusjon. Vedtak av generalforsamlingen i FHL/ Sjømat Norge, sak 7/201526.08.2015. Retrieved August 24, 2015, from http://sjomatnorge.no/resolusjon-om/

Tödtling, F., & Trippl, M. (2005). One size fits all? Towards a differentiated regional innovation policy approach. *Research Policy*, *34*, 1203–1219. doi:10.1016/j.respol.2005.01.018

UNCTAD. (2009). *World investment report. Transnational corporations, agricultural production and development*. New York, NY: Author.

UNCTAD. (2014). *World investment report 2014*. New York, NY: Author.

Vergne, J., & Durand, R. (2010). The missing link between the theory and empirics of path dependence: Conceptual clarification, testability issue, and methodological implications. *Journal of Management Studies*, *47*, 736–759. doi:10.1111/j.1467-6486.2009.00913.x

Watts, H. D. (1981). *The branch plant economy: A study of external control*. London: Longman.

White Paper 16 2014–2015/ Meld. St. 16 2014–2015.

Paving the way for new regional industrial paths: actors and modes of change in Scania's games industry

Johan Miörner and Michaela Trippl

ABSTRACT
Recent scholarly work has enhanced our understanding of how new path development activities are enabled or constrained by 'regional environments', made up of pre-existing industrial structures, knowledge organizations, support structures and institutional configurations. This paper moves beyond overly static views on regional environments. We develop a dynamic perspective by analysing conceptually and empirically how a constraining environment can be transformed into one that enables the development of new growth paths. The paper offers a typology of various modes of change, including layering, adaptation and novel application that are used by key actors to 'manipulate' the regional support structures to facilitate new regional industrial path development. The conceptual framework is applied to a case study of the digital games industry in the region of Scania, southern Sweden. Our findings suggest that the creation of a more enabling environment for the growth of the digital games industry has been the outcome of multi-scalar processes and combinations of various modes of change employed by a few key individuals operating in the newly emerging path.

1. Introduction

Explaining how new regional industrial growth paths emerge and develop over time has become a key focus of enquiries in economic geography. In the past decade, scholarly work has moved beyond old conceptualizations of path creation as outcomes of exogenous shocks, chance events and serendipity, emphasizing that pre-existing local economic structures, resources and competences constitute the regional environment in which path development activities take place (Martin, 2010; Neffke, Henning, & Boschma, 2011). This has shifted attention to regional factors and conditions and the ways by which they enable or constrain the development of new industrial growth paths, that is, the rise and evolution of new industries in a region.

We argue that there is a need to deepen our understanding of what factors in the regional environment are shaping the development of new industrial growth paths. The paper advocates a broad view and maintains that the regional environment in which new industrial paths emerge is not only made up of pre-existing industrial structures but also of historically grown organizational and institutional support arrangements.

Furthermore, the characterization of regional environments as enabling or constraining offers a static perspective on the relationship between new industrial path development and the regional context. New industrial growth paths often require a major reconfiguration of the regional organizational and institutional support structures (Martin & Simmie, 2008; Tödtling & Trippl, 2013). It is thus intriguing to explore how the transformation of regional support structures takes place and how these processes are shaped by key actors of change.

The role of actors of change, however, remains poorly understood in current accounts of new path development (Dawley, 2014). The literature has thus far been primarily concerned with the role of private actors involved in new firm formation and has only recently begun to examine how public actors influence new industrial path development (Dawley, 2014; Dawley, MacKinnon, Cumbers, & Pike, 2015; Sydow, Lerch, & Staber, 2010). It is necessary to consider the role of purposeful actors in a broader sense, as reproducing and transforming existing regional arrangements (Martin, 2010; Martin & Sunley, 2006) in addition to firm entrepreneurs mindfully deviating from existing paths (Garud & Karnøe, 2001).

The paper goes beyond overly static views on regional environments. We aim to contribute to the development of a more dynamic perspective by investigating conceptually and empirically how key actors induce changes in the regional environment, in order to 'turn' a constraining context into one that enables new industrial path development. Focusing on the organizational and institutional support structure as one important dimension of the regional environment, we address the following research questions: how can a regional environment be turned into being enabling for new industrial path development and what is the role of key actors in this process? By what modes do they change the regional environment?

The paper draws on recent scholarly work on the role of key actors in new path development. It offers a typology of various modes of change and seeks to explain the relation between different types of power held by key actors and the modes of changes that are employed to 'manipulate' the regional environment. The empirical part of the paper discusses findings from a case study of the digital games industry in Scania, an emerging industrial path that is geographically concentrated in the region's largest city, Malmö. Focusing on the regional organizational and institutional support structure, we demonstrate that reconfiguration processes of the regional environment have been the result of complex multi-scalar processes and combinations of various modes of change employed by key individuals operating in the digital games industry.

The remainder of the paper is organized as follows. Section 2 offers a review of the literature and provides a conceptual discussion of transformation processes of organizational and institutional set-ups, focusing particularly on key actors and modes of change. In Section 3 we present and discuss the findings of our empirical analysis. Section 4 summarizes our main results and draws some conclusions.

2. Turning constraining environments into enabling ones: key actors and modes of change

The past years have witnessed a growing interest in the question of how new growth paths emerge and develop in regional economies (Martin & Sunley, 2006). Recent contributions to the literature have challenged the traditional canonical model of path dependence and its focus on chance, historical accidents and exogenous shocks as a source of new path creation. New models foreground endogenous factors and mechanisms. Neffke et al. (2011, p. 261) noted that new regional growth paths 'do not start from scratch but are strongly rooted in the historical economic structure of a region'. In a similar vein, Martin (2010, p. 21) argues that new path development is shaped by 'preexisting resources, competences, skills and experiences that have been inherited from previous local paths and patterns of economic development'. New accounts thus highlight the (pre-existing) regional context in which path development takes place.

In the model suggested by Martin (2010), the development of new industries is both enabled and constrained by the environment inherited from previous regional industrial paths. However, there is a need to add more clarity and provide more detailed insights into 'what' constitutes an enabling or constraining environment (Dawley, 2014) and 'when and how', in the course of new regional industrial path development, the environment is exerting an influence.

Attempts have been made in the regional innovation system (RIS) literature to specify which regional conditions are most beneficial (and which ones provide the biggest challenges) to new industrial path development. The RIS approach takes into account not only the industrial structure of the region, but also the network configurations (nature and geography of knowledge flows) and the organizational and institutional support structures (i.e. knowledge organizations, support agencies and the institutional dimension). Isaksen and Trippl (2016) categorize RISs based on the level of organizational thickness and the degree of industrial specialization and argue that various RIS types differ in their capacity to promote the emergence of new industries in the region. Organizationally thin RIS and organizationally thick and specialized RIS are seen as offering rather unfavourable conditions for the rise of new growth paths due to thin structures or the lack of variety in the industrial, organizational and institutional set-ups. In contrast, thick and diversified RIS are described as providing excellent regional conditions for new industries to emerge and flourish, as they host a large variety of knowledge and support organizations and a heterogeneous industrial base. In addition, they display a strong capacity to attract new skills and competencies from outside the region (Trippl, Grillitsch, & Isaksen, 2015). However, there may also be constraining factors, including economic, institutional, cognitive and social ones (Simmie, 2012), that could hamper the development of new growth paths in organizationally thick and diversified regions.

2.1. Factors constraining the development of new growth paths

Constraints may be found in the private sector, the public support structure and the institutional setting of the RIS. The rise and evolution of a new industry can be held back by a lack of resources, competencies and experiences related to the newly emerging industry. Due to limited experiences among capital providers (e.g. venture capital firms, business angels and banks), entrepreneurs may face difficulties to draw on local sources to obtain seed funding. In thick and diversified regions there is plentiful public support for new firm formation (e.g. start-up grants and business incubators), but this is often adapted to the needs of existing industries and does not necessarily match the requirements of the new path. Low availability of finance and support for start-ups could thus be an obstacle for new path development (Gustafsson, Jääskeläinen, Maula, & Uotila, 2016). Another barrier might be the lack of specialized labour. Even if a thick and diversified region offers a pool of skilled labour in a variety of fields, employees with prior work experience in the emerging field may not be obtained locally. Relevant educational programmes at local universities or vocational schools may not exist (yet), or are too generic, resulting in a mismatch between required and available skills in the region. Similar arguments might hold true for research organizations and the knowledge they generate. Constraining factors might also be related to missing support for networking activities between firms operating in a newly emerging path, leading to low levels of collaboration and knowledge exchange necessary for positive lock-in and further growth of the new industry. Arguably, gaining support from public decision-makers (in the form of customized infrastructure such as cluster organizations, business incubators, funding of projects, etc.) can be essentially important for a new industry to grow.

Barriers to new path development might also be found in the institutional dimension of RIS. Institutions tend to change slowly, which can hold back new economic development processes (Boschma & Martin, 2010). In addition, some regulative, normative and cultural-cognitive institutions can hinder new path development processes by their very nature. This includes a lack of understanding among private actors and public authorities and uncertainties among new actors regarding future development prospects and policy support for the new path. Competition with well-established and other emerging paths in the region for human capital, infrastructure and other scare resources as well as for the attention and support of public policy may hamper the development of a new industry. Finally, 'political lock-in' (Grabher, 1993) could lead to a preference of supporting established players and paths rather than new developments.

2.2. From constraining to enabling environments: the role of key actors and modes of change

In the previous section, we argued that a variety of factors could constrain the development of new regional industrial paths. Little is still known about how a constraining environment can be transformed into an enabling one through intentional and purposive actions taken by key actors of change. This section synthesizes recent findings on key actors and different modes of change and applies them to the question of how regional institutional and organizational support structures are transformed to meet the needs of newly emerging industrial paths.

2.2.1. Actors of change

The role of key actors in new path development is, with some exceptions (see e.g. Dawley, 2014; Simmie, 2012; Simmie, Sternberg, & Carpenter, 2014; Sydow et al., 2010), an under-researched topic. Simmie's (2012) seminal contribution draws on work by Garud and Karnøe (2001) and Garud, Kumaraswamy, and Karnøe (2010) and approaches new path creation from a sociological perspective, arguing that through iteration and reflexive feedback loops actors are both embedded in the structures in which new paths emerge, and contribute to the creation of new development paths. Departing from the assumption that 'new pathways are not created by disembodied economic forces but by knowledgeable agents' (Simmie, 2012, p. 760) and using insights from the literature on institutional change (Streeck & Thelen, 2005), Simmie explains how new technological paths are created by agents. These agents can be both inventors (exploring new technologies) and innovators (exploiting new technologies). They deviate from past practices by conscious social actions with the intention of introducing and diffusing new technologies. To do so, they have to change the regional environment, particularly by overcoming barriers to new path creation (identified as the economic selection environment, technological paradigms, institutional hysteresis and technological regimes). In a later study, Simmie et al. (2014) apply this framework to the emergence of wind energy industries in Great Britain and Germany, adding more emphasis on the co-evolution between knowledgeable inventors and innovators, and initiatives by policy actors, in creating niche conditions supporting the emergence of new paths. This approach takes into account the social actions of intentional agents and how new paths through these actions change the environment, but is concerned mainly with the creation of new technological paths.

Dawley (2014) puts a more explicit focus on how agents deliberatively shape the regional environment to facilitate new path development. Taking on a multi-scalar and a multi-actor approach, he explores how regional and non-regional actors such as state agencies and public policy, experienced entrepreneurs and practitioners have shaped the development of the wind energy industry in Scotland by creating a favourable environment for its rise and further evolution. Policy actors played a role in promoting industry-relevant R&D and together with key entrepreneurs they had an influence on Foreign Direct Investment (FDI) promotion, processes of strategic coupling and supporting knowledge transfer between different but related industries (Dawley, 2014).

Sydow et al. (2010) make the purposiveness and intentionality more explicit and extend the analysis to include the later stages of path development, beyond path creation. Based on findings from a case study of the Berlin-Brandenburg optics cluster the authors argue that actors in the cluster engage in networks deliberately planning for positive lock-in. They do so through communication and exercising power and sanctions, influencing interpretative schemes, supporting facilities and informal institutions (Sydow et al., 2010).

Moving beyond studies explicitly examining the role of agency in new path development, other strands of literature dealing with purposive and intentional change of RIS elements can be of use when examining how regional actors transform the regional institutional and organizational set-up. The literature on institutional entrepreneurship can help to understand in greater detail how institutions are changed by key actors. First introduced by DiMaggio (1988), institutional entrepreneurs are actors who do not comply with current institutions but mobilize resources, competences and power for the purpose of creating institutions or transforming existing ones. Building on this definition, Battilana, Leca, and Boxenbaum (2009) argue that institutional entrepreneurs are change agents who initiate divergent institutional changes and who actively participate in the implementation of these. The institutional entrepreneurship concept has been used for example to explain how new beliefs, practices and activities are institutionalized within an RIS during the development of new regional industrial paths (Sotarauta & Mustikkamäki, 2015). It has also been shown that institutional entrepreneurs can play a role in bridging actors and resources at different spatial scales (Karlsen, Larrea, Wilson, & Aranguren, 2012).

Institutional entrepreneurs exercise different types of power when trying to change institutions, and power relations evolve over time with institutional change. Sotarauta and Mustikkamäki (2015) distinguish between three forms of power, that is, interpretative, network and institutional power. Interpretative power relates to the ability of actors to create a new vocabulary, promote new ways of looking at different functions in the RIS and lead a process of sense making around the particular institutional change. Network power is the power to remove obstacles for communication, information flows and collaboration. Institutional power is defined as the power to act, to make decisions, to create formal institutions and direct resources (Sotarauta & Mustikkamäki, 2015). Furthermore, Weik (2011) distinguishes between three types of institutional entrepreneurs: agents creating new institutions, removing existing institutions or changing established institutions.

Similar insights are offered by the literature on policy entrepreneurship. Policy entrepreneurs are individuals or organizations who are willing to invest own resources for seeking future returns, by attempting to initiate policy change (Edler & James, 2015; Mintrom & Norman, 2009). They are said to play a crucial role when it comes to identifying new opportunities for policy initiatives and mobilizing and linking interests of various stakeholders (Edler & James, 2015). Policy entrepreneurs are not only public actors but can as well be private actors mobilizing resources for policy change (Flanagan, Uyarra, & Laranja, 2011).

Arguably, different strands of literature emphasize different actors of change in creating a favourable environment for new path development and in transforming support structures. These structures consist of both organizational (knowledge organizations and support agencies) and institutional elements.

2.2.2. Modes of change: towards a typology

Drawing on the literature synthesized above, we acknowledge that actors of change range from inventors and innovators to policy actors and other stakeholders. These are intentional knowledgeable agents, but the purpose of their actions differs widely. Expressed in a stylized manner, some actors engage in the exploration and exploitation of opportunities for new path development (e.g. private actors through entrepreneurship) whilst others work to facilitate such processes (e.g. public actors through policy). Inspired by insights from the institutional and policy entrepreneurship literature, we argue that a more fruitful approach is to depart from what is subject to change and how key actors promote change processes, rather than looking at it from the perspective that different actors have different roles. Hence, actors belonging to different categories can have multiple roles and the scope for change depends on a number of factors, such as the type and degree of power held and exercised by the actors.

Departing from Mahoney and Thelen's (2010) work on different types of institutional change and its application by Martin (2010) to regional industries, we suggest a typology for how key actors transform a constraining environment into an enabling one. This usually means altering the regional environment by creating new structures or transforming existing ones, but could also imply that actors find new ways of using existing structures. We distinguish between three modes of change in the institutional and organizational support structure of regions, namely layering, adaptation and novel application. In a next step, we discuss these types in more detail and explain when and why the different modes occur, linking the characteristics of key actors to different modes of change.

'Layering' takes place when the support structure is gradually changed by adding new elements (such as policies and other institutions, and organizations). Layering processes are most likely to be initiated by actors with a high degree of power in their respective field. For example, public actors with a high degree of institutional power are likely to play a crucial role in creating new policy instruments whilst key entrepreneurs with a high degree of network and interpretative power could lead a sense-making process in which other actors are mobilized around a certain task. In turn, this could lead to direct layering processes by the creation of, for example, an industry organization or indirectly by influencing policy-makers through policy entrepreneurship. Thus, following insights from the institutional and policy entrepreneurship literature, different types of power can be substituted with each other and the need for the different types of power differs with regard to what type of actor is engaging in change of what domain.

'Adaptation' refers to change within or reorientation of existing institutions and organizations and occurs when the actors do not have the degree of power necessary to facilitate the creation of new ones. There is a range of adaptation processes requiring various degrees of power. For example, adapting a formal regulation will indeed require a higher degree of institutional power, whilst adapting existing activities in the support structure could be facilitated by an actor endowed with less power. Adaptation is thus a way for actors to transform the institutional and organizational support structure without having the power necessary to engage in the creation of new elements.

'Novel application' refers to the changed impact of existing elements due to new utilization of the existing support structure, for example by actors creatively using existing policies in new, unintended and possibly unforeseen ways. This is not to say that the degree of power is irrelevant, as actors will need some degree of interpretative power to effectively communicate, for example, the possibility of using existing policy initiatives in new ways among other actors in the industry. However, in this context, knowledge comes to play as an important factor. For example, an actor with a high level of knowledge about an emerging industry and the policy system, but with a low degree of power, might be able to identify possibilities for the existing structures to meet the needs of the emerging industry without actually engaging in either processes of layering or adaptation.

The different modes of changes to the regional institutional and organizational support structure identified above are summarized in Table 1.

Table 1. Power of actors and modes of change.

Actors of change	Mode of change	Change of regional institutional and organizational support structure
High degree of power	Layering	Introducing new institutions (regulations, standards, routines, procedures), particularly creating new policy instruments (e.g. funding for cluster programmes, networking arenas, incubators). Creating new organizations (e.g. industry organizations, cluster organizations, educational bodies)
Medium degree of power	Adaptation	Changing existing formal and informal institutions (e.g. regulations, perception of the industry), for example by re-aligning or replacing existing policy instruments (adaptation of existing initiatives and programmes, creation of sub-initiatives). Adaptation of activities within existing structures (e.g. adapted education programmes, tailored incubation activities)
Low degree of power	Novel application	Benefiting from existing institutions by strategic and creative use of resources (using regulatory arbitrages, exploiting public opinions and norms). Using existing policy instruments in new ways. Using existing organizations and their activities in new ways (e.g. identifying relevant existing educational programmes, using support targeting other industries, 'freeriding' on the image of other industry initiatives)

In a next step, the conceptual considerations outlined above will be applied to an empirical case study of the digital games industry in Scania.

3. Empirical analysis: actors and modes of change in Scania's digital games industry

Scania is the southernmost county of Sweden. The region has an organizationally thick and diversified RIS with a heterogeneous industrial structure and several well-established industrial growth paths (Business Region Skåne, 2016) and a strong endowment of universities and other knowledge-generating organizations. Scania also hosts more than 100 intermediary organizations that support innovation and entrepreneurship in the region. Partly following critique in the local media, regional policy actors have recently acknowledged the need to consolidate the regional support system by reducing the number of intermediary organizations. With this background, the RIS of Scania provides favourable conditions for new path development, though there is reluctance among policy-makers to further expand the public support structure to new areas of economic development.

The empirical analysis of actors and modes of change in Scania's digital games industry is based on qualitative research methods, including document studies and personal interviews with key actors. A number of 13 in-depth face-to-face interviews (lasting between 60 and 90 minutes) were conducted between October and December 2015. The interviews were transcribed and the data were triangulated with findings from policy reports and other publicly available secondary data. Seven interviews were with founders and CEOs of firms located in the region, two were with representatives of the public sector, one interviewee was from the educational system and three were industry experts belonging to local and national industry organizations. Interviewees were identified by a 'snowballing' technique, selecting the first key interview partners by identifying main firms and other key actors through document studies. By interviewing actors from different categories, including both interview partners identified as important actors of change and actors who have not been directly involved in change processes, the findings are based on the perspectives of a variety of different actors.

3.1. The digital games industry in Scania

The digital games industry in Scania is a rapidly growing new industrial path in the region. Today, the digital games industry in Scania consists of approximately 40 firms with 600–700 employees (Game City, 2015). The largest firms are Massive Entertainment (390 employees), King (80 employees) and Tarsier Studios (38 employees), representing a majority of the industry in terms of employment. In addition, there is a high number of start-ups and young small firms. More than half of the firms have been founded after 2010. Geographically, the industry is strongly clustered in Malmö (Game City, 2015).

The seeds for the emergence of a digital games industry in Scania were planted in the neighbouring region of Blekinge during the end of the 1990s. Many of Scania's leading games companies were founded in Blekinge at that time, as a result of a variety of factors creating favourable conditions for these firms to develop, including public support. In our interviews with representatives of the firms that later relocated to Malmö, GamePort (a game development branch of the NetPort incubator targeting the

ICT sector), game development education programmes at Blekinge Institute of Technology and the School of Future Entertainment (a vocational training school) were mentioned as being most important. At the beginning of the 2000s, several of the successful firms in Blekinge decided to relocate to Malmö. One important reason indicated by our interview partners was that in order to continue to grow, they needed to secure access to relevant competence, especially in terms of senior developers. As this was not available in Blekinge, the firms needed to either move to a location where competence was widely available or to a location which was attractive for alluring experienced talent from abroad (which was not the case with the peripheral region of Blekinge). Due to the latter, Malmö became the city of choice for some of the early movers in the industry. From originally being driven by the relocation of established firms, the digital games industry in Scania is now developing through spin-off and start-up activities in Malmö.

3.2. Constraining factors and the need for transformation

During the past decade, the development of the gaming industry has been hampered by a set of constraining factors in the regional support structure. It has only been recently that changes towards a more enabling regional context have taken place. In this sub-section, we shed light on the nature of constraints and concretize the problems emanating from these in relation to the digital games industry in Scania.

First, the higher education institutions present in the region have shown a limited capacity to satisfy the industry's need for young skilled talent. An education programme in game development launched by Malmö University College has been characterized by the interviewed firms as being 'too academic' and poorly equipped to meet the requirements of the industry. This holds true also for education programmes in software engineering and other related fields at the Faculty of Engineering at Lund University. This has resulted in a mismatch between the education offered by higher education institutions and the requirements of firms operating in the digital games industry.

Second, there was a lack of customized public initiatives for promoting networking activities, funding development projects and providing support services to start-ups and young firms. Public support for start-ups abounds in the region, with a number of both generic and specialized incubators and agencies providing start-up grants. However, the existing support does not fit the particular characteristics of the digital games industry. One concrete example is the MINC business incubator in Malmö which provides business development support and office space for new start-ups in a wide range of industries. However, it has so far not been able to 'reach' the digital game industry. This has been attributed to being a result of this cultural mismatch between individuals in the digital games industry and the support for entrepreneurial activity more in general. Existing structures providing support, for example, to the new media industry and cultural industries did not fit the needs of the digital games industry. Several of our interview partners expressed that game developers are different in terms of culture than people working in, for example, the new media industry, being less outgoing than the media entrepreneurs.

Third, there was (and still is) a lack of both private and public support for start-ups in the region. Private venture capital is scarce and firms in the digital games industry in Scania have to a large extent relied on organic growth, starting a firm with own money to growing larger through series of successful game development projects.

In addition, some interview partners have raised the lack of knowledge about the games industry among business support organizations as being a key barrier. For example, it is hard for business development support agencies such as ALMI (a publicly owned organization that provides loans, venture capital and advisory services to start-ups) to evaluate the business potential of new firms due to the 'single-project' nature of the digital games industry and a lack of documented experience among young developers.

Being a diversified region hosting many different industries and likely influenced by the public debate about the proliferation and fragmentation of the intermediary sector, policy actors have been reluctant to create new support organizations and initiatives for the digital games industry. Instead, they have argued that digital games firms should make use of existing support structures established for the new media industry. However, this view has not been shared by our interview partners, who argue that cultural differences and the broad focus of the new media sector makes it hard for game developers to get the support they need. Furthermore, the digital games industry has not been perceived as being 'serious business' by policy-makers or in the public opinion. This perception has been persisting despite the recent rapid growth in the industry, especially in terms of export, and high-profile acquisitions. The lack of understanding among public authorities of the potentials of the industry has thus reinforced their resistance to provide customized support. Finally, the large number of emerging paths and established industries in Scania, and the resulting competition for the attention of policy-makers, has been another reason for the absence of public support for the digital games industry at early stages of its development.

In the next section, we investigate how various key actors have employed different modes of change to overcome the constraints outlined above, leading to the creation of a more favourable environment for the growth of the digital games industry.

3.3. Reconfiguration of support structures and the role of key actors of change

Over the past few years the organizational and institutional support structures in the region have been reconfigured to facilitate new path development activities in the field of digital games. Our empirical study focuses on three new elements in the regional environment, that is, the Nordic Game Conference (NGC), the Game Assembly (TGA) and Game City. These have been highlighted by all interviewees as being particularly important for the development of the regional industry. In addition to the three cases presented below, we have found evidence of several smaller change processes, with less of an impact on the industry as a whole. For example, some small firms have secured funding from the national innovation agency Vinnova by aligning development projects with grand societal challenges, thus engaging in a novel application of existing structures. Another example involves networking activities among a handful of firms developing games for mobile platforms, representing a process of layering.

In the following sub-sections, we will investigate through which modes of change the three organizations and activities mentioned above came into being, paying particular attention to the role of key actors of change in their creation. Our empirical findings indicate that several of these actors were 'outsiders', or 'returnees' having moved from the region to other regions to study or work, bringing back competences or experiences from elsewhere. How they used this to influence the regional environment is investigated below.

3.3.1. The Nordic Game Conference

The NGC is an annual game development conference held in Malmö. It is among the largest conferences in this field in Europe. NGC benefits regional firms by providing networking opportunities, both with other regional actors and with extra-regional firms. Interviewees also pointed to NGC's role in marketing Scania as a 'game development region', increasing the attractiveness and thus making it easier to recruit foreign talent and to get access to funding opportunities such as venture capital.

3.3.1.1. Modes of change. The creation of NGC represents a case of layering in the regional support structure, but has been preceded by a process of adaptation at higher spatial scales. The conference was initially a way of disseminating the results of the Nordic Game Programme, a policy initiative funded by the Nordic Councils of Ministers intended to support the development of games in the Nordic languages. Forming NGC was not part of the initial project description, but was the outcome of an adaptation of the existing Nordic Game programme. Consequently, the creation of a new supporting element in the region took place with support from the Nordic level without any substantial involvement of regional stakeholders at the beginning.

More recently, through a process of novel application of existing regional structures, the conference has received financial support from the City of Malmö and Region Skåne, the highest elected regional government body. In order to access funding, the applications were written together with Media Evolution, a well-established support organization in Scania. This was accounted by one of our interviewees to be a result of policy-makers being reluctant to create new support structures. It was thus the use of existing policy instruments and organizational support structures in new, creative ways that secured funding for the conference at this stage.

3.3.1.2. Actors of change. Unlike most other policy programmes, the Nordic Game Programme was administrated by a private contractor based in Malmö through his existing company. This private entrepreneur has had a personal interest in the digital games industry since the mid-1990s, and had been engaged in mapping the industry both locally and nationally to increase awareness amongst policy-makers of its importance. In addition, he had experiences in working in the public sector, for example, by being involved in setting up a support agency for start-ups. Being deeply embedded in the digital games industry already at an early stage, the private entrepreneur approached the Nordic council of ministers and aided them in designing, and later administering, the Nordic Game Programme.

In the adaptation process of the existing programme, which led to the creation of NGC, the private entrepreneur played a crucial role. In terms of power, he had a high degree of interpretative power at the Nordic level, and expressed in our interview that his personal preference was to locate the conference permanently in Malmö. When convincing the council of ministers to adapt the existing programme he made use of his deep knowledge about the regional conditions, underlining the existence of a newly emerging vibrant industry in Scania.

However, the entrepreneur did not have enough institutional power at the regional level to permanently add new layers to or adapt the established public support structures, constraining his room for manoeuvre to the creative use of existing policy initiatives. However, even though this has secured public funding for the conference, it has not been followed by an adaptation of existing or introduction of new organizational or institutional set-ups at the regional level.

3.3.2. The Game Assembly

When the industry grew rapidly in the mid-2000s, the need for skilled workers became more pronounced. The firms recruited highly qualified senior game developers from abroad, but junior talent was missing in the region. This constraint has partly been overcome by the foundation of 'TGA' in 2008, an advanced vocational training school, providing education targeting the needs of the industry. It has been stressed by our interview partners as an important source of skilled junior talent in the region. For example, more than 70 employees of Massive Entertainment have been trained at TGA.

3.3.2.1. Modes of change. The creation of TGA represents a case of layering at the regional level, facilitated by a combination of adaptation and novel application of existing structures at other spatial scales. A firm operating vocational training schools in various sectors all over Sweden was approached by representatives of Massive Entertainment, and was presented with the plan to start an educational programme in Malmö in close connection with the local industry. They adopted the idea and study plans were written in collaboration with one of the lead programmers at Massive Entertainment, subsequently approved by the Swedish National Agency for Higher Vocational Education. TGA's early educational activities benefited from hiring staff who had previously been working at a vocational training school in Blekinge, where many of Scania's big gaming firms have their origin.

3.3.2.2. Actors of change. With knowledge obtained from experience with vocational training in Blekinge in combination with a deep knowledge about the needs of the regional industry, and a high degree of interpretative and network power within the industry, a private entrepreneur could approach an extra-regional educational body and convince them to establish a vocational training school in Malmö. In turn, this led to the involvement of other key actors and ultimately to the approval of the educational programme at the national level.

With the approval by the Swedish National Agency for Higher Vocational Education, key actors of change have mobilized power needed for the creation of TGA, a new organization offering new educational activities in the region. TGA thus represents a case of layering at the regional level, initiated by a key individual player who managed to access resources and power at other spatial scales to initiate the introduction of a new element to Scania's support structure.

3.3.3. Game City

Game City is a cluster initiative intended to coordinate firms and other actors in the industry, provide networking and other types of support and work with increasing the awareness of the digital games industry among regional policy-makers.

3.3.3.1. Modes of change. Representatives of the industry initially tried to start Game City within the existing cluster organization for the new media industry, Media Evolution. This attempt to adapt the existing support structure was, however, unsuccessful. At that time,

Media Evolution was still positioning itself as *the* new media support organization in the region, refusing provision of customized activities targeting the digital games industry. Instead, Game City was started as an independent initiative, by mobilizing support from within the industry and forming a cluster organization with involvement of big and many smaller game development firms. Thus, this resulted in a case of layering in the regional support structure.

Game City was unable to identify funding opportunities suitable for the organization. Due to the already large number of support bodies present in the region, Region Skåne was reluctant to fund an additional cluster organization (see Section 3.2). Things partly changed during spring 2015, when Game City received funding from the City of Malmö and Region Skåne for employing a person working 50% for one year in the organization. Since Region Skåne had a negative attitude towards establishing a new cluster organization, the solution was to find a joint cause together with Media Evolution and apply through the existing support structures. In this case, Game City wrote an application for a programme tackling youth unemployment together with Media Evolution and was granted public funding. Here, institutional constraints hindered layering of new policy initiatives to occur, which was however circumvented by a novel application of existing structures.

3.3.3.2. Actors of change. Throughout the process of creating Game City, incremental processes of adaptation of informal institutions took place. Key individuals engaged in public opinion forming, promoting the seriousness of the digital games industry as both an industry and a business opportunity. In our interviews, the importance of a small number of key actors has been stressed in this regard.

Furthermore, in the initial process of layering, one of the founders of Massive Entertainment played a key role. He was a board member of Media Evolution and according to out interviews, he tried to start Game City as a sub-organization of Media Evolution but was not successful (see above). Failing at initiating a process of adaptation, he approached a group of key actors in the industry and formed Game City as an independent, privately funded initiative. Thus, the lack of institutional and interpretative power within the existing support structures was compensated by a high degree of interpretative and network power at the industry level.

More recently, through the ongoing process of changing informal institutions and improving the perceived seriousness of the industry, Game City as an organization managed to gain enough interpretative power to make an impact also in the public sphere, overcoming a lack of institutional power. The reluctance and scepticism among policy-makers to fund a new cluster organization were circumvented by a novel application of existing funding opportunities, in agreement with policy-makers. By using Media Evolution as the channel and a scheme for tackling youth unemployment as the mean, Game City managed to secure funding without making substantial changes in the policy system, but with the result of taking small steps towards becoming a stronger player in the region.

Arguably, the NGC, TGA and Game City have different origins and they vary in terms of processes that have led to their establishment. However, all three cases show that changes in the organizational and institutional set-up have been initiated and implemented by a few individual key actors of change, who have, in the course of time, employed a mix of various modes of change to improve the conditions for growth of the digital games industry in Scania. Our analysis also suggests that the processes behind these changes have been multi-scalar in nature. Another common element is the close link between actor characteristics (power and knowledge) and the change mechanisms used by them.

4. Conclusions

Recent scholarly work has enhanced our understanding of how new path development activities are shaped by regional environments, made up of pre-existing industrial structures, knowledge organizations, support structures and institutional configurations. A distinction has been made between enabling and constraining environments, pointing to varying capacities of regions to provide favourable conditions for the rise and development of new growth paths.

The aim of this paper was to move beyond a simple characterization of regional environments as enabling or constraining and the static view it offers on the nexus between new path development and the regional context. We sought to develop a more dynamic perspective to highlight how a constraining environment can be transformed into a more enabling one, giving primary emphasis to the role played by key actors in such reconfiguration processes. Furthermore, borrowing ideas from the literature on institutional change we suggested a typology of various modes by which actors overcome constraining factors and contribute to the creation of a favourable environment for new growth paths. A distinction between three modes of change has been drawn, including the creation of new elements in the support structure ('layering') as well the 'adaptation' and 'novel application' of the existing support organizations and institutions. We advanced the argument that there is a close link between characteristics of key actors and the modes of change employed by them. Actors with a high degree of power can engage in layering processes, whilst actors lacking such power can only rely on adapting existing elements, or using existing structures in new, and possibly unintended or unforeseen, ways.

The conceptual framework has been applied to the digital games industry in Scania. We identified a set of factors constraining the development of this new growth path, including an insufficient supply of young skilled talent and a lack of customized policies to promote networking, new firm formation and development projects. It was found that these factors reflect and are closely related to path dependencies in the higher education and public policy and support systems, lacking experiences with and knowledge of the new industry as well as competition with other regional industries for policy support.

The paper investigated how key actors of change have overcome these constraints. In line with the conceptual framework we revealed that actors' degree of power had a strong influence on which modes of change are employed to reconfigure the regional environment. Furthermore, our study has shown that the key actors of change described in our case by no means are 'heroic individuals', but that changes in the organizational and institutional set-up have relied heavily on the mobilization of other actors. The results presented in this paper thus confirm the view from the literature that change processes are often a collective endeavour.

Our analysis also points to the need to extend the conceptual framework in several ways. The empirical findings presented above suggest that the creation of a more enabling environment for the growth of the digital games industry has been the outcome of a complex interplay of various modes of change, pointing to both simultaneous and sequential processes involving novel applications and adaptations of existing support structures and the creation of new ones. The question of when, why and how change modes are combined requires more conceptual and empirical research in the future.

Our study has also shown that change processes are multi-dimensional in nature, involving change in several dimensions (institutional, policy, industrial and organizational change) and have included key actors from different domains. In Scania, these actors have mainly belonged to the private sector.

Furthermore, the analysis of the digital games industry suggest that actors of change are navigating through different spatial scales in order to identify and source assets for inducing change at the regional level. Thus, our findings emphasize the role of regional key actors but acknowledge that these are not bound to use resources available only at the regional level. On the contrary, actors lacking the necessary power at the regional level are likely to search for opportunities for facilitating change in the institutional and organizational support structure by turning to existing structures and possibilities at other spatial scales. This implies that the multi-scalar perspective brought forward in previous studies should be further strengthened. In the case described in this paper, both sourcing of resources from other places and higher spatial scales and the transfer of knowledge and solutions learnt in other locations by key actors ('outsiders' or 'returnees') have been influential in the change processes analysed.

Finally, our study offered insights into the sustainability of the outcomes of different modes of change. There is no inherent hierarchy between the modes of change identified in this paper. A novel application of existing structures could be as beneficial as a layering of new elements in the regional environment.

Arguably, our findings are only based on one case and thus we do not claim that they are generalizable to other growth paths and regions. More conceptual and empirical research is needed to better understand how key actors of change influence the regional environment to establish more favourable conditions for the development of new industrial growth paths. One key issue that deserves more attention in future research is how key actors navigate through various spatial scales to mobilize resources for inducing change in the regional environment. Another core question concerns the interplay and interrelations of various modes of change and their relation to the knowledge and power of key actors employing these modes. A third remark is that our focus was on one particular aspect of the regional environment, that is, the organizational and institutional support structures present in the region. Future studies should direct attention to other elements of the regional environment to increase our knowledge of how regional conditions change to facilitate the rise and dynamic evolution of new regional industrial growth paths.

Disclosure statement

No potential conflict of interest was reported by the authors.

Funding

This work was supported by the Norwegian Research Council under the VRI programme [grant number 233737].

References

Battilana, J., Leca, B., & Boxenbaum, E. (2009). How actors change institutions: Towards a theory of institutional entrepreneurship. *The Academy of Management Annals, 3*(1), 65–107. doi:10.1080/19416520903053598

Boschma, R., & Martin, R. (2010). The aims and scope of evolutionary economic geography. In R. Boschma & R. Martin (Eds.), *The handbook of evolutionary economic geography* (pp. 3–39). Cheltenham: Edward Elgar.

Business Region Skåne. (2016). *Skåne developing with innovation arenas and clusters.* Retrieved February 24, 2016, from http://www.skane.com/en/skane-developing-with-innovation-arenas-and-clusters

Dawley, S. (2014). Creating new paths? Offshore wind, policy activism, and peripheral region development. *Economic Geography, 90*(1), 91–112. doi:10.1111/ecge.12028

Dawley, S., MacKinnon, D., Cumbers, A., & Pike, A. (2015). Policy activism and regional path creation: The promotion of offshore wind in North East England and Scotland. *Cambridge Journal of Regions, Economy and Society, 8*(2), 257–272. doi:10.1093/cjres/rsu036

DiMaggio, P.J. (1988). *Interest and agency in institutional theory. Institutional patterns and organizations: Culture and environment* (pp. 3–22). Cambridge: Ballinger.

Edler, J., & James, A.D. (2015). Understanding the emergence of new science and technology policies: Policy entrepreneurship, agenda setting and the development of the European Framework Programme. *Research Policy, 44*(6), 1252–1265. doi:10.1016/j.respol.2014.12.008

Flanagan, K., Uyarra, E., & Laranja, M. (2011). Reconceptualising the 'policy mix' for innovation. *Research Policy, 40*(5), 702–713. doi:10.1016/j.respol.2011.02.005

Game City. (2015). *Southern Sweden Games Industry Survey 2015.* Retrieved February 24, 2016, from http://www.gamecity.se/survey2015/

Garud, R., & Karnøe, P. (Eds.). (2001). *Path dependence and creation.* New York: Psychology Press.

Garud, R., Kumaraswamy, A., & Karnøe, P. (2010). Path dependence or path creation? *Journal of Management Studies, 47*(4), 760–774. doi:10.1111/j.1467-6486.2009.00914.x

Grabher, G. (1993). *The embedded firm* (pp. 255–277). London: Routledge.

Gustafsson, R., Jääskeläinen, M., Maula, M., & Uotila, J. (2016). Emergence of industries: A review and future directions. *International Journal of Management Reviews, 18,* 28–50. doi:10.1111/ijmr.12057

Isaksen, A., & Trippl, M. (2016). Path development in different regional innovation systems. In M.D. Parrilli, R.D. Fitjar, & A. Rodriguez-Pose (Eds.), *Innovation drivers and regional innovation strategies* (pp. 66–84). New York: Routledge.

Karlsen, J., Larrea, M., Wilson, J.R., & Aranguren, M.J. (2012). Bridging the gap between academic research and regional development in the Basque Country. *European Journal of Education, 47,* 122–138. doi:10.1111/j.1465-3435.2011.01512.x

Mahoney, J., & Thelen, K. (2010). A theory of gradual institutional change. In J. Mahoney & K. Thelen (Eds.), *Explaining institutional change: Ambiguity, agency, and power* (pp. 1–38). Cambridge: Cambridge University Press.

Martin, R. (2010). Roepke lecture in economic geography – Rethinking regional path dependence: Beyond lock-in to evolution. *Economic Geography, 86*(1), 1–27. doi:10.1111/j.1944-8287.2009.01056.x

Martin, R., & Simmie, J. (2008). Path dependence and local innovation systems in city-regions. *Innovation, 10*(2–3), 183–196. doi:10.5172/impp.453.10.2-3.183

Martin, R., & Sunley, P. (2006). Path dependence and regional economic evolution. *Journal of Economic Geography, 6*(4), 395–437. doi:10.1093/jeg/lbl012

Mintrom, M., & Norman, P. (2009). Policy entrepreneurship and policy change. *Policy Studies Journal, 37*(4), 649–667. doi:10.1111/j.1541-0072.2009.00329.x

Neffke, F., Henning, M., & Boschma, R. (2011). How do regions diversify over time? Industry relatedness and the development of new growth paths in regions. *Economic Geography, 87*(3), 237–265. doi:10.1111/j.1944-8287.2011.01121.x

Simmie, J. (2012). Path dependence and new technological path creation in the Danish wind power industry. *European Planning Studies, 20*(5), 753–772. doi:10.1080/09654313.2012.667924

Simmie, J., Sternberg, R., & Carpenter, J. (2014). New technological path creation: Evidence from the British and German wind energy industries. *Journal of Evolutionary Economics, 24* (4), 875–904. doi:10.1007/s00191-014-0354-8

Sotarauta, M., & Mustikkamäki, N. (2015). Institutional entrepreneurship, power, and knowledge in innovation systems: Institutionalization of regenerative medicine in Tampere, Finland. *Environment and Planning C: Government and Policy, 33*(2), 342–357. doi:10.1068/c12297r

Streeck, W. & Thelen, K. (2005). *Beyond continuity: Institutional change in advanced political economies,* Oxford: Oxford University Press.

Sydow, J., Lerch, F., & Staber, U. (2010). Planning for path dependence? The case of a network in the Berlin-Brandenburg optics cluster. *Economic Geography, 86*(2), 173–195. doi:10.1111/j.1944-8287.2010.01067.x

Tödtling, F., & Trippl, M. (2013). Transformation of regional innovation systems. In P. Cooke (Ed.), *Re-framing regional development: Evolution, innovation, and transition* (pp. 297–318). Oxon: Routledge.

Trippl, M., Grillitsch, M., & Isaksen, A. (2015). *External 'energy' for regional industrial change: Attraction and absorption of non-local knowledge for new path development (No. 2015/47).* CIRCLE, Lund University.

Weik, E. (2011). Institutional entrepreneurship and agency. *Journal for the Theory of Social Behaviour, 41*(4), 466–481. doi:10.1111/j.1468-5914.2011.00467.x

Regional agency and constitution of new paths: a study of agency in early formation of new paths on the west coast of Norway

Ann Karin T. Holmen and Jens Kristian Fosse

ABSTRACT

This article analyses regional agency in the early phases of new path constitution. We argue that the early stages of new path constitution can be explained by both structural factors and the strong presence of agency. With a specific focus on agency, this article contributes to the literature by providing a study of the role of agency at different stages of path constitution. The study shows that two types of agency operate together. Public policy agency is carried out through a common thrust for policy tools that can enhance the room to manoeuvre together. In addition, strong entrepreneurial agency functions as a locomotive for other firms which are important trigger points, and pushes the process forward. These two forms of agency need to be interrelated to constitute new paths.

1. Introduction

This article addresses the combination of agency and constitutive features in the early phases of regional path constitution. Agency has been suggested as the missing link in our understanding of regional growth processes (Rodriguez-Pose, 2013). The concept of agency seeks to supplement the systemic focus on regional innovation (Asheim & Gertler, 2005) in a bid to understand who the actors are and what they do when they aim to boost regional growth processes and, more specifically, new paths. Agency can appear through individuals, (teams of) entrepreneurs, firms and their leaders and public policy-makers who work as agents for a specific path. By combining agency and a more systemic focus on path constitution, this study contributes by giving greater attention to the role of human agents and the ways in which they affect the development of regional paths (Sydow, Windeler, Muller-Seitz, & Lange, 2012; Trippl, Grillitsch, Isaksen, & Sinozic, 2015).

The concept of path constitution refers to the establishment of new industry paths. New industry paths may be latent or develop from existing ones. There are several examples of how new industry paths build on the knowledge bases and institutions in existing paths (Klepper, 2007; Martin & Sunley, 2010). Martin and Sunley (2010) argue that existing paths as an enabling environment imply the reuse of competence and resources, or the transfer of technologies from a mature path to emerging paths. This is the situation in our study of the development of two new industry paths on the west coast of Norway. The study provides a deeper understanding of what Martin and Sunley refer to as the environment and explores the main mechanisms of the early path constitution phase, with special emphasis on the role of 'agency'. We pose the following research question: 'How do different types of agency play a role in the processes of path constitution?'

By agency we here refer to (a) regional policy agency and its contribution to creating functional frames for new industry paths, and (b) entrepreneurial agency, understood as private sector agents such as individuals, firms and firm leaders who use their power and resources to change the institutions that govern innovation systems in order to reach their goal. This approach to agency gives the opportunity to both capture and understand the interplay between public and private interest in the early phases of path constitution.

We present two cases of new paths on the west coast of Norway. The two cases differ in terms of the type of industry, but operate in a similar regional context where there is a need for the restructuring and reuse of the knowledge base from the oil and gas industry for new paths. The first case illustrates a new path in welfare technology, while the other is related to green maritime energy. Through the case studies, we identify the significance of agency in these processes and of a combination of different agency roles through the process. The study shows that changing regional environments (changing markets, changing needs and demands) provide conditions for agents to push new paths forward. In such conditions, there is regional legitimacy for change supported by policy and industry. We argue that proactive agency is multiple in the early phase and collaboration among these agents is crucial for path development.

The paper is organized as follows. The next section presents the theoretical framework of the study, drawing on the literature concerning the development of new paths for regional innovation systems in addition to agency. The subsequent section introduces the empirical case study and analysis, and also includes an outline of the research design and methods applied in the study. The paper ends with a discussion and conclusion section.

2. Theoretical framework

To develop an analytical framework for the role of agency in path constitution, we elaborate on the theories of path development with particular emphasis on the emerging phase. Based on a dynamic framework of different stages in the formation of new paths (Sydow, Schreyögg, & Koch, 2009), we add the constitutive features of paths (Sydow et al., 2012) to the different stages. Then based on these stages in path constitution and the features related to each stage, we develop our theoretical understanding of the role of agency.

2.1. Path constitution

The concept of path constitution refers to the establishment of new industry paths. The key issue is how new paths come into being. To integrate the concepts of path dependence and path constitution, Sydow et al. (2012) introduce the concept of 'path constitution'. Path constitution includes the definition of a path:

> ... as being a course of events interrelated on different levels of analysis, such as a single organization or an organizational or technological field, and in which one of the available technological, institutional or organizational options gains momentum in time-space, but cannot automatically be determined from the onset. (Sydow et al., 2012, p. 157)

Boschma and Frenken (2011) argue that the emergence of paths relates to previously developed local capabilities, routines and institutions. New industry grows out of existing technology and industrial structures through regional branching processes. Theories of path dependence have developed into a more nuanced and dynamic view on the constitution of paths (Sydow et al., 2009). In the following section, we address the literature on organizational path dependency, applying the dynamic framework of Sydow et al. (2009). We argue that the dynamic approach to the organizational level could be adapted to a regional/industry level as well. Sydow et al. (2012) present an analytical tool to study an early phase path. They suggest six indicators (path constitution analysis (PCA)) to identify, define and understand potential path constitution. The constitutive features identified by Sydow et al. (2012) also are presented in relation to different stages of path development (Sydow et al., 2009).

2.1.1. Preformation phase

The preformation phase is open-ended and includes a broad scope of actions. It relates, therefore, to features that trigger new actions. Sydow et al. argue that this development is triggered by certain actors or events, but that it is an empirical question whether a path 'is predominantly constituted by processes beyond the reach and consciousness of knowledgeable actors or by processes that are designed or shaped by powerful collectivities of actors' (2012, pp. 158–159). Path constitution entertains the possibility of a multiplicity of experiences associated with participation in action nets. As the journey unfolds, actors may develop new identities and frames of reference that allow them to imagine new future states and mobilize the past in new ways to accomplish their future goals and to reorganize their action nets (Karnøe & Garud, 2012). Based on this, path constitution can be considered as a more open approach, which may include emerging clusters. We explore path constitution processes by examining the emergence of two early cluster projects. Sydow et al. (2012) identify three constitutive features that we relate to the early phase of path constitution (preformation): level of interrelatedness, triggering events and non-ergodic process. 'Level of interrelatedness' refers to the contextual level of analysis in which the path develops. What are the significant industrial, technological, institutional, political, etc., factors affecting the path specifically? 'Triggering events' refer to observations of triggering events that initiate a path process. The observed events may come from actors involved in the path, and also from outside observers. 'Non-ergodic process' refers to a process of simultaneous and/or sequential events culminating in an outcome that is not automatically determined from the onset, but not arbitrary either. This feature can take place in all parts of the constitution process.

2.1.2. Formation phase

The formation phase ends the open-ended process identified in the preformation phase. According to Sydow et al. (2009), this phase is characterized by a new regime that takes the lead, and a more dominant action pattern emerges. This relates to a narrower range of options and the process seems irreversible when it comes to choice and action. Sydow et al. (2012) identify two constitutive features that we relate to the formation phase of path constitution: 'self-reinforcing processes and multiple types of actors'. 'Self-reinforcing processes' refer to positive feedback which drives the course of a path in the overall direction that is already being pursued. This mechanism comprises coordination and complementary and learning effects as well as adaptive expectations. 'Multiple types of actors' refer to multiple actors' influence on each other as well as upon the development of the path. An actor can be either an individual or a collective (e.g. an organization or a network).

2.1.3. Path lock-in phase

Sydow et al. (2012) identify lock-in as a constitutive feature that we relate to the final stage in path constitution. 'Lock-in' can be both negative and positive and refers to a situation or outcome whereby the trajectory of a path becomes confined to a single solution that agents have to follow. Such a lock-in may be of a predominantly cognitive, normative or resource-based nature. In this article, we relate to and observe 'positive lock-in', which relates to institutionalization and specialization and how the numbers of possibilities are narrowed down. This normally appears in the early stages of path development and is closely linked to the 'formation phase', while negative lock-in mainly appears in the later stages of path development (Martin & Sunley, 2006).

Sydow et al.'s (2012) PCA highlights process-related and relational features to 'integrate the concepts of path dependence and constitution' (p. 158). The approach is oriented towards organizational path dependence in contrast to the technological path dependency approach (Arthur, 1994) and elaborates on a more nuanced discussion of self-reinforcing dynamics. We add to this analytical framework by providing a closer attention to the inherent, but not explicitly discussed, role of agency. We thus elaborate on the role of agency as both public policy agents and entrepreneurial agents.

2.2. The role of agency in path constitution

The role of agency and how agency leads to changes provide a deeper understanding of push and pull factors in path constitution. Agency is said to play a crucial role in regional renewal, and in enabling regions to branch out into new paths (Sotarauta, Horlings, & Liddle, 2012). We approach the concept of proactive agency in regional development processes from two angles: agency as public policy and agency as institutional entrepreneurship.

'Public policy agency' in regional development processes refers to proactive agents representing the public sector that affect the early phases of new path constitution. Public authorities can take various roles in such a process (proactive and reactive). A proactive role requires a balanced role between too much and too little steering. Development of new paths is first of all industry/market driven, but policy agents can play an important role as regional partners and supporters in line with regional needs and challenges (Sørensen, 2006). Metagovernance, which refers to different ways of enacting the governing of governing (Kooiman, 2003), is a concept that captures this balanced agency role for public policy agents. It can be defined as 'coordinating the actions of self-governing actors' (Sørensen & Torfing, 2007, p. 169) and can be applied through four types of agency roles. The first type is 'framing', which refers to institutional design. An example of this may be political or administrative leaders who design a network or arena for dealing with policy issues outside/inside the traditional policy system. The second type is called 'storytelling', which emphasizes the idea that certain storylines and symbols create a frame of reference that then guides self-governing actions. The third type is 'support and facilitation'. Policy agents can provide support for or facilitate the constitution of an idea/network to achieve certain purposes. The fourth type is 'participation', which means direct participation in different processes and networks. These public agency roles may appear parallel and at different stages of the early phases of path constitution.

'Entrepreneurial agency' in the early phases of path constitution includes a more market-related agency role. Garud and Karnøe (2001) use the concept of 'mindful deviation' to illustrate processes of path constitution that are driven by the proactive agency of entrepreneurs.

> Entrepreneurs are embedded in structures where they attempt to mindfully depart in order to create new paths. Consequently, the endeavors to shape the institutional base for innovation systems reflect the many strategies adopted by relevant groups of actors aiming to break out from the past path and create new ones. (Battilana, Leca, & Boxenbaum, 2009, p. 68)

The result is often an entrepreneurial role that moves from a core business strategy for innovation towards an agency role affecting surrounding institutions, referred to as institutional entrepreneurs. Institutional entrepreneurs are agencies that use their power and resources to change the institutions that govern innovation systems in order to reach their goals (Sotarauta & Mustikkamäki, 2015). Institutional entrepreneurs are actors (firms and/or individuals), or groups of actors who not only introduce the required change/innovation, but also work to change the broader context so that the innovation has widespread appeal and impact. They have an interest in changing particular institutional arrangements and mobilizing resources, competences and power to create new institutions or to transform existing ones (Battilana et al., 2009; DiMaggio, 1988). Institutional entrepreneurs are considered as 'rule makers' as well as 'rule takers' in the process of shaping institutions (Streeck & Thelen, 2005).

2.3. Towards an analytical framework

Agency in regional development is related to both public policy and institutional entrepreneurship. On the regional level, we recognize the importance of both proactive organizations in taking the role of institutional entrepreneurs and proactive facilitators in public policy in the process of path constitution. The dynamic interplay between institutional entrepreneurs and public policy, however, seems unclear. To develop an analytical framework informed by theory, we therefore suggest a dynamic approach to the role of agency by connecting agency to the phases of path development identified by Sydow et al. (2009) (Figure 1).

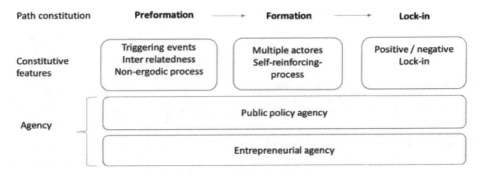

Figure 1. Constitutive features and phases towards new paths.

Through Sydow et al.'s constitutive features and phases towards new paths, we are able to describe the development of the two cases of new paths on the west coast of Norway. The role of agency is revealed through these case stories which enable us to analyse a combination of different agency roles and the interplay between them through the different phases of path constitution.

3. New paths on the west coast of Norway: cases and data material

The empirical context for the study is the west coast of Norway. This region specializes in some key industries such as energy production (both offshore fossil oil and gas production and renewable hydroelectric power), the maritime industry (construction/design, shipbuilding, maritime technology and shipowners) and the marine industry (fisheries and fish farming).

Some important international, national and regional trends influence the industry in the region. First, the 'green shift' has an increasing impact on the industries. Both the production of fossil energy and the problems of CO_2 emission from maritime shipping represent key issues in the global debate on sustainability. The industries are striving to meet new regulations in addition to developing new clean technologies to gain a competitive advantage for the future. Another challenging international trend is new technology for wealth and health, also called welfare technology. This trend is a result of an ageing population and the need to meet challenges related to care and health services. This trend addresses activity from both the public sector and industry more broadly (big data, IT/smart solutions, development of new technology solutions, etc.). Second, the falling price of crude oil on the international market due to overproduction has had a substantial influence on the Norwegian national and regional economy. The oil and gas industry is going through a significant restructuring process focused on efficiency and cost reduction. This restructuring process influences the economic activity in several other industries which are more or less dependent on the oil and gas industry. The close relation between parts of the maritime industry and the oil and gas industry has had a severe economic impact on several firms which specialize in offshore supply vessels. The west coast of Norway is the main region for these industries, and as a direct consequence, the registration of unemployed workers with higher education has increased by 100% from late 2014 (1091 persons) to late 2015 (2097 persons) in Rogaland County, and by almost

40% (from 1238 to 1723 persons) in Hordaland (Statistics Norway, 2015).[1] In the following presentation, we highlight both these contextual and more path-related events.

3.1. The smart care (welfare technology) case

The first emerging path presented in this paper is the case of the smart care path. The key actors are located on the south-west coast of Norway and represent a diversity of stakeholders which all relate to welfare, provision of services and technological solutions. It is a new mix of stakeholders responsible for service (such as municipalities, hospitals and private providers of services) and stakeholders developing or supporting product development. Additionally, there are stakeholders that enable financing, coordination, research and networking. This new mix of industries and public actors developed and created a common project through an ARENA project in 2013. ARENA projects are a national policy tool for cluster/path development in Norway. The project's main goal is to contribute to innovation, development and commercialization of new solutions within welfare technology. Their vision is to be a significant international player in providing health and welfare technologies. In 2016 the ARENA project involved 75 members, including public stakeholders such as municipalities, small and medium-sized business (ranging across a broad set of industry types) and research and development (R&D) organizations such as universities, research institutes and technology transfer organizations, and can be considered an early stage path which represents a radically new orientation of the industry in the region.

3.2. The maritime clean technology case

The second emerging path discussed in this paper is the case of the maritime clean tech path. The key actors are located on the south-west coast of Norway, between the two major cities in the region, Bergen and Stavanger. The maritime industry in the region has recently undergone big changes. From having focused on conventional maritime technology, the industry is now in the process of adopting a strong environmental profile. This profile was developed through an ARENA cluster project in 2011 by eight companies and was initiated by a regional development agency. It has since been embodied in the recent emergence since 2014 of the industrial cluster, NCE Maritime Clean Tech ('Norwegian Centre of Expertise Maritime Clean Tech'), which now consists of 51 actors, including several firms and R&D institutions working together to implement green solutions in the maritime sector. NCE Maritime Clean Tech is engaged in building arenas and networks for creating forward-looking, innovative and competitive solutions in the maritime sector that reduce environmentally harmful emissions in the air and sea. The activities seek to increase the competitiveness of the petro-maritime cluster in the region. While the emergence of this sustainability oriented maritime clean tech path in many ways represents a radically new orientation of the global maritime industry in general, its conception has not occurred in a vacuum. The region has a long tradition of shipbuilding, ship design and engine production, which, in a path-dependent way, have shaped the development of the regional maritime industry as we know it today. From a historical perspective, the maritime industry has a strong position in the area.

3.3. Methodology

The cases were selected based on indications of new emerging industry paths in the region. The chosen cases can be considered as two emerging paths which are characterized by industries with international significance, but which also address market needs and societal challenges at the national and regional levels. There is a need for regional industrial change in order to reduce dependency on the oil and gas sector. The market needs and societal challenges are related to renewable green energy and an ageing population with an increased need for services. Additionally, both cases can be considered as being influenced by proactive agency.

The empirical case study analysis is based on a qualitative data set consisting of policy documents and semi-structured interviews. The qualitative data set focuses on the early phase of these two paths. The regional policy for innovation and growth has been studied through policy documents for the region from 1990 to 2015. These documents address changes in regional priorities and focus areas over time. The collected documents include not only regional policy plans, but also priority areas for policy instruments such as R&D support and business support (small-medium sized enterprise). Additionally, 12 interviews (in each case) of stakeholders within a triple helix system (R&D, business and public sector) related to the new path were conducted. In the maritime clean tech case, interviews were conducted from the first initial phase in 2009 and on several occasions until late 2015. In the smart care case, interviews were carried out in the autumn of 2015. The individuals interviewed were involved with the path from different angles and with different interests. In the analyses, the policy documents not only function as support for describing the structure, but also indicate some of the most important agents during this first phase. Moreover, regarding agency, the interviews supplement and add a richer understanding of the different stakeholders' involvement during this first phase.

The data material was interpreted in light of the analytical framework to come up with causal explanations for the emergence of the paths and the role of agency. The framework on path constitution is used in this paper to describe the two emerging paths. Perspectives on agency are used to analyse the role of agency through the emerging process. The number of data sources makes it possible to cross-check information, while the theoretical framework is the filter for sorting out relevant empirical information for the discussion of the research question.

4. Emerging paths on the west coast of Norway

In the following section, we identify and describe constitutive features of the two cases through the different stages of path constitution.

4.1. The smart care path – constitutive features

Preformation phase: Surrounding this budding path there is an 'interrelated' context. The strong dependence on oil and gas has made the need to develop other industry bases very clear. An additional base will secure regional resilience and build competence and labour for an increasing population in this area. However, there was no connection between the oil and gas sector and the smart care path in the early initiating phase, which can be traced back to 2009.

From 2009, there was an increase in the development of technological products serving the household market in the region. A new gateway produced by the regional energy company – LYSE (owned by 16 municipalities) – provided a new possibility to serve all households in the city region with different technological solutions. This gateway was also available for other services provided by different businesses. The idea, and not least the access to households, gave a new business opportunity to several interests, providing an entry into the market of public-sector services and also addressing a field of international interest. In this period, LYSE developed a small-scale test project together with some municipalities. The goal was to test new technologies for safer homes, targeting citizens with cognitive impairment, mobility problems, chronic illness and the elderly.

Initiated by the mayor of Stavanger in 2012, a group of actors from the regional energy company LYSE, municipalities, the regional hospital, the regional university and a few private stakeholders gathered to discuss possibilities related to health technology (Hidle & Normann, 2013). The municipalities were under pressure on account of the fact that the number of elderly people and their need for healthcare will increase. It was necessary to think about healthcare in new terms in order to meet this coming challenge. At this time, this was also a growing thematic area internationally, where similar challenges and the need for smarter solutions were articulated. The group worked together and introduced several initiatives oriented towards EU and national network instruments, providing financial and administrative support to create projects in which the idea of the smart city/smart care was at the focus. These happenings are considered as 'triggering events', where resources to put this smart care initiative into a system and build a regional network more systematically were made available. The regional energy company LYSE, which on the one hand saw a business opportunity to develop their products and services, but on the other hand took an active locomotive role in broader regional development processes, was also an important triggering element.

Formation phase: A significant reinforcing event that affected the path process during the early phase was a drop in oil prices, which had a huge effect on oil- and gas-related businesses in the region – which is nearly all of them. The business downscaling and the loss of jobs have been significant – the registration of unemployed workers with higher education, for example, increased by almost 100% from late 2014 to late 2015 in Rogaland County. Consequently, competencies were made available and businesses were looking for new markets. Additionally, a significant focus on Medicare was reinforced through national and regional plans and the decision to build a new regional hospital located close to the university and science park being on the political agenda. These processes were said to bring positive energy to the path of smart care. We may consider these simultaneous events as 'non-ergodic processes', but also as affecting what Sydow et al. (2012) refer to as 'self-reinforcing processes'. The simultaneous challenges led to overall positive feedback from the industry, the public sector and the R&D sector. Multiple types of actors showed interest and got involved during the application process, which gave a positive push to the process.

Lock-in phase: The result of this collaborative process was positive and resulted in an international smart city network (Triangulum) granted in 2013 and a regional ARENA project called Smart Care Cluster granted in 2014. The ARENA project may also be considered a 'positive lock-in' situation where some priorities were decided and actors gathered around a common theme. The response from public and private stakeholders was significant. During the application period, a group of stakeholders was active, but along the way new partners wanted to join in. This trend continued when the ARENA project was established:

> This ARENA project gathered a mix of stakeholders that does not connect through the common NACE code. Still, they saw a potential to fit in with someone else in a common interest area – despite the fact that their motives and goals may be different. (Contributor in the application writing phase)

There has been, and still is today, strong and increasing support for the ARENA Smart Care Cluster which can be identified through public regional priorities and new initiatives related to the budding path. Still, the diversity of actors involved in this path implies that a narrower priority may evolve in the future. The Smart Care Cluster is at this point (summer 2016) still in a constitutive phase, but is supported by other initiatives. The region is now working towards a smart city path including not only smart care, but also other areas such as green technology, smart buildings and smart policy systems. Most of the stakeholders involved in the constitution of the Smart Care Cluster are still significantly involved. The path is, in this way, evolving gradually from a simple to a more complex form.

4.2. The maritime clean tech path – constitutive features

Preformation phase: The focal level of analysis is the collective actions of knowledgeable actors to develop an organizational process for strategic collaboration on maritime clean tech. This level 'interrelates' closely with a general call internationally for a green shift in the transport industry based on clean technology development and local actions taken by shipowners to implement new clean technology in new ships. What seems to be the most important 'triggering event' for a clean tech path in the maritime industry is the bold decision of a local shipowner to build an offshore supply vessel in 2009 based upon collaboration with a local supplier of new maritime clean technology. The Viking Lady[2] is specially designed to service offshore installations in the North Sea, and is the first commercial ship ever with a fuel cell technology specially adapted for marine use. The companies Eidesvik Offshore and Wärtsilä engaged in an entrepreneurial project resulting in significant political attention when the ship and new environmental technology were promoted and presented during the United Nations Climate Change Conference in Copenhagen (COP15) in 2009. This project paved the way for new clean tech projects in the industry based on the company's initiative. A survey of clean technology projects in the region in 2010[3] showed that around two-thirds of the projects were initiated by companies on their own, without a particular market demand (market pull) or new regulations and public financing of R&D (technology push). Similar results were found in a national survey in 2009 (Espelien, Grimsby, & Grünfeld, 2009). Several events followed in addition to the descriptive study and the cluster initiative that can be related to the 'non-ergodic processes' to which Sydow et al. (2012) refer. Key actors in the industry gained financial support from Innovation Norway for a new project in marine battery technology, and the cluster initiative became an ARENA project. These sequential events gave considerable momentum in line with the self-reinforcing processes identified by Sydow et al. (2012).

Formation phase: The NCE Maritime Clean Tech Cluster is based on its previous period as an ARENA cluster. Key actors engaged quickly when an ARENA cluster initiative was undertaken by the public–private development agency in the region in 2009 to conduct a pre-project in order to map the ongoing clean tech projects in the region. The aim of this descriptive study was to identify the scope of clean tech projects in the region within different industries, to support the establishment of a network among the companies and to provide a foundation for further priorities. The study revealed a wide range of clean tech projects within different industries, but the majority were in the maritime industry. A group of key actors selected the maritime industry and new clean technology as the base for further strategic industrial development. There was already a well-established clean tech project within the maritime industry and the key actors in this project became central in the further development of the maritime clean tech cluster in the region.

Lock-in phase: The cluster project represents also in this case a potential 'positive lock-in' regarding both the organizational processes (type of actors involved) and technology development (competing/alternative technologies). At the same time, the cluster project involves multiple actors collectively engaged in the development of the new industrial path. The maritime clean tech industry and the NCE cluster have had a significant impact on the political agenda. Issues such as change in public tenders for new maritime transport based on zero emission principles, new design concepts for urban sea shuttles and cargo handling, and broad public attention to new maritime clean technology have strengthened their position. This suggests that single actors or groups of actors can take a leading position regionally and, in addition, change the institutional system in order to promote a green technology shift in the maritime industry. The support and initiative for collaboration undertaken by the regional development agency were complementary to the action taken by the companies. Their actions led to the survey of clean tech projects in the region in 2010 and the establishment of the member organization called Maritime Clean Tech West in 2011, which included eight companies. Maritime Clean Tech West took on the role of network facilitator and of profiling the maritime clean tech industry to regional and national policy-makers. Through financial support from the public Norwegian Innovation Clusters programme, both as an ARENA cluster project and later as an NCE cluster project, the organization has grown from 8 to 51 members, and Maritime Clean Tech West has had a comprehensive influence on policy-making, regionally and nationally.

5. Agency in the process of path constitution

Sydow et al. (2012) argue that the development of new paths is triggered by certain actors or events, but that it is an empirical question whether a path 'is predominantly constituted by processes beyond the reach and consciousness of knowledgeable actors or by processes that are designed or shaped by powerful collectivities of actors' (p. 156). Through this section, we would like to elaborate on the role of agency understood as proactive – public policy agency and entrepreneurial agency – in the two path constitutions presented.

The process also implies that the role of agency is intertwined and changes through the stages from preformation to lock-in.

5.1. Public policy agency

Preformation phase: The initial preformation phase included ideas and arenas where common challenges and possible solutions were raised. Issues such as an ageing population and the need to meet challenges related to care and health services, and changes in public tenders for new ferries based on zero emission principles and broad public attention to new maritime clean technology, were significant public challenges to be solved. This is one of the reasons why public agents took a proactive role in the preformation phase. In both these cases, public agents acted through 'facilitation'. They supported and facilitated a common arena where ideas and possible solutions were discussed. Additionally, they acted through 'participation'. Both facilitation and participation can be considered hands-on public policy agency (Sørensen & Torfing, 2007). The municipality of Stavanger and its administrative resources were important drivers in this phase, in addition to the mayor who legitimized this priority politically. It was in these arenas that the idea of an ARENA application was decided. The inter-municipal development agency, SNU AS, took a proactive role in the early phase of the maritime clean tech case. Together with Innovation Norway and Bergen University College, a pre-project was established supported by the Program for Regional R&D and Innovation (VRI), founded by the Norwegian Research Council and Hordaland County. This facilitative and participating public policy agency was considered necessary to bring the process forward. No one had the power to instruct the others and they were all dependent on each other. Still, while those who participated in this early process influenced the scope and priorities of this path, it remained a situation in which none of the actors had the power to instruct the others, but instead it created a climate in which interdependent actors collaborated.

Formation phase: Agency through public policy added a new coordinative action to this phase – 'storytelling'. In both cases, the process of creating a shared platform through an ARENA/NCE application involved powerful political and administrative actors. Those involved in the application phase communicated broadly the idea and the possible impact on regional innovation. There was overall positive feedback from the industry, the public sector and the R&D sector. Storytelling is argued to be an important instrument to build support and legitimacy during such a process (Sørensen & Torfing, 2007). Multiple types of actors increased their level of interest and became involved during the application process, which gave the process a positive push. Additionally, public agency continued to facilitate and be a participant in arenas for involvement and also invested significant administrative resources into the process of creating the ARENA/NCE application.

Lock-in: In both cases, the lock-in phase included a change in public policy agency. Through the formation phase towards the positive lock-in, we observed a clear change in formal policy plans and strategies. Smart care/smart city and maritime clean technology had a significant impact on the political agenda and were included in formal policy priorities for the municipality and the region. Sørensen and Torfing (2007) refer to this as 'framing', which is a more indirect form of coordination. Framing is here brought about through clear regional political priorities, which lend legitimacy to supporting these budding paths. Additionally, public policy agents such as political and administrative leaders continued to support initiatives through 'storytelling' related to these budding paths. For both cases, the support and initiative for collaboration led to (a) an international smart city network (Triangulum) granted in 2013 and a regional ARENA project called Smart Care Cluster granted in 2014, and (b) the establishment of the member organization Maritime Clean Tech West which took a leading role as network facilitator and profiling industry, earning both an ARENA project and later a NCE project. During this period, a group of stakeholders was active, but along the way, new partners have joined in.

5.2. Entrepreneurial agency

Preformation phase: A strategy for innovation in regional companies was an important trigger event in this preformation phase. The entrepreneurial agents LYSE (regional energy company) in the first case, and Eidesvik Offshore together with Wärtsilä (offshore supply vessels and clean technology) in the second case were significant. We can observe strategic entrepreneurs moving from a core business strategy for innovation towards an entrepreneurial agency role affecting surroundings. On the one hand, the entrepreneurial agents saw a business opportunity to develop their products and services, but, on the other hand, they took an active locomotive role in broader regional development processes.

Formation Phase: The entrepreneurial agents took a leading role in the formation phase; they were proactive in all the prioritized activities and put administrative and economic resources into the process. In both cases, they contributed in different regional arenas regarding public policy and among a broad set of industries. The management teams of these companies were proactive in putting forward ideas and setting the regional agenda for this new industry path. At the same time, their entrepreneurial actions were accountable and inclusive, taking responsibility for actions to push the process forward. The kind of entrepreneurship demonstrated relates to Sotarauta and Mustikkamäki's (2015) reference to institutional entrepreneurship, whereby power and resources are used to change institutional arrangements that govern innovation systems to reach their goals. These individuals can be considered rule makers in the shaping of both new arenas and institutions. In both cases, they had a significant role in framing and enabling an initiative, with a broad invitation to join in and commit, and later give space, to other proactive stakeholders.

Lock-in: The lock-in phase included a change for the entrepreneurial agents. Regarding the smart care path, the granted ARENA project may be considered a 'positive lock-in' situation where some priorities were decided and actors gathered around a common theme. The fact that LYSE can be considered a hub company with core resources on which other stakeholders depended (such as technology, networks, competence and economy) made it necessary to secure broad anchoring and commitment for future activities. The ARENA project was organized as a cluster organization driven by the regional science park and by administrative recourses reconnected from LYSE in order to secure the strong inclusion and involvement of other regional stakeholders. As entrepreneurs, and further, institutional entrepreneurs, they paved the way for new institutional arrangements for innovation through mobilizing resources, competences and power. This finding is also evident in the clean tech path and the NCE. Maritime Clean Tech West took the role of network facilitator and of profiling the maritime clean tech industry. The organization has grown from 8 to 51 members, and Maritime Clean Tech West has had a comprehensive influence on policy-making, regionally and nationally. Entrepreneurial agency represents in both cases a strong strategic position in the further development of the two paths in the lock-in phase. These positions, as chair of the board or board members in the network organizations or key actors in significant innovation projects, represent the continuity of the entrepreneurial agency role beyond the initial phase of emergent new paths.

5.3. Interplay between agency roles

There is a clear interrelation between agency roles in these path constitution processes. Figure 2 illustrates how the two agency roles appear and change during the process.

A clear observation is the common need for and interest in a new industry path. Both agency roles are proactive and add significant efforts to the preformation phase. The formation phase also witnesses proactive, equal and engaged effort from both agency types. In this phase, a new institutional arena is constituted for future collaboration within the respective industry path. An interesting observation is the roles of agency in the lock-in phase. Once the institutional arrangements are in place, the agents pull back towards a more supportive and less dominating role, giving room for others and starting up new initiatives related to the path.

In both cases, the ARENA/NCE project functioned as a positive lock-in towards which the entrepreneurs and public policy agents could work. ARENA/NCE projects, arising from a national policy tool for cluster development, defined and demarcated a way to institutionalize and empower the initiative (Battilana et al., 2009). The support, development of the idea and approval of ARENA created a trajectory that defined a strategy and created a 'positive' lock-in which was not something imposed by others, but a shared interest. The fact that this was a situation in which none of the agents had the power to instruct the others meant that they all needed this common ground to reach their individual objectives – if they collaborated (Karlsen, Larrea, Wilson, & Aranguren, 2012). The development of

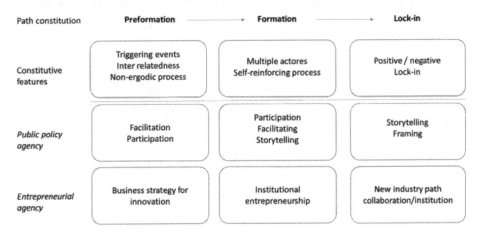

Figure 2. Constitutive features and agency.

the ARENA was influenced by those who participated, and in both cases, the regional support increased over time. In this way, it was not only the required innovation that was introduced, but work was also done to change the broader context so that the innovation had a widespread appeal and impact (Battilana et al., 2009).

Storytelling and self-reinforcing processes were important drivers during the process (Sørensen & Torfing, 2007; Sydow et al., 2012). Positive communication and feedback drove the course of a path in an overall direction which was already being pursued. Policy priorities were made in favour of the path and new stakeholders connected continually. In policy documents, regional policy and industry arenas, there was an increased interest in the idea, goal, technology and knowledge leading the path. These arenas were perceived as transparent and inviting. The self-reinforcing process of general support has been important to bring about the continuation of these budding paths. Proactive public policy agency in the early phase gave legitimacy and contributed to this broad support. Still, both cases illustrate the need for a locomotive, someone in front taking risks and with the initiative to do something different. The regional energy company and the local shipowner can be considered as such entrepreneurial agents. They took a leading position regionally in the early phases and acted as institutional entrepreneurs. The interplay between the two agency types affected the institutional system in order to promote a shift in focus which affected regional policy priorities, providing an arena for developing new solutions in the public sector (transport and healthcare) and contributing to a new market for diversity in industry stakeholders in the region. Both agency roles manoeuvred in a landscape consisting of politics, public services, new technology and combinations of ideas in order to create a common platform based on collaboration.

6. Conclusion

This article addresses the combination of agency and constitutive features in the early phases of regional path constitution. The study provides a deeper understanding of the 'missing link' in our understanding of regional growth processes (Rodriguez-Pose, 2013), by asking 'how different types of agency play a role in the processes of path constitution'. Combining the literature related to path constitution and agency-related perspectives, the analytical framework provides a dynamic approach. Through this, the analysis captures different agency roles, how they change and interact during the constitutive process.

The empirical context, the 'smart care path' and the 'maritime clean tech path', are two emerging paths which are characterized by industries with international significance, but which also address market needs and societal challenges at the national and regional levels. The two cases are presented as part of the same historical and present empirical context. They are both situated in the context of a need for regional industrial change to reduce dependency on the oil and gas sector. Still, they differ with regard to industry type and how the industry is related to the existing dominant industry.

The study indicates that a decline in dominant regional industries triggers possibilities for new paths and triggers agents to reorient. New competencies are made available, more generic industries turn their interest towards other markets and policy priorities change; there is a climate for new initiatives. However, for new initiatives to materialize, there is a need for entrepreneurial agency. These agents represent a person, organization or a network moving from a core business strategy for innovation towards an agency role affecting surrounding institutions. They are ready to take risks and use their time to change the institutional understanding of regional industry priorities. We find that such entrepreneurs are important triggers and drivers during the constitutive phase, but this alone is not sufficient. A common interest and a strong interdependency between entrepreneurial agency and public policy agency are significant for pushing a path process forward. Both paths comprised services that the public sector needed to develop. The innovation strategy raised by the entrepreneurial agents had, in this way, an effect reinforced by its relationship to international trends, business opportunities and regional needs which further strengthens legitimacy, general regional support and positive reactions.

This study adds to the literature on path constitution by illustrating how different types of agency operate together through the different stages of the constitutive process. Public policy agency is carried out through a common thrust for policy tools that can enhance the room to manoeuvre together. In addition, strong entrepreneurial agency functions as a locomotive for other firms. Sydow et al. (2012) are building bridges between Garud and Karnøe's (2001) focus on entrepreneurship and path constitution, on one hand, and path dependence (structure and history), on the other hand. This study illustrates that a collective organization through cluster projects created a common arena enabling entrepreneurial agents to push an initiative forward and public policy agents to be supportive. It also assures 'proliferation' and mobilization of various actors – industrial, public and political.

The early stages of new path constitution can be explained and understood by both structural factors and the strong presence of agency. The policy lesson stemming from the analytical framework in this article is to stimulate path emergence through the notion that policy matters. But, policy only matters if it is supported by significant industry partners which may function as locomotives. Public policy agency and entrepreneurial agency are interdependent and intertwined during the constitutive process. Due to this, there is a need for policy stakeholders to work closely with entrepreneurial agents to both control and support actions towards regional path development.

Notes

1. http://www.ssb.no/arbeid-og-lonn/statistikker/regledig/aar.
2. www.vikinglady.no.
3. Environmental Technology in Sunnhordland and Haugesundsregionen. Høgskolen i Bergen.

Disclosure statement

No potential conflict of interest was reported by the authors.

Funding

This work was supported by the Norwegian Research Council, the Regional Council of Agder, Rogaland, Hordaland and Troms, through the project VRI.

References

Arthur, W. B. (1994). *Increasing returns and path dependency in the economy*. Ann Arbor: University of Michigan Press.

Asheim, B. T., & Gertler, M. (2005). The geography of innovation: Regional innovation systems. In J. Fagerberg, D. Mowery, & R. Nilsen (Eds.), *The Oxford handbook of innovation* (pp. 291–317). Oxford: Oxford University Press.

Battilana, J., Leca, B., & Boxenbaum, E. (2009). How actors change institutions: Towards a theory of institutional entrepreneurship. *The Academy of Management Annals*, 3, 65–107. doi:10.1080/19416520903053598

Boschma, R., & Frenken, K. (2011). Technological relatedness and regional branching. In H. Bathelt, M. P. Feldman, & D. F. Kogler (Eds.), *Beyond territory. Dynamic geographies of knowledge constitution, diffusion and innovation* (pp. 64–81). London: Routledge.

DiMaggio, P. J. (1988). Interests and agents in institutional theory. In L. G. Zucker (Ed.), *Institutional patterns and organizations* (pp. 3–22). Cambridge, MA: Ballinger.

Espelien, A., Grimsby, G., & Grünfeld, L. A. (2009). *[Miljøteknologi] Potensial og hindre for utvikling av norske konkurransedyktige bedrifter*. MENON-publikasjon nr. 7.

Garud, R., & Karnøe, P. (2001). Path constitution as a process of mindful deviation. In R. Garud & P. Karnøe (Eds.), *Path dependence and constitution* (pp. 1–38). New York, NY: Erlbaum.

Hidle, K., & Normann, R. (2013). Who can govern? Comparing network governance leadership in two Norwegian city-regions. *European Planning Studies*, 21(2), 115–130. doi:10.1080/09654313.2012.722924

Karlsen, J., Larrea, M., Wilson, J. R., & Aranguren, M. J. (2012). Bridging the gap between academic research and regional development in the Basque Country. *European Journal of Education*, 47, 122–138. doi:10.1111/j.1465-3435.2011.01512.x

Karnøe, P., & Garud, R. (2012). Path constitution: Co-constitution of heterogeneous resources in the emergence of the Danish wind turbine cluster. *European Planning Studies*, 20(5), 733–752. doi:10.1080/09654313.2012.667923

Klepper, S. (2007). Disagreements, spinoff and the evolution of Detroit as the capital of the US automobile industry. *Management Science*, 53, 616–631. doi:10.1287/mnsc.1060.0683

Kooiman, J. (2003). *Governing as governance*. London: Sage.

Martin, R., & Sunley, P. (2006). Path dependence and regional economic evolution. *Journal of Economic Geography*, 6(4), 395–437. doi:1093/jpg/lbl012

Martin, R., & Sunley, P. (2010). The place of path dependence in an evolutionary perspective on the economic landscape. In R. Boschma & R. Martin (Eds.), *The handbook of evolutionary economic geography* (pp. 62–92). Cheltenham: Edward Elgar.

Rodriguez-Pose, A. (2013). Do institutions matter for regional development? *Regional Studies*, 47 (7), 1034–1047. doi:10.1080/00343404.2012.748978

Sørensen, E. (2006). Metagovernance: The changing role of politicians in processes of democratic governance. *American Review of Public Administration*, 36(1), 98–114. doi:10.1177/0275074005282584

Sørensen, E., & Torfing, J. (2007). Theoretical approaches to metagovernance. In E. Sørensen & J. Torfing (Eds.), *Theories of democratic network governance* (pp. 25–42). Basingstoke: Palgrave Macmillan.

Sotarauta, M., Horlings, L., & Liddle, J. (2012). Leadership and sustainable regional development. In M. Sotarauta, L. Horlings, & J. Liddle (Eds.), *Leadership and change in sustainable regional development* (pp. 1–29). Abingdon: Routledge.

Sotarauta, M., & Mustikkamäki, N. (2015). Institutional entrepreneurship, power and knowledge in innovation systems: Institution of regenerative medicine in Tampere, Finland. *Environment and Planning C: Government and Policy*, 33, 342–357. doi:10.1068/c12297r

Statistics Norway. (2015). *Labour force survey, registered unemployed, 2015*. Retrieved from www.ssb.no

Streeck, W., & Thelen, K. (2005). Introduction: Institutional change in advanced political economies. In W. Streeck & K. Thelen (Eds.), *Beyond continuity: Institutional change in advanced political economies* (pp. 1–39). Oxford: Oxford University Press.

Sydow, J., Schreyögg, G., & Koch, J. (2009). Organizational path dependence: Opening the black box. *Academy of Management Review, 34*(4), 689–709. doi:10.5465/AMR.2009.44885978

Sydow, J., Windeler, A., Muller-Seitz, G., & Lange, K. (2012). Path constitution analysis: A methodology for understanding path dependence and path constitution. *German Academic Association for Business Research, 5*(2), 155–176. doi:10.1007/BF03342736

Trippl, M., Grillitsch, M., Isaksen, A., & Sinozic, T. (2015). Perspectives on cluster evolution: Critical review and future research issues. *European Planning Studies, 23*(10), 2028–2044. doi:10.1080/09654313.2014.999450

Regional skill relatedness: towards a new measure of regional related diversification

Rune Dahl Fitjar ⓘ and Bram Timmermans

ABSTRACT
This paper proposes a novel index of regional skill-relatedness and calculates this measure for all Norwegian labour-market regions. Studies of regional related diversification rely on measures of related variety, which build on the industry classification hierarchy. However, the growing literature identifying similarities in knowledge and competences across industries demonstrates that these classifications fail to identify a great deal of actual skill relatedness, and that measures based on empirical measures of industry relatedness are required. The skill relatedness measure builds on labour mobility flows across industries to develop a relatedness matrix for Norwegian industries. It further uses social network analysis to identify the number of other regional industries to which each industry in a particular region is related. Comparing this measure to the related variety index, the analysis shows that the two measures are highly correlated, but that the regional skill relatedness index is able to identify more of the relatedness across industries. In particular, the related variety index tends to underestimate the level of relatedness in many of Norway's most technologically sophisticated manufacturing regions, whereas these rank highly in the regional skill relatedness index. Consequently, the regional skill relatedness index represents a promising new tool for identifying relatedness in regional systems.

Introduction

Since Frenken, Van Oort, and Verburg (2007) introduced the concept of related variety in the regional studies literature, scholarly and policy interest in the approach has rapidly gained momentum. The core idea in this literature is that higher levels of regional related diversification, which means the extent to which industries in a particular region build on closely related skills and competences, leads to more local knowledge spillovers across industries. Ultimately, this will enhance regional growth and employment. In its wake, a range of studies have confirmed the positive effects of regional related diversification on employment growth (Boschma & Iammarino, 2009; Boschma, Minondo, & Navarro, 2012; Frenken et al., 2007), resilience (Diodato & Weterings, 2015) and innovative performance (Antonietti & Cainelli, 2011; Castaldi, Frenken, & Los, 2015; Tavassoli & Carbonara, 2014), demonstrating the utility of this approach.

Most studies of regional related diversification have so far applied the measure of related variety by Frenken et al. (2007), which relies on the hierarchical structure of the NACE industry classification system. However, co-classification of two industries within the NACE system does not necessarily imply that these build on related knowledge, as the classification hierarchy is not based on considerations of the type of knowledge used in different industries. Furthermore, and more commonly, industries in completely different industry classes might be related even though they are not classified in the same industry class. Reflecting these problems, recent research has proposed better measures of relatedness across industries, focusing on co-occurrences, similarities, or flows between industries on input and output factors (e.g. traded goods, labour, machine, technologies and products) (Essletzbichler, 2015; Neffke & Henning, 2013). The underlying argument of these approaches is that relatedness across industries reveals itself in high levels of co-occurrence, similarity and/or resource flows between industries, which will only occur consistently over time if these industries are related. Compared to the hierarchical approach, these measures allow for the identification of relatedness between industries that are categorized in different higher level industry classes, as well as for the possibility that co-classified industries may not always build on related knowledge. The strength of this method has been demonstrated in studies of regional industrial dynamics, which have found a consistent relationship between entry and exit of industries and, for example, the skill relatedness of regional industries (Boschma, Minondo, & Navarro, 2013; Essletzbichler, 2015; Neffke, Henning, & Boschma, 2011). However, studies of skill relatedness have mainly focused on the industry level and have so far not been extended to a region-wide measure of relatedness across all regional industries. Consequently, studies at the regional level have been limited to the related variety measure based on co-classification as the only available approach. This paper addresses this shortcoming by proposing a novel regional skill relatedness measure based on mobility flows between industries, using social network analysis to develop an index of the overall level of relatedness across all industries in each region.

The empirical setting of the study is Norway, where we construct both the traditional measure of related variety and a new regional skill relatedness measure to analyse relatedness at the level of Norwegian regions. To identify the industrial composition of Norwegian regions, we rely on register data from Statistics Norway. This database also allows us to identify longitudinal employer–employee linkages, which can subsequently be used to identify industry affiliation and intra-industry mobility rates. The data on industry affiliation are used to calculate related variety, while labour mobility is used to measure skill relatedness across industries. The data on intra-industry mobility and industry affiliation are further combined in a novel measure of regional skill relatedness in Norwegian economic regions.

Comparing the related variety and regional skill relatedness measure, we find that the two measures are strongly correlated. However, the second approach identifies a lot more relatedness across industries in Norwegian regions than the traditional related variety measure would have us believe. A visual inspection of the two measures provides an indication that regional skill relatedness might better illustrate the industrial relatedness structure of a region compared to the traditional related variety measure. Furthermore, the related variety measure tends systematically to underestimate relatedness in certain types of regions, in particular those specialized in manufacturing industries. Notably, the related variety index is negatively correlated with the share of employees in manufacturing industries, while the regional skill relatedness index is not correlated with the region's share of manufacturing employment. This produces low scores on the related variety index for many of Norway's most innovative manufacturing regions, while the regional skill relatedness index identifies a high level of relatedness in these regions.

The remainder of this paper is structured as follows. In the next section, we start with a literature review presenting an overview of studies that have used the concept of related variety to explain regional economic performance and the shortcomings of this measure. Thereafter, we present an alternative method of regional skill relatedness that can address some of these shortcomings. The empirical strategy will be presented in more detail in the method section after which we present the results, comparing the related variety index with the regional skill relatedness measure separately for large, medium-sized and small city regions, as well as for rural regions. The last section concludes.

Related variety, skill relatedness and regional economic growth

Overview of the literature

There has been a long-standing interest in understanding the link between the industry structure of a region and regional economic performance. Two ideal types of industry structures have dominated this line of research (Van der Panne, 2004). On the one hand, agglomeration externalities that emphasize the importance of regional specialization, often referred to as Marshall–Arrow–Romer (MAR) externalities (Glaeser, Kallal, Scheinkman, & Shleifer, 1992). Such regional specialization leads to thick and specialized labour markets, access to specialized suppliers and large markets, and promotes regional knowledge spillovers, as firms rely on similar knowledge, skills and competences. Conversely, a different school of thought emphasizes agglomeration externalities as the result of diversified regional structures, that is, Jacobs externalities (Jacobs, 1969). In such a regional structure, diversity is the trigger of new ideas, which would lead to new economic activities and subsequent regional economic growth. Diversity could be expected to lead to more radical innovation (Castaldi et al., 2015), while specialization predominantly produces incremental innovation. Empirical research has demonstrated positive and negative effects of both types of externalities on innovation performance and activities (Feldman & Audretsch, 1999; Paci & Usai, 1999; Shefer & Frenkel, 1998).

Frenken et al. (2007), by introducing the concept of related variety, provided a more nuanced perspective on how specialization and diversity affect regional economic performance. They positioned themselves in between the two schools, arguing that knowledge spillovers that are useful for innovation mainly take place across industries which are different, but also not completely unrelated. Knowledge spillovers are not expected between all sectors, as some level of complementarity in competences is required or at least beneficial for knowledge spillovers. However, too much proximity potentially hampers interactive learning and innovation as well (Boschma, 2005; Fitjar, Huber, & Rodríguez-Pose, 2016; Nooteboom, 2000). Consequently, neither regional diversity nor regional specialization is beneficial for innovation and regional development per se. Interactive learning, innovation and regional development will most likely occur when knowledge flows between sectors that are technologically related, but not identical. Thus, related variety leads to more knowledge spillovers, which will enhance regional growth and employment. On the other hand, unrelated variety, which means that there are no apparent or only limited complementarities between sectors, may have a portfolio effect that protects regions against the impacts of economic shocks, mitigating unemployment growth. However, more recently, studies have argued that such portfolio effects might also be achieved in a setting of related variety if the related sectors are subject to different business cycles (Boschma, 2015; Diodato & Weterings, 2015).

The concepts of related and unrelated variety have lent themselves well to empirical testing. Over the last couple of years, many studies of the effects of related and unrelated variety in industry structure have emerged. These studies have investigated how related and unrelated variety affect a range of regional economic performance indicators, including employment and unemployment growth, productivity, value-added growth and regional innovation capabilities (Bishop & Gripaios, 2010; Boschma & Iammarino, 2009; Boschma et al., 2012; Falcıoğlu, 2011; Frenken et al., 2007; Hartog, Boschma, & Sotarauta, 2012; Tavassoli & Carbonara, 2014; Van Oort, de Geus, & Dogaru, 2015). Others have used these concepts to explain national growth rates (Saviotti & Frenken, 2008) and more recently, firm-level performance, using indicators such as innovation and productivity growth (Aarstad, Kvitastein, & Jakobsen, 2016; Antonietti & Cainelli, 2011).

Frenken et al. (2007), upon introducing these concepts, investigated the impact of related and unrelated variety on regional economic development in the Netherlands. The paper examined whether there was a potential spillover effect of related variety, which would create jobs, and a portfolio effect for unrelated variety, which was better able to sustain economic shocks and therefore dampen unemployment. This study concluded that related variety positively affects employment growth, which was corroborated in studies in Italy (Boschma & Iammarino, 2009) and Spain (Boschma et al., 2012). Despite the general character of the theory, there is considerable heterogeneity between sectors in the size of this effect (Bishop & Gripaios, 2010). In particular, the effect is typically stronger for high-tech industries (Hartog et al., 2012). Furthermore, there was an additional positive effect when the region had high levels of related trade variation, that is, when it interacted with regions whose industry structures can be characterized as related, rather than similar or unrelated (Boschma & Iammarino, 2009). Meanwhile, unrelated variety had a negative or non-significant effect on regional employment growth (Boschma et al., 2012; Frenken et al., 2007). However, unrelated variety tends to dampen unemployment growth (Frenken et al., 2007), although these results are not robust for a wider set of European regions (Van Oort et al., 2015).

Measuring related variety

In order to measure related variety, research tends to rely on the hierarchical structure of the industrial classification system (Essletzbichler, 2015; Neffke & Henning, 2013). Industrial classification systems like NACE and SIC have various levels of aggregation. These are often utilized to measure related variety. The underlying assumption is that all lower level categories within a higher level category are related. To illustrate, the low-level industry class 'manufacturing of batteries and accumulators' is considered related to the low-level industry class 'manufacturing of electricity distribution and control apparatus' since these classes are both part of the higher level industry category 'manufacturing of electrical equipment'. However, these industries are not related to the manufacturing of fluid power equipment, which belongs to a different higher level industry category ('manufacturing of machinery and equipment not elsewhere classified'). This approach has several properties that make it an interesting approach for research. First, these classification systems are internationally harmonized, allowing for international comparison and thus for comparative studies of the impact of related variety (Van Oort et al., 2015). Second, similar approaches can be, and have been, applied to other hierarchical classification systems like patents (Castaldi et al., 2015), education, occupations and product classes. Third, the aggregated nature of the data needed to investigate this form of relatedness is often readily available from statistical offices.

However, the downsides of this approach are also obvious as, for example, Neffke and Henning (2013) and Essletzbichler (2015) stress. The classification of industries is not based on considerations of relatedness across them, meaning industries that have little in common are sometimes grouped together. For example, 'manufacturing of medical and dental instruments and supplies' is part of the same two-digit category as 'manufacturing of games and toys', and 'transportation via pipelines' is part of the same category as 'taxi operation'. In addition, and perhaps more commonly, it also fails to capture apparent relatedness across the higher level categories. For example, one might argue that industries within the same supply and value chain (e.g. 'manufacturing of computer, electronic and optical products' and 'computer programming, consultancy and related activities') are related, as they both rely on the same skills, competences and technologies. But given that these are in different two-digit industry classes, this type of relatedness is not identified using the traditional co-classification measure.

The concept of skill relatedness

Some of these shortcomings of using the hierarchical method of related variety can be dealt with by measuring relatedness based on flows of resources between different types of industries. Common approaches are to look at input–output tables to identify the presence of strong trade linkages between industries, or, in an approach developed more recently, and which this paper applies, at labour mobility flows (Boschma et al., 2013; Neffke et al., 2011; Neffke & Henning, 2013; Timmermans & Boschma, 2014; Timmermans & Fitjar, 2015). Labour mobility flows provide an indicator of relatedness because workers are more inclined to move to employers who value their skills and competences and reward them according to their human capital. Thus, workers tend change to employers either in the same industry or in industries that rely on similar skills and competences. We thus expect mobility between industry pairs to be more frequent when skills and competences are transferable to another industry. Consequently, higher levels of mobility between industry pairs is a sign that these industries are more related. This measure has been used to predict the entry and exit of new industries, that is, regional branching, in Sweden (Neffke, Henning, & Boschma, 2012), Spain (Boschma et al., 2013) and the US (Essletzbichler, 2015). Furthermore, this indicator of relatedness has also proven useful to explain resilience of Swedish and German shipbuilding industries

(Eriksson, Henning, & Otto, 2016) and labour productivity growth of Danish plants (Timmermans & Boschma, 2014).

Overall, this measure provides useful information on how individual industries, or firms within a particular industry, are related to other firms and industries in a particular geographic context. Skill relatedness measures have mainly been used to explain industry dynamics and labour market dynamics of particular industries in conjunction with their related industries and individual firm or plant performance. However, as far as we could identify, this industry skill relatedness measure has not yet been aggregated to a regional level and as such has not been compared to the measure of related variety.

Method

Data

This study investigates the link between regional skill relatedness and related variety as introduced by Frenken et al. (2007) in the context of Norway. We calculate relatedness across regional industries for Norwegian regions using two measures: Frenken et al.'s (2007) measure of related variety, and the novel regional skill relatedness measure which we develop in this paper. Both measures are created based on data from the Norwegian registers. The data contain detailed universal and longitudinal information on the workplace, industry and work location of individuals for the period 2008–2011. From this register, we first build a data set of the number of workers per industry in each economic region of Norway. Industries are identified at the five-digit NACE level. Second, we build a separate data set of inter-industry mobility across industry pairs in Norway, which we subsequently use to construct our skill relatedness measure. Finally, the two data sets are combined to create the regional skill relatedness measure, to which we will return shortly.

We calculate the measures of related variety and skill relatedness for labour-market regions, which in Norway correspond mostly to the statistical category economic regions. Economic regions are officially defined by Statistics Norway (2000) and represent NUTS 4 regions[1] at the level between the counties and municipalities, which are the official political and administrative units.[2] However, we merge integrated labour markets on the basis of Gundersen and Juvkam's (2013) analysis of labour market flows.[3] This gives a total of 78 regions, which we further classify as large cities, medium-sized cities, small cities, and rural regions, again following Gundersen and Juvkam's (2013) classification based on population size and availability of services.

Related variety

To measure related variety, we follow the same approach as Frenken et al. (2007) of analysing the industrial structure in each region, making a distinction between the higher (two-digit) and lower level (five-digit) NACE industry classification. All five-digit industry classifications i fall under a two-digit industry classification S_g, where $g = 1, \ldots, G$. The share of employees in each two-digit industry class (P_g) can be calculated by summing the five-digit sub-disciplines (p_i). Summing all employment shares in the various industries within a region will add up to 1. The level of unrelated variety in the region is calculated as an entropy of the distribution of industry classes. This measure is calculated as follows:

$$\text{URV} = \sum_{g=1}^{G} P_g \log_e \left(\frac{1}{P_g} \right).$$

Related variety is calculated as the weighted entropy index for lower level five-digit NACE industry classes in each of the two-digit industry classes, indicating the diversity within the lower levels.

$$\text{RV} = \sum_{g=1}^{G} P_g H_g,$$

where

$$H_g = \sum_{i \in S_g} \frac{p_i}{P_g} \log_e \left(\frac{1}{p_i/P_g} \right).$$

Regional skill relatedness

In order to examine the regional skill relatedness in each region, we further develop the measure of skill relatedness between industry pairs based on labour mobility patterns, as developed by Neffke and Henning (2013). To measure this relatedness, we rely on the unique person and workplace identifiers from the register data. These allow us to identify mobility patterns between employers and industries. We use information on nationwide individual workers' mobility between industries to measure skill relatedness across Norwegian four-digit industries.[4] When observing more mobility than expected between industries, these industries are considered related, as they can be expected to build on similar human capital. We measure the skill relatedness between two industries i and j as follows:

$$\text{SR}_{ij} = \frac{F_{ij}/F}{(F_i/F)(F_j/F)} = F_{ij} \frac{F}{F_i F_j}.$$

In this equation, F_{ij} is the total number of employees moving from industry i to industry j; F is the total number of employees who change employers in any given year; F_i is the number of individuals who leave a firm in industry i; and F_j is the number of employees who enter a firm in industry j. We furthermore standardize the measure to a range between -1 and $+1$ using the formula

$$\widehat{\text{SR}}_{ij} = \frac{\text{SR}_{ij} - 1}{\text{SR}_{ij} + 1}.$$

In order to create a general measure of skill relatedness across industries, we combine data for all regions over a four-year period. This is done to reduce the impact of random noise on the measure, so that only industry pairs which consistently across time and space display higher inter-industry mobility rates than what would be expected due to chance are considered skill-related. Consequently, we apply a four-year measure of skill relatedness in the whole of Norway to identify regional skill relatedness in one particular region[5] at a particular point in time. Two industries are considered related if $\widehat{SR}_{ij}$ is higher than 0.25 for the period 2008–2011 as a whole, and higher than 0 in at least two of the four years. In total, 6614 industry pairs are related, representing 3% of all possible industry pairs and 14.5% of all empirically observed industry pairs. A more detailed description of the method, along with the full relatedness matrix for Norwegian industries, is presented in Timmermans and Fitjar (2015).

These skill relatedness measures only provide an indication of whether particular industry pairs are related and do not provide an overall regional measure of skill relatedness as such. For this purpose, we apply social network analysis in which we combine data on regional employment and skill relatedness to construct network measures for each region. The network analysis is used to measure the number of regional industries related to each industry i by calculating the number of ties between i and all other industries j present in the region. As the relatedness of larger industries is of greater importance for the possibility for local knowledge spillovers, we weight the industry's number of ties by the square root of its share of regional employment. As an overall measure of regional skill relatedness, we measure the average number of weighted ties for all industries in the region.[6] The introduction of the weight makes the measure sensitive to the overall distribution of regional employment.[7] Hence, we further standardize the measure by dividing the score with the regional average of this weight term. This ensures that the regional skill relatedness index is determined exclusively by the number of ties and not by the distribution of regional employment (and hence by the level of specialization in the region). The regional skill relatedness (RSR) is calculated as follows:

$$RSR_r = \frac{(\sum_{i=1}^{n} (d_i/2)\sqrt{P_{ir}})/N_{ir}}{(\sum_{i=1}^{n} \sqrt{P_{ir}})/N_{ir}},$$

where P_{ir} is industry i's share of total regional employment in region r, N_{ir} is the number of industries present in region r, and d_i is the sum of incoming and outgoing ties for industry i to other industries in region r. The weighted numbers of ties are summed over all n industries present in each region r.

Regional skill relatedness and related variety

In order to compare the regional skill relatedness measure to the related variety measure, we compare the scores and rankings of Norwegian regions on the two measures. Overall, the two indices are highly correlated with a Pearson's R of 0.79. The concurrent validity of the measure is therefore high. However, there are also some notable discrepancies between the two indices. For instance, the related variety index is significantly negatively correlated with the share of manufacturing employment in the region ($R = -0.40$), whereas the regional skill relatedness index is not significantly correlated with manufacturing employment ($R = -0.03$). This suggests that the regional skill relatedness index might be less sensitive than the related variety index to certain types of regional industrial structures, for example, manufacturing regions.

We further examine the face validity of the regional skill relatedness measure through visual inspection of a series of network graphs, focusing on regions in each category where there are discrepancies between the indices. These graphs show the size and relatedness ties across industries in one region which ranks higher on the regional skill relatedness measure than on the related variety index, and one region where the opposite is true. Examining the underlying data on which the measure is calculated will give an indication of which types of regional industry structures would produce higher or lower scores on the regional skill relatedness measure.

The possibilities for skill relatedness are highly correlated with region size, that is, the more economic activities there are in a region, the more regional diversity there will be, including related variety and regional skill relatedness. Hence, the bivariate correlation between employment size and regional skill relatedness is 0.59, while the correlation between employment size and related variety is 0.46. To account for this, we conduct the comparisons both across the two indices and across regions which differ in their rankings on the two measures separately for regions of different sizes, looking in turn at large cities, medium-sized cities, small cities and rural regions.

Large cities

It is not surprising that the largest city regions are among the regions with highest level of regional skill relatedness and related variety, and that Oslo tops the regional ranking for both measures (see Table 1). The three remaining large city regions are more comparable to each other. However, the ranking of the three is reversed in the regional skill relatedness index compared to the related variety index. In the former, Stavanger is second with Bergen close behind, while Trondheim clearly has a lower score. In the related variety index, Trondheim ranks second, followed closely by Bergen, while Stavanger is trailing by a margin. Furthermore, none of the three regions has particularly impressive scores on the related variety index. Indeed, 5 of the medium-sized city regions discussed below have higher scores than Trondheim on this index, and 12 out of 16 medium-sized city regions have higher scores than Stavanger. This raises the question: Are Norway's large cities outside the capital region characterized by related variety, as the regional skill relatedness measure would suggest, or are they not, as suggested by the related variety index?

Figure 1 demonstrates the differences between Trondheim and Stavanger in greater detail. The network graphs show all relatedness ties between industries. The size of the nodes indicates the share of regional employment in this industry. Both regions have dense networks, reflecting that Stavanger and Trondheim are among the regions with the most regional skill relatedness in Norway. Both regions are, however, also specialized in some industries that are not related to any other industries in the region, shown as isolated nodes to the right.

The Stavanger region, which is heavily reliant on the oil and gas industry, has an industry structure that could be characterized as more specialized. However, the oil and gas

Table 1. Large cities, regional skill relatedness and related variety scores.

	RSR		RV	
	Score	Rank	Score	Rank
Oslo	16.69	1	1.47	1
Stavanger	14.82	2	1.02	4
Bergen	14.74	3	1.17	3
Trondheim	14.19	4	1.24	2

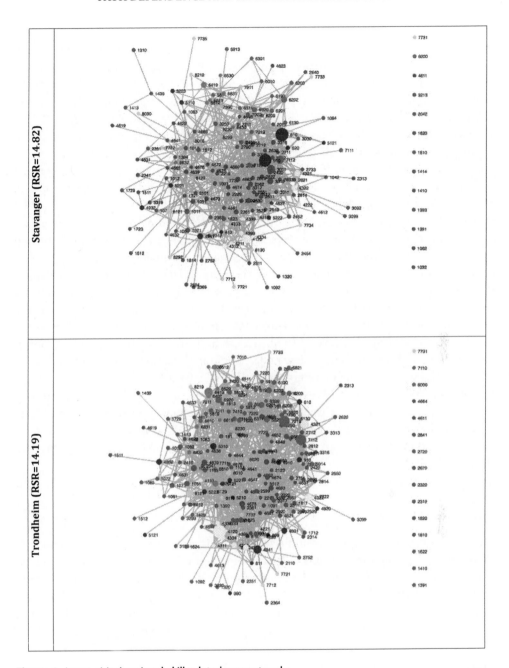

Figure 1. Large cities' regional skill relatedness networks.

industry is composed of various sub-industries specializing in different aspects of the production of oil and gas (e.g. extraction of oil and gas, oil and gas services and various manufacturing and service industries), and the complete value chain within the upstream part of the industry is represented in the Stavanger region (Fitjar & Rodríguez-Pose, 2011). Hence, the region also has a fairly diversified industry structure within oil and gas. Arguably, this is precisely what the concept of related variety is meant to capture – a series of different industries that are connected through a common knowledge core, in this case, engineering knowledge, particularly in fields such as chemistry, geology and construction. However, as the oil and gas industry is spread over several two-digit industry codes, covering mining, manufacturing and services, a lot of the relatedness across different subsectors of the oil and gas industry is not picked up by the traditional related variety index. The related variety score is therefore lower than in the other city regions.

The oil and gas industry in Stavanger is clearly presented with the two largest nodes in the map (shown in purple). These are related not only to each other but also to many smaller sectors in the region. Notably, several of the major manufacturing sectors (red nodes) in Stavanger are related to oil and gas and tend to cluster close to the oil and gas industries on the map. The effect of this is that larger nodes are placed in close proximity on the map, which indicates that there are relatively strong relatedness ties among larger industries in Stavanger. Conversely, the industries (including manufacturing) located further away from this cluster tend to be smaller. Compared to Stavanger, Trondheim has fewer major nodes, reflecting that the region is less specialized than Stavanger. Furthermore, the largest nodes are in some cases located on opposite edges of the network and are unrelated to each other. Scientific and technical consultancy services (brown nodes) are located in the upper right-hand corner of the map, surrounded by many smaller manufacturing and service (pink nodes) industries. In the opposite corner of the map is a set of construction (yellow nodes) and transportation (blue nodes) industries that have a large share of regional employment, but benefit little from the region's strength in scientific and technical services (an exception is the electrical installation industry, shown as a large yellow node close in the upper right section, close to scientific and technical consultancy). The same could be said for the financial sector (orange nodes) in the upper left part of the map. Trondheim's score on the regional skill relatedness measure is therefore lower than Stavanger's.

Medium-sized cities

Table 2 shows the ranking of medium-sized cities. In most cases, the rankings tend to be quite similar. The top three regions in the regional skill relatedness index are also the top three in the related variety index. There are also low-ranking regions on both measures, such as Molde, Bodø, Gjøvik and Lillehammer. However, there are also some discrepancies, which tend to follow along a clear geographical pattern: While the medium-sized coastal cities in Eastern Norway (Drammen, Tønsberg, Fredrikstad, Sandefjord and

Table 2. Medium cities, regional skill relatedness and related variety scores.

	RSR		RV			RSR		RV	
	Score	Rank	Score	Rank		Score	Rank	Score	Rank
Drammen	14.00	1	1.42	1	Hamar	12.00	9	1.22	6
Tønsberg/Horten	13.38	2	1.33	3	Ålesund	11.94	10	1.13	9
Fredrikstad/Sarpsborg	12.93	3	1.39	2	Molde	11.64	11	1.01	14
Kristiansand	12.86	4	1.12	10	Moss	11.60	12	1.26	5
Sandefjord/Larvik	12.72	5	1.26	4	Gjøvik	11.34	13	1.07	11
Skien/Porsgrunn	12.51	6	1.17	7	Tromsø	10.89	14	1.15	8
Haugesund	12.18	7	0.90	16	Bodø	10.85	15	1.01	13
Arendal	12.08	8	0.98	15	Lillehammer	8.83	16	1.07	12

Skien) tend to do well on both measures, the southwestern cities Haugesund, Kristiansand and Arendal all score much higher on the regional skill relatedness than on the related variety index. Kristiansand is fourth on the regional skill relatedness index, but only tenth on the related variety index. Similarly, Haugesund and Arendal are both above the median in this category for regional skill relatedness, but occupy the two lowest places in the related variety index ranking. Conversely, another group of cities in Eastern Norway – Moss, Hamar, Gjøvik and Lillehammer – all rank higher on the related variety than on the regional skill relatedness index, as do the Northern Norwegian cities Tromsø and Bodø.

How can this be accounted for? To examine this, Figure 2 shows the skill relatedness maps for Haugesund and Tromsø, which moved in opposite directions on the two indices. The two regions are similar in size, with a population in 2008 of 99,000 and 78,000, respectively, although Haugesund has a higher share of private sector employment, translating into a private sector workforce that was 55% higher than Tromsø's in the industries considered. The industrial structures of the two regions are also quite different. As the maps show, Haugesund relies much more on manufacturing (red nodes) than Tromsø. The two largest industries in Haugesund are both in manufacturing (shipbuilding and aluminium production). Both of these are also located quite centrally in the map and are surrounded by several smaller manufacturing industries. This includes various metal products and machine production industries, which – as they are in different two-digit categories – are not picked up by the related variety index as being related to either of the two largest industries. This is also true for other large industries in Haugesund, such as the sea freight industry (blue node at the top) and the oil and gas industries (purple nodes). The related variety index therefore fails to detect a lot of the relatedness across industries in Haugesund, while the regional skill relatedness measure picks up much more of these linkages.

The manufacturing industries in Tromsø are much smaller and also more dispersed throughout the map. Tromsø's major specializations include the construction (yellow nodes) and transport (blue nodes) industries, which form two separate clusters in the upper right and left parts of the map, respectively. The industries within these sectors tend to be skill-related, but this kind of relatedness is to a greater extent also picked up by the related variety index, as construction and transport both cover a limited number of two-digit industries (3 and 5, respectively, compared to 24 in manufacturing). Being host to a research university, Tromsø also has a set of scientific and technical service industries (brown nodes) which cluster at the bottom of the map. However, as in Trondheim, these industries are somewhat disconnected from other large industries in Tromsø, although they are related to a series of smaller information and communication services (pink nodes) and financial services (orange nodes) industries in Tromsø. Overall, however, the division between two or three relatively unrelated specializations in construction, transport and scientific/technical services translate into a fairly low level of regional skill relatedness in Tromsø.

Small cities

Moving to smaller city regions (see Table 3), a similar pattern emerges. The top of the two rankings is once more identical, with the same two regions occupying the first two

Figure 2. Medium cities' regional skill relatedness networks.

positions in both rankings. However, also in this category, there is a group of manufacturing-oriented regions with very high scores in the regional skill relatedness index, which are in the bottom places on the related variety index. This includes the third-ranking region Sunnhordland and fifth-ranking Kongsberg, as well as Egersund, Sogndal/Årdal, Halden and Mo i Rana. All of these regions are mainly specialized in one or more manufacturing industries, which tends to result in lower related variety scores due to the limited number

Table 3. Small cities, regional skill relatedness and related variety scores.

	RSR		RV			RSR		RV	
	Score	Rank	Score	Rank		Score	Rank	Score	Rank
Askim/Mysen	10.56	1	1.21	1	Orkanger	8.21	16	0.73	23
Kongsvinger	10.17	2	1.08	2	Narvik	8.19	17	0.92	14
Sunnhordland	10.02	3	0.66	28	Mandal	8.12	18	0.80	22
Hønefoss	9.75	4	0.92	13	Alta	8.11	19	1.03	3
Kongsberg	9.69	5	0.68	27	Namsos	7.96	20	0.93	11
Kristiansund	9.52	6	0.97	5	Sogndal/Årdal	7.91	21	0.65	29
Steinkjer	9.19	7	0.95	9	Mosjøen	7.23	22	0.82	20
Levanger/Verdalsøra	9.02	8	0.83	18	Lofoten	7.22	23	0.80	21
Halden	8.90	9	0.70	25	Florø	7.13	24	0.68	26
Harstad	8.85	10	0.93	10	Ørsta/Volda	7.09	25	0.83	17
Notodden/Bø	8.71	11	0.95	8	Hammerfest	6.98	26	0.88	15
Mo i Rana	8.45	12	0.82	19	Voss	6.82	27	0.93	12
Elverum	8.39	13	0.99	4	Finnsnes	6.53	28	0.87	16
Egersund	8.38	14	0.65	30	Sandnessjøen	5.90	29	0.73	24
Førde	8.35	15	0.95	7	Kirkenes	5.61	30	0.96	6

of four-digit industries normally present within each two-digit manufacturing sector in most regions. Conversely, several regions in Northern Norway score much higher in the related variety than in the regional skill relatedness index also in this category. This includes regions such as Alta and Kirkenes, both in Finnmark, which are third and sixth, respectively, in the related variety index, while they are nineteenth and rock bottom, respectively, in the regional skill relatedness index. Other northern regions, such as Hammerfest and Finnsnes, also move in the same direction. Much like Tromsø, these regions tend to be much more dominated by the construction and transportation services sectors.

To illustrate this, Figure 3 shows the network graphs for Kongsberg in Eastern Norway and Kirkenes in Finnmark. Kongsberg is fifth in the regional skill relatedness measure, but third from bottom in the related variety index. The opposite is the case for Kirkenes, which is sixth in the related variety index, but last in the regional skill relatedness index. The dominance of manufacturing industries in Kongsberg is clear from the large red nodes in the upper left part of the network. Kongsberg has emerged in recent years as one of the major high-technology manufacturing regions in Norway, home to the Subsea Valley oil and gas technology cluster, as well as leading weapons manufacturers (Isaksen, 2009; Onsager, Isaksen, Fraas, & Johnstad, 2007). The three largest nodes in Kongsberg are shipbuilding, weapons manufacturing and instrument manufacturing, which all belong to different two-digit NACE industries, but are clearly skill-related as shown by the links between them as well as their proximity in the map. Most other manufacturing industries in Kongsberg are also located close to the largest industries, while the service industries tend to be fairly detached from this cluster. Overall, however, the relatedness ties among all three dominant industries, as well as the many ties between these and other industries in Kongsberg, lead to a high regional skill relatedness score for Kongsberg.

Kirkenes is also specialized in a manufacturing industry, in this case, ship repairs. This industry also has a central position in the regional network, although with few other manufacturing industries nearby. However, the construction and transportation industries are much more important in Kirkenes than in Kongsberg, as shown by the larger yellow and blue nodes. In particular, many of the construction industries are in the two-digit category specialized construction, while many of the transportation industries are in storage or land

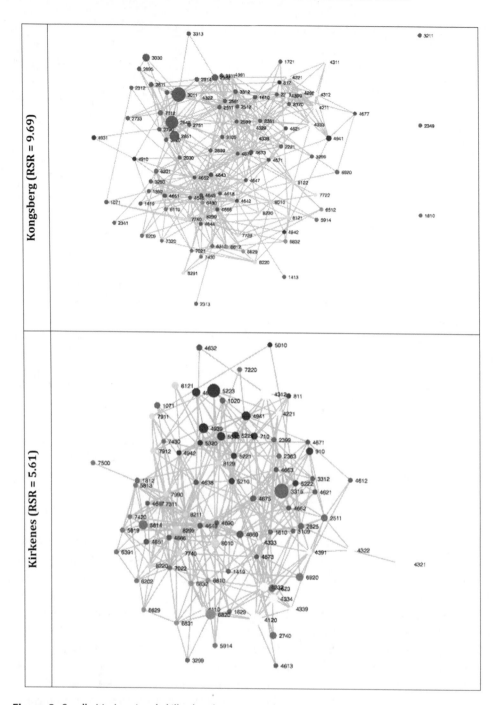

Figure 3. Small cities' regional skill relatedness networks.

transport, leading to a high score on the related variety index. However, particularly in the case of construction, these industries are not skill-related, as the network map shows. For instance, the large node in electrical installations is only related to one other industry in Kirkenes and is therefore on the periphery of the network, even though there are several other specialized construction industries in the region. In this case, therefore, the related variety index might have, in some cases, overestimated relatedness across industries in Kirkenes. Meanwhile, the largest nodes are spread out in different parts of the regional network, with large nodes in the top, bottom, right and centre of the network. Few large industries are located in the vicinity of other large industries in Kirkenes. This results in a low regional skill relatedness score.

Rural regions

Finally, the classification for rural areas tends to show the largest discrepancies. While there are certainly many regions that are at the top or, especially, at the bottom of both indices, this is the only category where the top of the two lists looks quite different. In particular, the top-ranking region for regional skill relatedness, Ulsteinvik, is nearly at the bottom of the related variety index. Conversely, a region in Finnmark once more stands out with a much higher score in the related variety index than in the regional skill relatedness measure: Vadsø is second for related variety, compared to its twelfth place in the regional skill relatedness index. Nonetheless, there are also similarities. In particular, several inland regions in Eastern Norway, such as Hadeland, Hallingdal and Valdres, do well on both measures, while the smallest regions are at the bottom in both indices, as would also be expected (Table 4).

Figure 4 shows the network maps for Ulsteinvik and Rørvik, which have similar related variety scores (0.63 and 0.60, respectively), even though Ulsteinvik's regional skill relatedness score is more than double that of Rørvik. Ulsteinvik is a heavily manufacturing-oriented region which hosts world-leading and highly technologically sophisticated shipbuilding firms (Karlsen, 2005). Its largest sectors are shipbuilding (red node) and ship transportation (blue node). Shipbuilding in particular is related to a large number of other manufacturing industries in Ulsteinvik, mostly in the machine or metal products manufacturing sectors. Consequently, most manufacturing industries in Ulsteinvik are located in close proximity on the map, linked by a large number of relatedness ties. This results in a high score on the regional skill relatedness index. However, many of these linkages are not picked up by the related variety index, as shipbuilding belongs to

Table 4. Rural regions, regional skill relatedness and related variety scores.

	RSR		RV			RSR		RV	
	Score	Rank	Score	Rank		Score	Rank	Score	Rank
Ulsteinvik	8.90	1	0.63	24	Surnadal	6.10	15	0.67	22
Nordfjord	8.55	2	0.95	3	Tynset	6.03	16	0.80	11
Vesterålen	8.18	3	0.91	6	Andselv	5.97	17	0.76	15
Hadeland	7.97	5	1.05	1	Odda	5.90	18	0.74	17
Valdres	7.66	4	0.93	5	Oppdal	5.70	19	0.77	12
Hallingdal	7.46	6	0.94	4	Høyanger	5.66	20	0.42	27
Nord-Gudbrandsdalen	7.19	7	0.86	10	Sunndalsøra	5.46	21	0.39	28
Lyngdal/Farsund	7.17	8	0.76	14	Røros	5.34	22	0.68	21
Flekkefjord	6.85	9	0.72	18	Brønnøysund	5.14	23	0.71	19
Midt-Gudbrandsdalen	6.83	10	0.90	7	Setesdal	4.94	24	0.74	16
Risør	6.62	11	0.86	9	Nord-Troms	4.70	25	0.76	13
Vadsø	6.34	12	0.95	2	Rjukan	4.53	26	0.64	23
Brekstad	6.34	13	0.71	20	Rørvik	4.18	27	0.60	25
Vest-Telemark	6.20	14	0.87	8	Frøya/Hitra	4.10	28	0.42	26

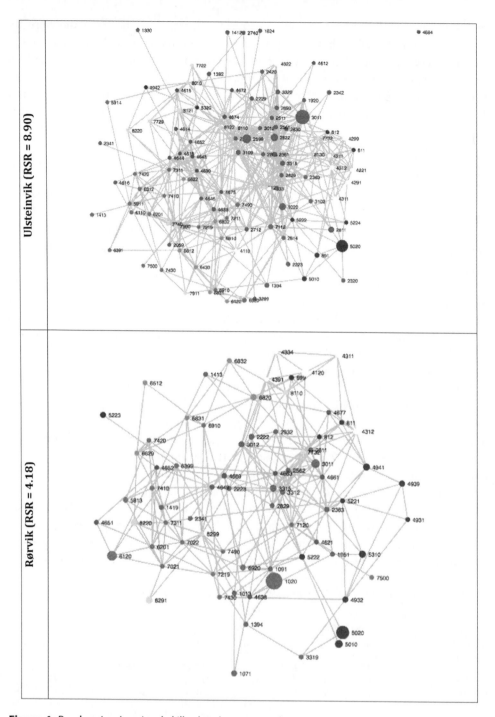

Figure 4. Rural regions' regional skill relatedness networks.

a different two-digit category (manufacture of transport equipment) than machine or metal products manufacturing. Ulsteinvik's score on the related variety index is therefore much lower.

Ostensibly, the industry structure in Rørvik is similar to that of Ulsteinvik, although the region is much smaller. Its largest industries are also ship transportation – as in Ulsteinvik – and a manufacturing industry. However, in this case, the manufacturing specialization is fish processing, which has less to do with ship transportation than Ulsteinvik's shipbuilding industry. Fish processing also has fewer ties to other industries in Rørvik in general, with only a few other small food production industries related to it. The other manufacturing industries in Rørvik are located in a different part of the map, and are mostly quite small. Furthermore, ship transportation is only related to three other industries in Rørvik, whereas the same industry has seven related industries in Ulsteinvik. Despite being one of the least densely populated regions in Norway, Rørvik also has a small concentration of IT industries (pink nodes), the largest being wireless telecommunications. However, this is located in a different part of the network from the other large industries in the region. Overall, there are also considerably fewer ties across industries in Rørvik than in Ulsteinvik, as the density of linkages on the two maps illustrates. This results in a low score for Rørvik on the regional skill relatedness index.

Conclusion

Understanding how the different industrial structures of regions create or deter opportunities for knowledge flows between industries has long been a topic of interest for academics and policy-makers. During the last 10 years, the concept of related variety, which takes into account the extent to which industries in a given region build on related knowledge, has gained momentum as an approach to explaining regional economic performance. Existing empirical research tends, with some exceptions, to support this idea. However, the empirical support for the benefits of related variety has relied mainly on studies using indices which build on the co-classification of industries in the NACE hierarchical industry classification system. In the meantime, new measures of industry relatedness have been introduced which are in many cases clearly better at identifying relatedness between industries. In particular, such measures are able to capture links between industries that build on related knowledge, but which are classified in different parts of the NACE system. However, these measures tend to focus on individual industries rather than regional systems. A macro-level measure of relatedness at the regional level has hitherto not existed.

In this paper, we have created such a measure. The paper proposes a measure of regional skill relatedness based on empirical measurement of relatedness ties across regional industries as identified by labour mobility flows. We create and calculate this measure for all Norwegian regions using social network analysis, building on the comprehensive linked employer–employee data available from Statistics Norway. We further compare the measure to the related variety measure as introduced by Frenken et al. (2007). When comparing these measures, we see some notable discrepancies between them. Relatedness between industries appears to be underestimated for most regions in the related variety index. This underestimation is mainly driven by the failure of the related variety index to identify a large number of linkages between industries belonging to different two-digit NACE codes. Relying exclusively on related variety as identified by the classification hierarchy would particularly be problematic for smaller regions, where many industries are not co-located with other industries in the same two-digit NACE category. The measure of regional skill relatedness identifies these industries more clearly, thus highlighting a larger number of industries that can (potentially) benefit from being co-located in the same area. Furthermore, while the sheer number of relatedness linkages is underestimated in all regions, this is particularly a problem in manufacturing-oriented regions. The correlation analysis demonstrates a negative correlation between the share of employees active in manufacturing industries and related variety, and this is also apparent in several of the individual regions shown in the analysis. A consequence of this is that regions specializing in manufacturing tend to score lower on the related variety index than on the regional skill relatedness index in all size categories. Consequently, the level of related variety in many of Norway's most technologically sophisticated and export-oriented manufacturing regions is severely underestimated by the related variety index, including large cities such as Stavanger, medium-sized cities such as Kristiansand and Haugesund, small cities such as Sunnhordland, Kongsberg and Halden, and rural regions such as Ulsteinvik. Conversely, the proposed regional skill relatedness index picks up more of the relatedness across industries in these regions, placing many of them close to the top of the rankings in the respective categories.

This has implications for regional policy building on the concept of relatedness, also beyond the Norwegian context. If the related variety index tends to underestimate relatedness, in particular in manufacturing regions, entrepreneurial discovery processes (Foray, 2015) may simply fail to identify many promising combinations of existing regional skills and competences. Policy-makers thus need to include a broad variety of indicators in their analyses and build on empirical measures of industry relatedness rather than co-classification. The analyses of Norwegian regions also show that there are highly different relatedness patterns, even across regions of similar size. While there is clearly more relatedness in large urban regions than in smaller and more peripheral ones, there are also large differences across regions within each category. An effective regional policy for Ulsteinvik would likely look very different from an effective policy for Rørvik, and Kongsberg has very different needs from Kirkenes. Hence, we should be cautious of policy approaches that treat all rural or peripheral regions as the same, or indeed which dish out the same policy solutions for all large urban regions. One size does not fit all, even if they are all peripheral, to paraphrase Tödtling and Trippl (2005). The development of appropriate regional policies has to depart from specific analyses of the regional context in each individual region.

Our analysis comes with some limitations. First, our proposed measure needs to be fine-tuned further, as it is strongly correlated with the size of the region. A consequence of this is that it is challenging to investigate how well this measure can explain regional economic performance beyond general centralization trends. Second, the Norwegian context is one of the factors that should be considered. Our findings thus provide a call for future research to investigate the robustness of our proposed regional skill relatedness measure, not only compared to the Norwegian setting, but also to existing measures of regional industrial diversity. The oil and gas industry plays an important role in the Norwegian economy as it provides jobs for a diverse labour force, paying high wages. As such, labour mobility patterns and subsequent related variety might be to some extent affected by the strong dominance of this industry. Furthermore, Norway's main industries are in many cases distributed across different NACE categories. This is the case for oil and gas, but also for maritime industries as the examples discussed in the paper have shown. This might lead the related variety index into greater problems in Norway than in industrial settings that conform more to the logic of the classification hierarchy. Third, relatedness based on labour mobility patterns is only one way to empirically measure industry relatedness. Other measures could also be aggregated into regional indices (see Neffke and Henning (2013) and Essletzbichler (2015) for a more detailed discussion on the type of relatedness measures that can be constructed). However, this paper has provided a first step towards developing an overall regional measure of relatedness which relies on empirical industry relatedness rather than on the classification hierarchy.

Notes

1. Norway, with its population of 5.2 million inhabitants, is among the most sparsely populated countries in Europe. Consequently, economic regions are highly dispersed in both geographic size and population size, and the NUTS 3 regional classification is relatively large. Smaller Norwegian NUTS 3 regions are often the same size as NUTS 2 regions in other European countries, while regions located in the north are similar in geographical extent to the countries of Denmark, the Netherlands or Belgium. Hence, NUTS 4 regions is the best equivalent of functional economic regions. As we question the validity of these knowledge spillover dynamics in regions which cover very large areas, we rely on NUTS 4 regions in our analyses.
2. However, many economic regions are also represented by organizations such as regional councils or regional development agencies, which are normally joint ventures by several neighbouring municipalities with responsibilities especially for development policy.
3. The following economic regions are identified as part of the same labour market by Gundersen and Juvkam (2013) and are therefore classified as one region: Oslo, Follo, Bærum/Asker, Lillestrøm and Ullensaker/Eidsvoll; Drammen and Sande/Svelvik; Tønsberg/Horten and Holmestrand; Skien/Porsgrunn and Kragerø; Kristiansand and Lillesand; Stavanger/Sandnes and Jæren; Haugesund and Søndre Sunnhordland; Trondheim and Stjørdalshalsen; and Namsos and Grong.
4. When calculating the regional skill relatedness index, industries are measured at the four-digit level in order to retain a reasonable number of employees in each industry. While the related variety index is measured at the five-digit level for consistency with Frenken et al.'s (2007) approach, we have also tried calculating this at the four-digit level with no meaningful differences in the results.
5. Of course, labour mobility could be higher (or lower) between an industry pair in a particular region, leading these industries to be related in this region even if they are not related at the national level (or vice versa). However, the intention here is to identify industries which are related in a more general sense of building on the same skills, and we therefore calculate a national measure where industries are only considered related if the mobility levels between them are high across the whole country. It is thus not possible to determine from the relatedness maps whether there are actually high levels of mobility between any two industries in an individual region, only that these industries are related in the sense of building on the same skills as evidenced by higher than expected mobility at the national level.
6. The analysis focuses on employment in the private sector only. Following Frenken et al. (2007), we further exclude the primary sector industries agriculture and fisheries from the analysis. We also exclude retail, hotels and restaurants, as well as temp agencies. The three former industries are excluded, as they include lots of temporary workers, while the latter is excluded, as it mainly acts as a channel to place workers in other industries; consequently, the knowledge and skills that are being transferred are not specific to the temp agency industry, but related to the industries in which temp agencies place workers.
7. The sum of all industries' employment shares is by definition 1 in all regions. However, the root transformation implies that the sum of the weights will be higher for regions with more diversified industrial structures than for more specialized regions.

Acknowledgements

Earlier drafts of the paper have been presented at workshops in Stavanger and Oslo. The authors are grateful to all participants at these events for their helpful comments and suggestions.

Disclosure statement

No potential conflict of interest was reported by the authors.

Funding

This work was supported by the Research Council of Norway (Norges Forskningsråd) under the programmes Demosreg, grant no. 209761, and VRI, grant no. 233737. The relatedness matrix and regional industrial statistics were analysed in the former project based on data from Statistics Norway, and the relatedness matrix developed in this project is available in Timmermans and Fitjar (2015). The regional skill relatedness method was further developed in the latter project.

ORCID

Rune Dahl Fitjar ⓘ http://orcid.org/0000-0001-5333-2701

References

Aarstad, J., Kvitastein, O. A., & Jakobsen, S. E. (2016). Related and unrelated variety as regional drivers of enterprise productivity and innovation: A multilevel study. *Research Policy, 45*(4), 844–856. doi:10.1016/j.respol.2016.01.013

Antonietti, R., & Cainelli, G. (2011). The role of spatial agglomeration in a structural model of innovation, productivity and export: A firm-level analysis. *The Annals of Regional Science, 46*(3), 577–600. doi:10.1007/s00168-009-0359-7

Bishop, P., & Gripaios, P. (2010). Spatial externalities, relatedness and sector employment growth in Great Britain. *Regional Studies, 44*(4), 443–454. doi:10.1080/00343400802508810

Boschma, R. (2005). Proximity and innovation: A critical assessment. *Regional Studies, 39*(1), 61–74. doi:10.1080/0034340052000320887

Boschma, R. (2015). Towards an evolutionary perspective on regional resilience. *Regional Studies, 49*(5), 733–751. doi:10.1080/00343404.2014.959481

Boschma, R., & Iammarino, S. (2009). Related variety, trade linkages, and regional growth in Italy. *Economic Geography, 85*(3), 289–311. doi:10.1111/j.1944-8287.2009.01034.x

Boschma, R., Minondo, A., & Navarro, M. (2012). Related variety and regional growth in Spain. *Papers in Regional Science, 91*(2), 241–256.

Boschma, R., Minondo, A., & Navarro, M. (2013). The emergence of new industries at the regional level in Spain: A proximity approach based on product relatedness. *Economic Geography, 89*(1), 29–51. doi:10.1111/j.1944-8287.2012.01170.x

Castaldi, C., Frenken, K., & Los, B. (2015). Related variety, unrelated variety and technological breakthroughs: An analysis of US state-level patenting. *Regional Studies, 49*(5), 767–781. doi:10.1080/00343404.2014.940305

Diodato, D., & Weterings, A. B. (2015). The resilience of regional labor markets to economic shocks: Exploring the role of interactions among firms and workers. *Journal of Economic Geography, 15*(4), 723–742. doi:10.1093/jeg/lbu030

Eriksson, R. H., Henning, M., & Otto, A. (2016). Industrial and geographical mobility of workers during industry decline: The Swedish and German shipbuilding industries 1970–2000. *Geoforum, 75*, 87–98. doi:10.1016/j.geoforum.2016.06.020

Essletzbichler, J. (2015). Relatedness, industrial branching and technological cohesion in US metropolitan areas. *Regional Studies, 49*(5), 752–766. doi:10.1080/00343404.2013.806793

Falcıoğlu, P. (2011). Location and determinants of productivity: The case of the manufacturing industry in Turkey. *Emerging Markets Finance and Trade, 47*(suppl. 5), 86–96. doi:10.2753/REE1540-496X4706S506

Feldman, M. P., & Audretsch, D. B. (1999). Innovation in cities: Science-based diversity, specialization and localized competition. *European Economic Review, 43*(2), 409–429. doi:10.1016/S0014-2921(98)00047-6

Fitjar, R. D., Huber, F., & Rodríguez-Pose, A. (2016). Not too close, not too far: Testing the Goldilocks principle of 'optimal' distance in innovation networks. *Industry & Innovation, 23* (6), 465–487. doi:10.1080/13662716.2016.1184562

Fitjar, R. D., & Rodríguez-Pose, A. (2011). Innovation in the periphery: Firms, values and innovation in Southwest Norway. *European Planning Studies, 19*(4), 555–574. doi:10.1080/09654313.2011.548467

Foray, D. (2015). *Smart specialisation: Opportunities and challenges for regional innovation policy.* London: Routledge.

Frenken, K., Van Oort, F., & Verburg, T. (2007). Related variety, unrelated variety and regional economic growth. *Regional Studies, 41*(5), 685–697. doi:10.1080/00343400601120296

Glaeser, E. L., Kallal, H. D., Scheinkman, J. A., & Shleifer, A. (1992). Growth in cities. *Journal of Political Economy, 100*(6), 1126–1152. doi:10.1086/261856

Gundersen, F., & Juvkam, D. (2013). Inndelinger i senterstruktur, sentralitet og BA regioner. NIBR-rapport 2013-1.

Hartog, M., Boschma, R., & Sotarauta, M. (2012). The impact of related variety on regional employment growth in Finland 1993–2006: High-tech versus medium/low-tech. *Industry and Innovation, 19*(6), 459–476. doi:10.1080/13662716.2012.718874

Isaksen, A. (2009). Innovation dynamics of global competitive regional clusters: The case of the Norwegian centres of expertise. *Regional Studies, 43*(9), 1155–1166. doi:10.1080/00343400802094969

Jacobs, J. (1969). *The economy of cities.* New York: John Wiley.

Karlsen, A. (2005). The dynamics of regional specialization and cluster formation: Dividing trajectories of maritime industries in two Norwegian regions. *Entrepreneurship & Regional Development, 17*(5), 313–338. doi:10.1080/08985620500247702

Neffke, F., & Henning, M. (2013). Skill relatedness and firm diversification. *Strategic Management Journal, 34*(3), 297–316. doi:10.1002/smj.2014

Neffke, F., Henning, M., & Boschma, R. (2011). How do regions diversify over time? Industry relatedness and the development of new growth paths in regions. *Economic Geography, 87*(3), 237–265. doi:10.1111/j.1944-8287.2011.01121.x

Neffke, F. M. H., Henning, M., & Boschma, R. (2012). The impact of aging and technological relatedness on agglomeration externalities: A survival analysis. *Journal of Economic Geography, 12*(2), 485–517. doi:10.1093/jeg/lbr001

Nooteboom, B. (2000). Learning by interaction: Absorptive capacity, cognitive distance and governance. *Journal of Management and Governance, 4*(1-2), 69–92. doi:10.1023/A:1009941416749

Onsager, K., Isaksen, A., Fraas, M., & Johnstad, T. (2007). Technology cities in Norway: Innovating in glocal networks. *European Planning Studies, 15*(4), 549–566. doi:10.1080/09654310601134896

Paci, R., & Usai, S. (1999). Externalities, knowledge spillovers and the spatial distribution of innovation. *GeoJournal, 49*(4), 381–390. doi:10.1023/A:1007192313098

Saviotti, P. P., & Frenken, K. (2008). Export variety and the economic performance of countries. *Journal of Evolutionary Economics, 18*(2), 201–218. doi:10.1007/s00191-007-0081-5

Shefer, D., & Frenkel, A. (1998). Local milieu and innovations: Some empirical results. *The Annals of Regional Science, 32*(1), 185–200. doi:10.1007/s001680050069

Statistics Norway (2000). *Classification of economic regions. Official statistics of Norway C-616.* Oslo: Statistics Norway.

Tavassoli, S., & Carbonara, N. (2014). The role of knowledge variety and intensity for regional innovation. *Small Business Economics, 43*(2), 493–509. doi:10.1007/s11187-014-9547-7

Timmermans, B., & Boschma, R. (2014). The effect of intra-and inter-regional labour mobility on plant performance in Denmark: The significance of related labour inflows. *Journal of Economic Geography, 14*(2), 289–311. doi:10.1093/jeg/lbs059

Timmermans, B., & Fitjar, R. D. (2015). *Skill relatedness in Norway.* University of Stavanger Working Papers in Economics and Finance, no. 20/2015.

Tödtling, F., & Trippl, M. (2005). One size fits all? Towards a differentiated regional innovation policy approach. *Research Policy, 34*(8), 1203–1219. doi:10.1016/j.respol.2005.01.018

Van der Panne, G. (2004). Agglomeration externalities: Marshall versus Jacobs. *Journal of Evolutionary Economics, 14*(5), 593–604. doi:10.1007/s00191-004-0232-x

Van Oort, F., de Geus, S., & Dogaru, T. (2015). Related variety and regional economic growth in a cross-section of European urban regions. *European Planning Studies, 23*(6), 1110–1127. doi:10. 1080/09654313.2014.905003

Public policies and cluster life cycles: insights from the Basque Country experience

Aitziber Elola, Jesus M. Valdaliso, Susana Franco and Santiago M. López

ABSTRACT

This paper contributes to the study of the role of public policies in the origins and evolution of clusters. Building on the existing literature, we set up a taxonomy of nine public policies that may have an impact on the emergence and evolution of clusters. Based on in-depth case studies of six clusters of the Basque Country, particularly representative of the industrial history of the region, we analyse the relevance of the different types of policies both in the emergence and evolution of clusters over time. In agreement with cluster literature, the paper concludes that public policies seem to have played only an indirect role across clusters and over their life cycles. Moreover, it points to the necessity of taking history and context into account, as most of the important policy measures highlighted by cluster literature today do not fit well with the previous policy and economic context. Finally, it also concludes that for cluster policies to be effective, the stages of the life cycle should be taken into consideration.

1. Introduction

In general, there is wide agreement in the literature on cluster evolution for the necessity of an evolutionary and contingent approach (Boschma & Fornahl, 2011; Fornahl, Hassink, & Menzel, 2015). Cluster life cycles are determined by path-dependent forces, among which public policies and local institutions stand out (Elola, Valdaliso, Aranguren, & López, 2012; Martin & Sunley, 2006, 2011; Menzel & Fornahl, 2010).

The policy implications of the cluster life cycle framework, however, is a scarcely addressed topic by cluster literature (Boschma & Fornahl, 2011), even if this is important to identify the best timing for these interventions and the form they should take (Landabaso & Rosenfeld, 2009). Among the few exceptions, two different approaches have been taken, one theoretical by Brenner and Schlump (2011), and other empirical, by Van Klink and De Langen (2001), and Shin and Hassink (2011). The latter ones point to the necessity of taking context, and history, into account: 'No blueprints of cluster policies can be given, simply because different contexts require different policies' (Van Klink & De Langen, 2001, p. 454), and a recent work by Njøs and Jakobsen (2016) also highlights this idea that 'no one size fits all'.

This paper contributes to the recently emerging literature on cluster life cycles and policy issues, examining the role of public policies in the origins and development of clusters. For that purpose, and building on the existing literature we first set up a taxonomy of nine policy measures that are likely to have an impact on the emergency and evolution of clusters (education, public research, supporting R&D and innovation, start-up support, network organization and cooperation support, infrastructure and local conditions, trade policies, demand-side policy instruments and other). We then analyse the effective role of these policies in a multiple-case study of six industrial clusters of the Basque Country, particularly representative of the industrial history of the region in the nineteenth and twentieth centuries. Although, with a single exception, policy measures were not the key drivers of cluster origins and evolution, the paper attempts to assess their suitability and, if possible, impact over the different phases of cluster life cycles.

The case of the Basque Country is of great interest for several reasons. First, it epitomizes the experience of old industrialized European regions that were ravaged by the economic crisis of the 1970s and since then have achieved considerable success in transforming their industrial and productive structure in the last 30 years. Second, the Basque Country was one of the first European regions, along with Scotland, that applied a cluster-based competitiveness policy in the early 1990s, following explicitly Porter's model, with proven and recognized results in R&D, innovation, cluster development and competitiveness (Aranguren & Navarro, 2003; Ketels, 2004; OECD, 2007, 2011). Finally, the Basque Country is a region with significant autonomy in the field of industrial policy, having exclusive powers of the regional government in very different areas (Aranguren, Magro, Navarro, & Valdaliso, 2012; OECD, 2011).

The paper is divided into four parts. The first discusses literature on cluster policies and their impact on the evolution of clusters over time, e.g. across the different phases of their life cycle. The second presents the methodology employed and describes the six clusters studied. Then follows a discussion of the main findings of the empirical analysis; and finally, the last section offers some concluding remarks.

2. Theoretical background: public policies and cluster life cycles

Even if there is no conclusive evidence on the long-term impacts of clusters (Uyarra & Ramlogan, 2012), they are generally seen as conductive for economic development (Delgado, Porter, & Stern, 2010, 2014; Franco, Murciego, & Wilson, 2014; Malmberg & Maskell, 2002; Martin & Sunley, 2003; Porter, 1998). It is not surprising then that cluster policies have flourished over the last decades to encourage the emergence of clusters and support their development, both in developed and in developing countries (Ketels, Lindqvist, & Sölvell, 2006).

As the cluster idea encompasses a wide variety of phenomena, cluster policies may also take different shapes and follow different objectives (Commission of the European Communities, 2008; Nauwelaers & Wijtnes, 2008). In this regard, two different approaches to cluster policy could be distinguished. The narrow approach to cluster policy implies the existence of policies designed with the explicit purpose of directly supporting clusters, and those policies are in most cases supported and implemented by specific cluster programmes. On the contrary, the broad approach to cluster policy would reflect the systemic, multi-actor and multi-level nature of cluster policy, by considering the broader set of activities influencing clusters, without being necessarily designed with this purpose (Borrás & Tsagdis, 2008; Nauwelaers & Wijtnes, 2008; Uyarra & Ramlogan, 2012). This last approach recognizes that, while important, the influence of policy may often be indirect, driven by policies such as infrastructure, research, education and training rather than policies directed at clusters per se (Uyarra & Ramlogan, 2012). Although 'cluster policies' (in the narrow sense) may be mostly focused on supporting existing clusters (and industries), 'broad-based general policies' may encourage the appearance of new clusters and industries in a given region (Asheim, Isaksen, Martin, & Trippl, 2015). In this paper, we consider both the impact of cluster policies and broad-based general policies in the emergence and evolution of clusters.

Based on that, in order to establish a taxonomy of policies that may affect the emergence and evolution of clusters, we consider the model developed by Brenner and Schlump (2011), where they analyse, on one hand, the impact that different policies exert at different stages of the cluster life cycle and, on the other, in which areas government support should focus in order to be more effective. Based on their review of the literature, they suggest six categories of policies:

- 'Education', which encompasses different interventions aimed at improving the knowledge base and skills, either in a broad sense or narrowly focusing on the skills relevant to particular clusters. Human capital formation is considered an important element throughout the whole cluster life cycle and therefore these policies are to be present in all stages.
- 'Public research', as a means to increase knowledge, training of qualified workforce and possible breeding ground for future entrepreneurs. It is found to be more relevant in the initial stages of clusters, but it might also help to avoid the decline of mature clusters.
- 'Supporting R&D support and innovation culture' – in contrast with public research policies, these measures focus on private firms, but they are also purported as being more critical in the early stages, as well as contributing to prevent the decline of clusters.
- 'Start-up support' is included due to the need to develop a local firm base. In different countries, these measures have been applied in all stages of cluster life cycles.
- 'Network organization and cooperation support' is frequently a focal point of what is usually named as cluster policies by governments, given that collaboration is seen as a main strength of clusters. Hence, it generally constitutes the core of cluster policies in a narrow sense and usually takes place at the early initial and expansion stages, in order to establish the connections that will link the different actors. Support for cooperation and for the creation of new networks (or the redefinition of existing ones) might also be necessary in order to trigger the renewal of clusters.
- 'Infrastructure and local conditions' – their improvement is considered to be particularly important in emerging and development stages, in order to adjust to the cluster changing needs. However, they are more likely to happen at a mature stage, when the cluster is more influential.

Besides those six categories, all of them supply-side policies, and we consider three further categories. First, **trade policies** aimed at protecting local industries through tariffs and import quotas, or fostering export-orientation of local firms, through export subsidies and other measures. Second, **demand-side policy instruments**, such as public

procurement, regulation standards, policies supporting private demand and systemic policies that may also have an impact on the evolution of clusters (Edler & Georghiou, 2007;
Izsak & Edler, 2011). Third, we also add a general category termed 'other', in order to consider the rest of the policies that may also have an impact on clusters (promotion of
national champions, fiscal policies, …).

As already mentioned, 'network organization and cooperation support' is generally the
core of what is usually named as cluster policies by governments. For the rest of the categories included in our taxonomy, these type of policies might be cluster-specific, i.e. narrowly defined, or, more frequently, broad measures applied to the whole regional or even
national economy, but having significant impact on particular clusters, contributing to
create the conditions for their emergence, expansion, maturity and eventually decline or
renewal. Table 1 summarizes the nine different categories of policies that may have an
impact of clusters in our study.

Public policies, however, cannot be depicted as tools taken from a toolbox according to
a theoretical rationale and then implemented; they are very sensitive to context-specific
differences and show a great variation over time and space. Moreover, policy measures
co-evolve with the political and economic cycle and with the issues and actors they try
to shape (Flanagan & Uyarra, 2016; Uyarra & Ramlogan, 2012). They unfold over time
and are, themselves, affected by path dependence (Flanagan & Uyarra, 2016; Valdaliso,
Magro, Navarro, Aranguren, & Wilson, 2014).

As regards clusters, there is an increasing recognition of the necessity of dynamic
approaches that can explain not only their origin and current performance but their
long-term evolution as well (Fornahl et al., 2015; Trippl, Grillitsch, Isaksen, & Sinozic,
2015). Regardless of whether cluster evolution can be framed in the stylized life cycle
model (Menzel & Fornahl, 2010) or in the adaptive life cycle model (Martin & Sunley,
2011) all the authors reckon that clusters can take multiple development paths that are
shaped, but not determined, by their previous trajectory (e.g. history); and by the co-evolution of actors, institutions (such as public policies) and networks at different scales and
levels (Fornahl et al., 2015; Njøs, Jakobsen, Aslesen, & Fløysand, 2016; Trippl et al., 2015).
If both public policies and clusters unfold over time and co-evolve with each other and
with other factors, it seems therefore quite clear that every policy measure can have a
different impact over cluster evolution depending on the particular stage of the cluster
life cycle.[1] Policy measures, then, should be adapted to the different stages of such

Table 1. Public policies that affect clusters.

Policies	Description
Education	Policy measures aimed at improving the knowledge base and skills of human capital
Public research	STI policy (public institutions, research centres, universities)
Supporting (private) R&D	STI policy (tax exemptions, R&D subsidies, research projects …)
Supporting start-ups	Measures to support new firm creation, SMEs
Supporting networks and cooperation	Supporting cluster initiatives/associations, measures to encourage inter-firm collaboration
Infrastructure and local conditions	Measures aimed at improving physical infrastructure and factor conditions (labour and capital)
Trade policies	Tariffs, import quotas, export subsidies, export promotion
Demand-side policy instruments	Local content (of MNEs production), public procurement
Other	Promotion of national champions, fiscal policies, internationalization …

Source: Authors' elaboration.

cycles (Aragón, Aranguren, Diez, Iturrioz, & Wilson, 2011; Flanagan & Uyarra, 2016; Ketels et al., 2013; Shin & Hassink, 2011; Van Klink & De Langen, 2001). However, our current empirical knowledge about the real impact of public policies on cluster evolution is still too scarce and the few empirical meta-studies available suggest that policy measures had an indirect impact on clusters (Brenner & Mühlig, 2013; Uyarra & Ramlogan, 2012; Van der Linde, 2003). What we attempt to do in this paper is to examine this co-evolution of public policies and cluster life cycles over a very long period of time on an empirical sample of six clusters of the Basque region in Spain.

3. Methodology and context

This paper draws on in-depth longitudinal studies conducted by the authors on six Basque industrial clusters particularly representative of the industrial development of the region in the nineteenth and twentieth centuries: papermaking, maritime industries, machine tool, energy, electronics and ICTs, and aeronautics. The former three belong to industries of the first industrial revolution that trace back their origins to the nineteenth century, and have followed an entire life cycle of emergence, development, maturity, and decline or transformation or renewal. The energy cluster dates back to the first years of the twentieth century, linked to the spread of electricity in the region. During the 1980s, while the cluster was still in a development stage, it got into a transformation or renewal stage, prior to getting into a mature stage. The last two correspond to young industries and clusters that have emerged in the second half of the twentieth century and are still in a development phase.[2]

Before discussing the policies, a brief description of the six clusters is provided in Table 2. Their current size is quite heterogeneous, ranging from over 300 firms in the maritime industries and energy clusters to 20 firms in the papermaking cluster. In terms of employees and turnover, the biggest cluster is that of energy, with 23,336 employees and 15,943 million euros and the smaller ones are the aeronautics and papermaking clusters, with around 4000 and 1650 employees, respectively, and a turnover between 600 and 800 million euros. As to their competitive position, the maritime industries, aeronautics

Table 2. Main figures of the Basque clusters c. 2012.

	Firms (number)	Employment (number)	Turnover (million €)	Exports (million €)	R&D expenses (million €)	Exports/ Turnover (%)	R&D/ Turnover (%)
Aeronautics and space	60	4142	771	694	195	90.0	25.3
Electronics and ICT	289	11,900	2950	1210	122	41.0	4.1
Maritime industries	350	6430	985	837	n.a.	85.0	n.a.
Paper making[a]	20	1650	614	302	n.a.	49.2	n.a.
Energy	350	23,336	15,943	n.a.	253	c.36	1.6
Machine tool[b]	108	5762	1107	846	n.a.	76.4	5.0

Notes: SPRI, *Observatorio de Coyuntura Industrial* 2013-I; and ACE, *Panorama del Clúster de Energía del País Vasco 2011*, for the energy cluster; data on turnover, exports and R&D expenditures, in million euros; unless otherwise stated, figures refer to facilities located in the Basque Country.
[a]Figures refer to 2010 and to the firms affiliated to the cluster association, which represents about 50% of the whole cluster.
[b]R&D/turnover ratio corresponds to 2011.

and machine tool clusters are the most export oriented (more than 70 per cent of their turnover was sold abroad in 2012). R&D data are not available for all clusters, but vast differences among those where comparison is possible are observed: the figures range from 1.6% of turnover in the case of the energy cluster to more than 25% in the research-intensive aeronautics cluster.

Following Menzel and Fornahl (2010), the first step was to set up the different phases in the life cycle of each cluster, based on quantitative (number of firms and employment) and qualitative (cluster and industry life cycle and cluster diversity) indicators (see Elola et al., 2012 for details about the methodology and specific sources for the analysis of each cluster). Then, a qualitative meta-study approach (Belussi & Sedita, 2009; Elola et al., 2012; Van der Linde, 2003) was employed selecting, for each cluster, the policies that played a more important role in each phase of its life cycle. The selection criteria were based on qualitative information taken from each study (e.g. whether a policy measure was considered to have played a triggering effect by the different actors involved in the cluster or not) and/or on the authors' criteria, particularly if the former information was not available. Policies are classified according to the nine categories presented in Table 1.[3]

The information thus collected is summarized in Table 3, showing the number of clusters that applied each type of policy in each phase in order to assess the type of policies more prevalent in each period and, conversely, whether any given policy is more widely used in one phase or in others. Given that clusters with very different life-spans are considered, a more chronological explanation is also required to assess whether the use of policies was linked to the phases of the clusters or whether they were generally used at any given time. For such a purpose, Table 4 summarizes the policies that had an impact on each cluster over time.

Table 3. Use of the various policy measures in the different phases of the cluster life cycle.

POLICY MEASURES	Origins (6)	Development (6)	Maturity (3)	Decline, transformation or renewal (4)
Education	4	6	3	4
Public research	1	2	1	3
Supporting R&D	3	3	1	4
Supporting start-ups	0	2	0	2
Supporting networks	1	2	0	4
Infrastructures	3	3	1	2
Trade policies	5	5	3	3
Demand-side policy instruments	3	3	2	2
Other	2	4	3	4

Source: Authors' calculation.
Note: Between parentheses, the number of clusters analysed in each phase. Shadings refer to the intensity in the use of policies in the different phases of the cluster life cycles. White shading is used when no cluster applied that policy, while black shading refers to all clusters applying the policy.

Table 4. Policies that have had an impact on clusters over time.

	1800-1850	1850-1875	1875-1900	1900-1910	1910-1920	1920-1930	1930-1940	1940-1950	1950-1960	1960-1970	1970-1980	1980-1990	1990-2000	2000-2009
Paper-making	7	7	67	67	1 67	67	1 67	1 7 9	1 7 9	1 7 9	7 9	1 3 5 7 9	1 3 5 7	1 3 5 7
Maritime industries				678	678	1 78	1 78	1 78	1 78	1 6789	6789	123 567 9	123 567 9	123 567 9
Machine tool				1 7	1 7	1 7	1 7	1 3 5 7	1 3 5 7	1 3 5 7	123 78	123 789		
Electronics and ICTs								1 3 7	1 3 7	1 3 7	1 3 7	123456789	123456789	123456789
Aeronautics												23 56 89	23 56 89	12345	9
Energy				1 7	1 7	1 67	1 67	1 7 9	1 67 9	1 6789	1 6789			

Legend: Formation / Emergence — Development — Maturity — Decline — Transformation/Renewal

Source: Authors' elaboration (see main text for further references).
Notes: 1. Education; 2. Public research; 3. Supporting R&D; 4. Supporting start-ups; 5. Supporting networks; 6. Infrastructures; 7. Trade policies; 8. Demand-side policy instruments; 9. Other.

4. Discussion

As some other meta-studies have emphasized (Belussi & Sedita, 2009; Brenner & Mühlig, 2013; Van der Linde, 2003), and in agreement with the literature on cluster policy (Uyarra & Ramlogan, 2012), public policies do not seem to have played a key role in the origin of five out of six of the Basque clusters studied. Local demand and factor conditions along with entrepreneurship and the inflow of external knowledge and technology, plus historical legacy, are the most important explanatory factors. Only in the case of the aeronautics and aerospace cluster was the Basque Government's strong support a key driving force behind its emergence in the early 1990s.[4] Cluster evolution through the different life cycles is explained by path-dependent mechanisms linked to both the cluster and region evolution (development of cluster specific factors, dynamic external economies) and to the clustered firms (strategic, dynamic and absorptive capacities); as well as by demand conditions (either local or international) (see Elola et al., 2012; Elola, Valdaliso, Franco, & López, 2017; Valdaliso et al., 2016).

Having reckoned this, however, this section further examines the main policies applied across the sample of Basque clusters over their different life cycles and their impact on cluster origins and evolution.

4.1. Description of policies affecting each cluster

4.1.1. Papermaking cluster

Tariffs (in place at least since 1780 to shelter the Spanish market from foreign competition) were one of the factors that accounted for the origins of the papermaking cluster (c. 1779–1870s) along with other measures that facilitated the import of new technology and expertise. Those tariffs were still in place during its development phase (1870s–1930s), but the clustered firms also benefited from improvements in transport infrastructures (railways and ports) that strengthened location advantages (better access to markets and to imported raw materials). During this phase, the emergence of training centres promoted by firms, but supported by local and regional governments, constituted a significant element of government support to the sector. The support to specific training was strengthened in the maturity phase (1940s–1970s), with the creation of a technical paper school, a private specialized training centre that was publicly funded. Protectionist policies were also predominant, with a period of extreme market regulation and autarky (1940s and 1950s) and a return to tariffs afterwards, but with a progressive openness of the domestic market. There were also fiscal policies that negatively impacted on the sector, through the excessive taxes imposed on it. The last phase (the 1980s to this day) saw a wider range of policies affecting the cluster, though they were not able to avoid cluster decline. On the education side, the government continued its support to the Paper School that became a government school, but still suffered from a decline in student numbers. Moving away from the protectionist measures that had been sheltering domestic production, the accession of Spain to the European Economic Community (EEC) marked a progressive external openness from 1986 onwards. The sector also had to cope with increasing environmental requirements. During this phase, the Basque Government started its cluster policy, and the papermaking cluster association was eventually integrated within the Basque cluster programme in 1999. However the scope and extent of its activities along with its representativeness over the whole population of firms remained limited, at least in comparison with other clusters. Some firms and technology centres collaborated to get hold of R&D funds from the Basque Government (Valdaliso et al., 2008, 2016).

4.1.2. Maritime cluster

The maritime cluster benefited in its origins (1880s–1910s) from a growing domestic market protected by tariffs, too. Other policies that had a positive impact on the sector were: on the one hand, modern port infrastructure was built up in the region and, on the other, the government passed the so-called *Ley de Escuadra* in 1887 that resulted in an increased demand of warships to be built in Spanish shipyards. During the following developmental phase (1920s–1950s), protectionist measures were still prevalent and domestic demand was stimulated through cheap public capital offered to Spanish shipowners. The support to education comes with the transfer of the School of Naval Engineers of the Spanish Navy (1914) to the Ministry of Education in 1933 and the creation of a new technical degree in marine engines by the Nautical School of Bilbao in 1924. During the maturity phase (1960s–1970s) the educational, protectionist and demand stimulus policies continued. They were complemented by other measures that included shipbuilding and export subsidies as well as the promotion of national champions that were partly state-owned, such as AESA, the merger of the three largest Spanish shipyards, in 1969. During the decline and renewal phase (the 1980s to this day) a wider array of policies were adopted. Spanish accession to the EEC resulted in the liberalization of the Spanish market and the sector underwent an important restructuring, both of the large shipyards in the 1980s (heavy cuts on capacity and employment, with key financial support of the Spanish government) and of the small & medium shipyards in the 1990s (with modest support of the Basque Government). This period has also seen a renewed interest in infrastructures, with investments in big and small ports. Specialized education has also been supported both by the regional government and the EU. The maritime cluster association, thanks to the efforts of a previous business association (ADIMDE), was eventually integrated within the cluster programme of the Basque Government in 1999 (who had not originally envisaged it), which also put forward policies to foster R&D. These included the creation of generic technological centres that carry out research in several areas and, specifically, the establishment of Azti-Tecnalia, a technological centre specialized in marine technologies. The Basque Government also subsidized private R&D projects (Valdaliso et al., 2010, 2016).

4.1.3. Machine tool cluster

Even if tariffs were also present during the origins of the machine tool cluster (1900s–1930s), they do not seem to be a key factor. The clustered firms did benefit from the creation of secondary schools with the support of firms themselves and local governments. During the developmental phase (1940s–1960s) protectionist policies continued, as well as policies to support the schools created during the previous phase, now transferred to the national government. The first measures to foster R&D started during this period. They helped to create the first laboratories and testing facilities and a specific R&D association, INVEMA, in 1968. The national government gave generous export subsidies and supported AFM's (the industry association created in 1946) efforts to go abroad (trade missions to foreign countries) and its initiative to create the BIEMH (International Machine Tool Exhibition) in Bilbao, both in the 1960s. During the maturity phase (1970s–1980s), the technology policies of the Basque and Spanish governments (R&D subsidies and creation of a network of technological centres) promoted firms' R&D activities. There were several programmes from the Spanish and Basque governments to encourage demand, fostering the acquisition of computer numerical control (CNC) machine tools. The Basque Government also fostered the restructuring and grouping of the sector in the 1980s through the *Plan de Relanzamiento Excepcional* (PRE), which gave generous subsidies to the companies so as they could cope with the crisis. In the same decade, in the area of education, the IMI programme of the Basque Government, directed to promote the use of microelectronics in the industry, particularly impacted in the machine tool sector, contributing to start a new phase of transformation (the 1990s to this day). The support to education continued during this phase with its funding of the Machine Tool Institute (IMH), as well as the support to public R&D, with the creation of technological centres and CICs (Centers for Collaborative Research). It is hardly surprising that AFM was one of the first cluster associations reckoned by the Basque government in the early 1990s. The NanoBasque strategy adopted by the regional government in 2008, which cut across several of the policy categories considered in this paper, has had an important impact on the sector: strengthening of R&D capacities, supporting the creation of start-ups, creation of networks and public-private collaboration. The cluster has also benefited from the internationalization policies of the Spanish and Basque governments.

4.1.4. Energy cluster

Public policies played a very limited role in the origins of the energy cluster in the Basque Country, linked to hydroelectricity, and explained by the existence of a strong and dynamic regional demand, along with local entrepreneurship and technicians, and an active involvement of local banks in financing this new sector. The Spanish government offered several incentives to promote new private investments in hydroelectric plants in the 1920s and to foster railways' electrification, but with very limited effects. Much more important, however, were the results of protectionist trade policies that, on the one hand, reserved the electrical sector to national firms and, on the other, imposed high tariffs on the imports of electrical parts and equipment (and resulted in the entry of American and German multinational firms in Spain, associated with local partners). This picture did not change substantially during the development phase, from the 1940s to the 1970s, although state intervention increased via regulated prices and the appearance of big state-owned firms in this sector. However, the renewal of the energy cluster, from the 1980s onwards, is strongly associated with a wide array of public policies displayed in several areas. To begin with, the sector was affected by the liberalization of the Spanish electricity sector and the change in regional policies, from promoting energy efficiency to efficiency and conservation. In the infrastructures category, it is worth mentioning the setting up of REE (Spanish Electrical Grid), a public company dedicated to the transmission of electricity and the operation of electricity systems. The creation of EVE (Basque Energy Board), a Basque governmental agency aimed at promoting energy efficiency and diversifying the energy sources, and the main shareholder of other agencies and companies (CADEM, Naturgas), was also particularly relevant during this period.

R&D subsidies started in the 1980s, but were intensified in the 1990s and the 2000s and have been complemented with the creation, by EVE, of the CIC EnergiGune, a public research organization. A handful of long and short grades on renewable energies have been launched at the universities and the Energy Cluster Association was created in 1996. The general policies of the Basque Government to support start-ups have aided the emergence of new firms responding to the increased demand for subsidized energy production companies that benefited from incentives to increase the market share of renewable energies from 1991 up to 2012, when these incentives had been suspended (Valdaliso et al., 2016).

4.1.5. Electronics and ICT cluster
The electronics and ICT cluster has only gone through two phases up to now. During its origins (1940s–1970s), it benefited from an internal market protected from foreign competition by tariffs and from the creation of specific educational facilities, at both secondary and tertiary levels. Support to R&D efforts was also present during this period, via research associations and laboratories created under the initiative of the Ministries of Education and Science, and Industry. During the developmental phase (the 1980s to this day) the support to education continued through the adaptation of the training programmes, the creation of new schools of computing and engineering and the aforementioned IMI programme of the Basque Government. Similar to the machine tool cluster, the NanoBasque strategy has also contributed to strengthen R&D capacities, to create start-ups and to develop networks and public-private collaboration in the cluster. Other policies (such as the PIE or the support to the industry association, later cluster association) have also contributed to the formation of networks, and public R&D has been promoted in technological centres and CICs. On the infrastructures side, the cluster has benefited from the development of telecommunication infrastructures and the creation of technology parks that have provided the space for the installation of ICT companies. Demand has been stimulated through public procurement (given that the public administration is an important client of ICT products) and the general promotion of the Information Society and the setting of a Digital Agenda by the Basque government (Elola, Valdaliso, & López, 2013; López et al., 2008; Valdaliso et al., 2016).

4.1.6. Aeronautics cluster
Finally, the aeronautics cluster has also gone through two phases. During its origins (1980s–1990s), the cluster benefited from different national and regional policies supporting private R&D and the public research carried out in different technology centres and, particularly in the Aeronautical Technologies Centre (CTA) established in 1996. The cluster was also helped by the unambiguous and strenuous efforts of the Basque Government to support this sector, commissioning a report on the viability of the cluster in 1992 and fostering collaboration through the creation of the *Comité de Tecnología del Cluster* (COMTEC) in 1993, which became HEGAN (the cluster association) in 1997. Other policies included special credit lines of the Basque government to the cluster's tractor firms in the 1990s; demand-side policies through CASA (a public company that belongs to Airbus), a main client of the clustered firms, and the FACA and Eurofighter national programmes in 1986 and 1988; as well as SEPI's participation in the ITP Project, later SOCADE's (both state-owned firms of the national and Basque governments,

respectively); and Basque Government investment in technology parks to attract companies. During the developmental phase (the 2000s to this day), the Basque Government has continued its support to HEGAN and the cluster has also benefited from the general policies of the regional government for R&D purposes and start-up support. Specific courses on aeronautics have also been developed at the universities (Elola et al., 2013; López et al., 2012; Valdaliso et al., 2016).

4.2. Life cycle stages and policy measures

The use of different types of measures is summarized in Table 3, with the number in each cell indicating the clusters that applied that type of policy in each phase. The darker the cell background, the more widespread its use is. Trade policies (mainly tariffs) appear as the most important policy measure behind cluster origins. As it can also be observed in Table 4, this is strongly linked to the long life history of the Basque clusters: four out of six appeared before the 1980s, when the Spanish economy was either protected from foreign competition or even (in the 1940s and the 1950s) closed. Tariffs did still matter in the development phase, but seemed to be less relevant than in the origins, and were combined with export subsidies and other measures aimed at increasing export orientation of the Spanish industry. However, after 1986, once Spain entered the EEC, clusters had to cope with a totally different scenario, characterized by an increasing economic openness and a much fiercer global competition (Valdaliso et al., 2016). Education policies became then paramount: in all cases, once the cluster entered the developmental phase, specific formation was developed to cater for the needs of specialized human resources. This confirms Brenner and Schlump's (2011) results on this matter. Policies to support R&D and networks have also been quite prevalent during the development phase, thus contradicting Brenner and Schlump's propositions. R&D subsidies had been applied since the 1960s in some clusters (for instance in the machine tool, and electronics and ICT clusters). However, they increased substantially since the 1980s, as a horizontal policy applied to all clusters independently of the phase they were going through. The support of networks that also started quite early in time in the machine tool cluster has also been an across-the-board policy of the Basque Government since the 1990s, as a pillar of its cluster policy.

Only half of the clusters considered have gone into the maturity phase. This affects the numbers in Table 3. The three clusters were influenced during this phase by other type of policies that do not fit in the categories described: fiscal measures negatively affecting the papermaking cluster; shipbuilding and export subsidies, as well as promotion of national champions in the maritime cluster; and the regional government's PRE aimed at restructuring the Basque industry in the 1980s and which exerted a particularly strong impact on the machine tool sector. Within the categories described, trade policies also occurred during this phase in the three cases, with a combination of protectionist measures at the beginning and progressive openness towards the end. Education policies also continued to be quite prevalent, along with demand-side policy instruments (through cheap public capital to build ships in the shipbuilding sector in the 1960s–1970s and programmes to foster the acquisition of CNC machine tools in the 1980s). Finally, the increasing importance of 'other' measures in the last phases has to be explained on account of the reconversion programmes of the national and regional governments in the 1980s and the 1990s (that affected the clusters of maritime industries and machine tools).

After reaching the maturity phase, these three clusters have followed different paths: while the papermaking cluster has not been able to avoid decline, the shipbuilding cluster, after a couple of decades of decline, seems to have managed to enter a new phase of renewal with the turn of the twenty-first century, and the machine tool cluster has even managed to upgrade and transform itself without going through a period of decline. The same goes for the energy cluster, which has experienced a thorough process of transformation since the 1980s while still being within a development stage. As the detailed case studies show, these diverse trajectories are due to different reasons. On the one hand, and within an increasing global and open market, each cluster is affected by the different impact that globalization and technological change exert on the industry, in general, and on the clustered firms in particular (Valdaliso et al., 2016). On the other, the types of policies applied are also relevant. Each type of policies applied in the paper-making cluster has also been implemented in at least two of the other three clusters. However, the real impact of every policy varied across clusters. For example, the four clusters were regarded as strategic by the Basque government, who supported the creation of cluster associations over the 1990s. However, only the clusters with previous business associations, such as those of machine tools and maritime industries, were earlier able to leverage on the advantages of networking and inter-firm cooperation. On the contrary, inter-firm collaboration did hardly develop in the papermaking cluster, in spite of the efforts of its cluster association. Finally, there is one type of policy that, while being present in the three transformed or renewed clusters, is missing from the declining one: public research. This corresponds with Brenner and Schlump's (2011) work, which points to public research as the only definite type of measure indicated to trigger the re-emergence of clusters. The fact that it is lacking in the papermaking cluster might be one of the reasons that are preventing this cluster from turning itself around.

5. Conclusions

This paper contributes to the study of the role of public policies in the origins and evolution of clusters, drawing on six case studies of Basque industrial clusters. The adoption of a longitudinal perspective, highly demanded by the literature (Boschma & Fornahl, 2011; Fornahl et al., 2015), although mainly based on qualitative empirical information, offers some findings that partially agree with the hypothesis of previous theoretical works, but also casts some doubts on others, and suggests new questions that deserve further inquiry.

The first conclusion is that public policies have played a secondary, indirect role in the emergence and subsequent development of industrial clusters in the Basque Country during the nineteenth and twentieth centuries, with the exception of the aeronautics and aerospace cluster. Path-dependent mechanisms linked to cluster and region evolution, clustered firms' resources and capabilities, and demand conditions seem to have been more influential (Elola et al., 2012, 2017; Valdaliso et al., 2016). As suggested by Asheim et al. (2015), broad-based general policies rather than cluster policies had a greater influence on the emergence of these clusters. To some extent, this has to do with the broad scope of policies until the appearance of the so-called cluster policies in the 1990s: classic industrial policies were aimed at promoting industries and sectors, not clusters, whereas framework policies were designed to improve the general conditions of the (national) economy. However, both types of policies conditioned cluster evolution.

The second conclusion is that history matters. Most of the important policy measures highlighted by cluster literature today do not fit well with the policy and economic context of the nineteenth century or even to that of the first half of the twentieth century. For example, trade and demand-side policies were more important in the origins of the oldest clusters whereas in the newest ones supply-side policies predominated. This has to do with the fundamental changes that policy discourses and rationales – at international, national and regional level – have experienced over time. In general, policy measures seem to have become more numerous and important in recent times than in earlier periods (something that Brenner & Mühlig, 2013 also indicate), something, again that is related to the emergence of new industrial policies at regional level in Europe (STI policies, cluster policies) since the 1980s. At least in the Basque case, however, all of these policy measures, and particularly cluster policies, have been designed to be applied equally in all clusters, without taking into consideration the phase they were at. Clusters with previous business associations, such as those of machine tools, maritime industries and electronics, were able to benefit earlier and deeper from cluster policies. In short, there is a virtuous circle between public policies and initiatives of companies in favour of clustering processes, but if business initiatives do not appear then policies alone are not enough to start a cluster.

There are also some conclusions in relation with the specific policy measures studied. Although Van Klink and De Langen's (2001) aforementioned caveat should be kept in mind, still, the empirical evidence presented in this paper reveals some findings. Protectionist measures, in times where their use was possible, provided a captive market that contributed to the emergence of the oldest clusters but then they tended to lose importance and even were counterproductive as clusters developed, being complemented by others aimed at increasing export orientation. Once the clusters entered the developmental phase, the support to specialized education was clearly endorsed by the government, thus contributing to provide the specific human resources required by the clusters to grow. At least with regard to education and trade policies, it seems quite clear that they co-evolved with the cluster life cycle and with the general framework of policy setting at national and regional levels. As the literature suggests, this paper also confirms that public research might play a significant role for clusters to renew themselves: turning around clusters that are already declining or helping mature clusters to move into new areas might require a research and innovation effort that companies alone might not be able to accomplish. Klepper (2016) shows this situation for many high-tech industries in the case of clusters in North America.

In each period the policy mix has been different. Therefore, an issue that deserves further attention is the interaction between the different categories of policies, both 'cluster policies' and 'broad-based general policies', in order to define a coherent policy mix in accordance with the wider territorial strategies. This is something that is currently being addressed in the Basque Country, where cluster policy is being reassessed in order to be better integrated within the broader framework of smart specialization strategies. The implication is that cluster policy needs to be coordinated with the broader policy in order to be more effective.

Policy measures, thus, can play a driving role in cluster evolution, but always along with other factors. However, the different impacts of these policies according to the technological level of every cluster have not been addressed here and deserve further attention. As

Brenner and Mühlig (2013) found out, policy measures had a stronger impact on high-tech industries (clusters) than on low-tech ones. The evidence presented in this paper with regard to the mature clusters of papermaking, maritime industries and machine tools, so far, points in this direction, but needs a more thorough analysis.

Work in progress on other Basque clusters will help to reinforce or refute all of these questions. Although Shin and Hassink (2011, p. 1400) emphasized that 'The exact course of a cluster life cycle and its characteristics vary from case to case and is therefore an empirical question', the use of broad samples of cases will make it easier to infer stylized facts or empirical regularities on this topic.

Notes

1. In this paper, we distinguish between five stages in cluster life cycles: origins, development, maturity, decline and transformation/renewal. For further details on different approaches to the analysis of cluster life cycles and their stages, see, for example, Valdaliso, Elola, and Franco (2016).
2. These clusters, along with other six (on the automotive industry, home appliances, environment, media and port of Bilbao), were considered strategic by the cluster policy implemented by the regional government in the 1990s, who supported the creation of cluster-associations to promote inter-firm collaboration. The six clusters selected, along with that of the automotive industries, are particularly representative of the industrial fabric of the Basque Country in the nineteenth and twentieth centuries. Every case study draws on a wide scope of quantitative and qualitative information (e.g. statistics of the industrial sectors included in every cluster, archival sources, firms' and business associations' annual reports, and secondary literature, among the most important). See López, Valdaliso, Elola, and Aranguren (2008), López, Elola, Valdaliso, and Aranguren (2012), Valdaliso, Elola, Aranguren, and López (2008), Valdaliso, Elola, Aranguren, and López (2010) and Valdaliso et al., (2016) for further details.
3. Notice that not all general or framework policies have been considered a priori, although they may affect each cluster differently. For instance, the availability of highly qualified human capital, and outcome of educational policies carried out by the Basque Government from the 1980s, is more important for 'high-tech clusters' such as electronics or aeronautics than for 'low-tech ones' such as papermaking. However, others, such as trade policies, have been taken into account because they have exerted a strong influence on cluster evolution.
4. Public intervention was particularly appropriate in this case due to the combination of other factors: increased demand for aircraft production caused by deregulation of world air traffic and existing knowledge and skills in the companies in terms of new materials and electronics (López et al., 2012).

Disclosure statement

No potential conflict of interest was reported by the authors.

Funding

This work was supported by Ministerio de Ciencia e Innovación under grant [HAR2009-09264]; Ministerio de Economía y Competitividad under grant [HAR2012-30948],VRI under grant [233737] and SPRI – Gobierno Vasco (Competitiveness Observatory Project).

References

Aragón, C., Aranguren, M. J., Diez, M., Iturrioz, C., & Wilson, J. (2011, April). *The importance of context: Lessons from a participatory cluster policy evaluation.* Paper presented at RSA Annual International Conference, Newcastle-upon-Tyne.

Aranguren, M. J., Magro, E., Navarro, M., & Valdaliso, J. M. (2012). *Estrategias para la construcción de ventajas competitivas regionales: el caso del País Vasco.* Madrid: Marcial Pons.

Aranguren, M. J., & Navarro, I. (2003). La política de cluster en la CAPV: una primera valoración. *Ekonomiaz, 53,* 90–113.

Asheim, B. T., Isaksen, A., Martin, R., & Trippl, M. (2015). The role of clusters and public policy in new regional economic path development (Papers in Innovation Studies, no. 2015/44). Circle/ Lund University.

Belussi, R., & Sedita, C. (2009). Life cycle vs. multiple path dependency in industrial districts. *European Planning Studies, 17*(4), 505–528. doi:10.1080/09654310802682065

Borrás, S., & Tsagdis, D. (2008). *Cluster policies in Europe: Firms, institutions, and governance.* Cheltenham: Edward Elgar.

Boschma, R., & Fornahl, D. (2011). Cluster evolution and a roadmap for future research. *Regional Studies, 45*(10), 1295–1298. doi:10.1080/00343404.2011.633253

Brenner, T., & Mühlig, A. (2013). Factors and mechanisms causing the emergence of local industrial clusters: A summary of 159 cases. *Regional Studies, 47*(4), 480–507. doi:10.1080/00343404.2012.701730

Brenner, T., & Schlump, C. (2011). Policy measures and their effects in the different phases of the cluster life cycle. *Regional Studies, 45*(10), 1363–1386. doi:10.1080/00343404.2010.529116

Commission of the European Communities. (2008). *The concept of clusters and cluster policies and their role for competitiveness and innovation: Main statistical results and lessons learned.* Brussels: Commission of the European Communities, Commission Staff Working Paper Number SEC (2008) 2637.

Delgado, M., Porter, M. E., & Stern, S. (2010). Clusters and entrepreneurship. *Journal of Economic Geography, 10*(4), 495–518. doi:10.1093/jeg/lbq010

Delgado, M., Porter, M. E., & Stern, S. (2014). Clusters, convergence, and economic performance. *Research Policy, 43,* 1785–1799. doi:10.1016/j.respol.2014.05.007

Edler, J., & Georghiou, L. (2007). Public procurement and innovation – Resurrecting the demand side. *Research Policy, 36,* 949–963. doi:10.1016/j.respol.2007.03.003

Elola, A., Valdaliso, J. M., Aranguren, M. J., & López, S. (2012). Cluster life cycles, path dependency and regional economic development. Insights from a meta-study on Basque clusters. *European Planning Studies, 20*(2), 257–279. doi:10.1080/09654313.2012.650902

Elola, A., Valdaliso, J. M., Franco, S., & López, S. (2017). Cluster life cycles and path dependency: An exploratory assessment of cluster evolution in the Basque Country. In J. L. Hervas & F. Belussi (Eds.), *Unfolding cluster evolution.* Oxford: Routledge.

Elola, A., Valdaliso, J. M., & López, S. (2013). The competitive position of the Basque aeroespatial cluster in global value chains: A historical analysis. *European Planning Studies, 21*(7), 1029–1045. doi:10.1080/09654313.2013.733851

Flanagan, K., & Uyarra, E. (2016). Four dangers in innovation policy studies – And how to avoid them. *Industry and Innovation, 23*(2), 177–188. doi:10.1080/13662716.2016.1146126.

Fornahl, D., Hassink, R., & Menzel, M. P. (2015). Broadening our knowledge on cluster evolution. *European Planning Studies, 23*(10), 1921–1931. doi:10.1080/09654313.2015.1016654

Franco, S., Murciego, A., & Wilson, J. R. (2014). *Methodology and findings report for correlation analysis between cluster strength and competitiveness indicators* (European Cluster Observatory Report).

Izsak, K., & Edler, J. (2011). *Trends and challenges in demand-side innovation policies in Europe* (Thematic Report 2011). INNO Policy TrendChart/ERAWATCH.

Ketels, C. (2004). European clusters. In T. Mentzel (Ed.), *Structural change in Europe 3-innovative city and business regions* (pp. 1–5). Boston, MA: Harvard Business School.

Ketels, C., Lindqvist, G., & Sölvell, Ö. (2006). *Cluster initiatives in developing and transition economies*. Stockholm: Center for Strategy and Competitiveness.

Ketels, C., Nauwelaers, C., Harper, J. C., Lindqvist, G., Lubicka, B., & Peck, F. (2013). *The role of clusters in smart specialization strategies*. Brussels: European Commission.

Klepper, S. (2016). *Experimental capitalism. The nanoeconomics of American high-tech industries*. Princeton, NJ: Princeton University Press.

Landabaso, M., & Rosenfeld, S. (2009). Public policies for industrial districts and clusters. In G. Becattini, M. Bellandi, & L. De Propis (Eds.), *A handbook of industrial districts* (pp. 739–753). Cheltenham: Edward Elgar.

López, S., Elola, A., Valdaliso, J. M., & Aranguren, M. J. (2012). *El clúster de la industria aeronáutica y espacial del País Vasco: orígenes, evolución y trayectoria competitiva*. San Sebastian: Eusko Ikaskuntza-Orkestra Instituto Vasco de Competitividad.

López, S., Valdaliso, J. M., Elola, A., & Aranguren, M. J. (2008). *Los orígenes históricos del clúster de electrónica, informática y telecomunicaciones en el País Vasco y su legado para el presente*. San Sebastian: Eusko Ikaskuntza-Orkestra Instituto Vasco de Competitividad.

Malmberg, A., & Maskell, P. (2002). The elusive concept of localization economies: Towards a knowledge-based theory of spatial clustering. *Environment and Planning A, 34*, 429–449. doi:10.1068/a3457

Martin, R., & Sunley, P. (2003). Deconstructing clusters: Chaotic concept or policy panacea? *Journal of Economic Geography, 3*, 5–35. doi:10.1093/jeg/3.1.5

Martin, R., & Sunley, P. (2006). Path dependence and regional economic evolution. *Journal of Economic Geography, 6*, 395–437. doi:10.1093/jeg/lbl012

Martin, R., & Sunley, P. (2011). Conceptualizing cluster evolution: Beyond the life cycle model? *Regional Studies, 45*(10), 1299–1318. doi:10.1080/00343404.2011.622263

Menzel, M. P., & Fornahl, D. (2010). Cluster life cycles – Dimensions and rationales of cluster evolution. *Industrial and Corporate Change, 19*(1), 205–238. doi:10.1093/icc/dtp036

Nauwelaers, C., & Wijtnes, R. (2008). Innovation policy, innovation in policy: Policy learning within and across systems and clusters. In C. Nauwelaers & R. Wintjes (Eds.), *Innovation policy in Europe: Measurement and strategy* (pp. 225–268). Cheltenham: Edward Elgar.

Njøs, R., & Jakobsen, S.-E. (2016). Cluster policy and regional development: Scale, scope and renewal. *Regional Studies, Regional Science, 3*(1), 146–169. doi:10.1080/21681376.2015.1138094

Njøs, R., Jakobsen, S.-E., Aslesen, H. W., & Fløysand, A. (2016). Encounters between cluster theory, policy and practice in Norway: Hubbing, blending and conceptual stretching. *European Urban and Regional Studies, 23*. Retrieved from http://eur.sagepub.com/content/early/2016/07/05/0969776416655860.refs. doi:10.1177/0969776416655860

OECD. (2007). *Competitive regional clusters*. Paris: Author.

OECD. (2011). *OECD reviews of regional innovation: Basque Country, Spain*. Paris: Author.

Porter, M. E. (1998). *On competition*. Boston, MA: Harvard Business Review Press.

Shin, D.-H., & Hassink, R. (2011). Cluster life cycles: The case of the shipbuilding industry cluster in South Korea. *Regional Studies, 45*(10), 1387–1402. doi:10.1080/00343404.2011.579594

Trippl, M., Grillitsch, M., Isaksen, A., & Sinozic, T. (2015). Perspectives on cluster evolution: Critical review and future research issues. *European Planning Studies, 23*(10), 2028–2044. doi:10.1080/09654313.2014.999450

Uyarra, E., & Ramlogan, R. (2012). *Cluster policy: A review of the evidence*. Report of the compendium of evidence on the effectiveness of innovation policy intervention. Project funded by the National Endowment for Science, Technology and the Arts (NESTA).

Valdaliso, J. M., Elola, A., Aranguren, M. J., & López, S. (2008). *Los orígenes históricos del clúster del papel en el País Vasco y su legado para el presente*. San Sebastian: Eusko Ikaskuntza-Orkestra Instituto Vasco de Competitividad.

Valdaliso, J. M., Elola, A., Aranguren, M. J., & López, S. (2010). *Los orígenes históricos del clúster de la industria marítima en el País Vasco y su legado para el presente*. San Sebastian: Orkestra-Eusko Ikaskuntza.

Valdaliso, J. M., Elola, A., & Franco, S. (2016). Do clusters follow the industry life cycle? Diversity of cluster evolution in old industrial regions. *Competitiveness Review*, *26*(1), 66–86. doi:10.1108/CR-02-2015-0006

Valdaliso, J. M., Magro, E., Navarro, M., Aranguren, M. J., & Wilson, J. R. (2014). Path dependence in policies supporting smart specialization strategies. Insights from the Basque case. *European Journal of Innovation Management*, *17*(4), 390–408. doi:10.1108/EJIM-12-2013-0136

Van der Linde, C. (2003). The demography of clusters – Findings from the cluster meta-study. In J. Bröcker, D. Dohse, & R. Soltwedel (Eds.), *Innovation clusters and interregional competition* (pp. 130–149). Berlin: Springer.

Van Klink, A., & De Langen, P. (2001). Cycles in industrial clusters: The case of the shipbuilding industry in the northern Netherlands. *Tijdschrift voor economische en sociale geografie*, *92*, 449–463. doi:10.1111/1467-9663.00171

Index

Note: Page numbers in *italics* refer to figures
Page numbers in **bold** refer to tables

Comité de Tecnología del Cluster (COMTEC) 195
commercialization, support system 7–8, 31, 150
competition and coopetition 26
contextual resilience 74, 78, 80, 82–5
continuum, concept of 57, 109–10, 112, 123
creativity 37, 74, 85–6
cross-industry innovation capability (CIIC):
  analytical model 35; case regions, comparison
  of 39; competence base 37–8; concept 35–6;
  creativity and idea management 37–8; culture
  and climate 37–8; data-analysis table 42;
  definition 36–7; drivers and indicators 35–6;
  indicators 38, 43–44; innovative firm 37–9;
  major elements 37; organizational intelligence
  37–8; path creation 40, 46; path renewal 35–6,
  40, 45–7; regional context 39–40, 44–5; research
  design 40–2; structure and systems 37–8;
  technological management 37–8; vision and
  strategy 37–8

de-locking 56, 91, 103
demand-side policy instruments, clusters 186, 187,
  196
developmental phase, clusters 193, 195–6, 198
Digital Agenda 195
Doloreux, David 9–10, 17–32
DUI (doing, using and interaction) 37–9, 43
Dun & Bradstreet industry database 50, 54, 58–9, 66

economic crisis 2008 34
economic decline 44–6
elasticity, clusters 31
electronics and ICT cluster 195, 196
Elola, Aitziber 12, 185–99
embedded agents 3
emerging industry 4, 53, 129, 133, 151
energy cluster 189–90, 194–5, 197
entrepreneurial agency 12, 144–5, 148, 154, 156–7,
  159
entrepreneurial industry structure, in Southwest
  Norway: bank's role 62–5; dimensions of 57;
  implications and limitations of research 67–8;
  macroeconomic environment 59–61; path
  dependence 54–5; path diversification 56–8;
  path extension 56; regional context 53–4;
  related and unrelated variety 57–9, 60; research
  methodologies 58–9; seed money 65–6; venture
  capital investments 65–6
entrepreneurial path dependence 10, 55, 59–61, 67
European Economic Community (EEC) 192, 193,
  196
European Technology Platforms (ETPs) 46
evolutionary economic geography (EEG) 1, 36,
  108–9
export subsidies 187, 188, 193, 196
external knowledge 90, 103, 192

financial institutions: role in path dependence 10,
  17, 53–6, 58–9, 62, 66–7, 120; role of banks

62–65; seed funds 65–66; venture capital funds
  65–66
Finnmark region: governmental enterprise 109,
  121; mining industry 115, 119–20; oil and gas
  industry 118–19; rural 177
Fitjar, Rune Dahl 12, 162–81
flexibility, organization 42, 74, 81–2, 94, 103
Fløysand, Arnt 1, 5–6, 11, 108–23
foreign direct investment (FDI) 11; benefits
  111–12; co-evolution of material outcomes
  110–11, 122; definition 113; as discursive
  process 113, 113–14; in Finnmark 118–20; in
  Hordaland 115–16; industry renewal and
  110–18; investment objectives 113, 113–14; as
  material outcome 111–13; mining industry
  119–20; MNC practice 108–9; oil and gas
  industry 118–19; path renewal and 109, 114–15,
  121, 123; regional development 108–23; salmon
  farming industry (Hordaland region) 115–16;
  selection of regions and industries 115; stock of
  114–15, 115
formation phase: path constitution 147, 152,
  154–7
FORNY programme 7–8
Fosse, Jens Kristian 12, 144–59
Franco, Susana 12, 185–99

Game Assembly (TGA) 136, 138
Game City 134, 136, 138–9
game industry, Scania, Sweden 134–6, 166
gatekeepers 13, 27, 28
Gjelsvik, Martin 10, 52–68
Global Centres of Expertise (GCE) 8–9, 40, 44,
  117
global innovation networks (GINs) 89–97, 100,
  102–4; see also multinational companies
  (MNCs)
globalization 85, 197
global production networks (GPN) 90
green shift policy 149
growth paths 1–4, 7, 11–12, 31, 86, 127–30, 140–1

Hauge, Elisabet S. 10, 34–47
HEGAN (cluster association) 195–6
higher education institutions (HEI) 27
high-tech industries 2, 165, 175, 198
Holmen, Ann Karin T. 12, 144–59
Hordaland: CIIC 40–1, 43–5; FDI narratives
  115–16; oil and gas industry 53; private
  enterprise culture 109, 121; RISs 40–1, 44;
  salmon farming industry, production system
  115–16; subsea industry 115, 117–18
human agency 3–4, 72, 91
human resources 2, 73, 94, 196, 198
Hydle, Katja Maria 11, 89–104

import quotas 187
individual actors 3–4, 6
industry paths 2, 9, 11–12, 56, 122, 144–5, 151